GULAG TO RHAPSODY

Dear Dr Laudone ;

Enjoy reading my Story

Paul Tarko

GULAG TO RHAPSODY

a survivor's journey

By

Paul Tarko

With Mason Loika

Gulag to Rhapsody

Printed in USA. First printing 2002.
Library of Congress Cataloguing-in-Publication Data
Paul Tarko
Gulag to Rhapsody: A Survivor's Journey

ISBN 0-9726148-0-X

Published and distributed in USA by:
Tarko Publishing
383 S. Main Street
Windsor Locks, CT 06096

10 9 8 7 6 5 4 3 2 1

Manufactured by King Printing Company, Inc.

This book is dedicated to my grandmother, Hermina Vereb, who taught me how to survive

Acknowledgments

Many thanks to the friends who helped to get this book published, including Mark and Rose Horan; my wife, Margit; and Maria Hawes.

In memory of my cousin, Thomas Vereb, whose bones are buried somewhere in Tigyina, southern Russia

Contents

PART V

AFTERWARD

LOOKING BACK   257

MY PLEA   262

GLOSSARY   267

Introduction

Tarko family at Nagylak Railroad Station. From left to right, Paul at age 17, Papa, Mama, Grandma, Baba and Geza.

APATFALVA ON A SUMMER'S DAY

Clickety-clack. Clack-clack-clack. Clickety-clickety-click-click. Clack.

The hypnotic sound and erratic movement of my passenger car on the train soothed my spirit, since I had enjoyed this trip hundreds of times before. The dependable diesel motor was hurrying me and other compatriot Hungarians to the town of my birth, Apatfalva!

As the train whisked across the ever-changing panorama, fields of three-inch stubble recalled fresh harvests across billowing fields of wheat. Through an open window, I felt the summer breeze of days long ago, skipping across my memory like a carefree child.

The sky was a deep, deep blue — bluer than blue, actually — and the sun shone bright enough to warm the soul as well as the body.

How long had I been back from Siberia? Two weeks, but it seemed like yesterday. My pulse quickened as the train squeakily complained about the brakes being applied.

I peered ahead of the train as I looked out the window. The sweet smell of vegetable fields infused my nostrils. Onions! Parsley! I believe I can even smell the carrots!

I didn't need to pinch myself. I could feel my homeland and the place of my birth surrounding me. And before my eyes unfolded a once-familiar tableau: the Apatfalva train station! The restaurant I spent hours in! And its attendant 30-foot oak tree in full summer greenery!

My heart was full.

My real-life reverie continued as the beige stucco walls identifying the Hungarian railway station came into view. Only a few minutes away were the hustle and bustle of a perfect Saturday in Apatfalva!

The train's movement slowed to a crawl, and finally I felt the jolt of the double-reverse bump that signaled that we had stopped.

I paused to permit the impatient people to traverse the aisles ahead of me. After all, I was free! Free, free, free!

Auntie Margit didn't know I had survived, and I couldn't wait to see her face when I showed up!

Most of the male passengers were wearing various shades of beige or white pants and white-linen button-up shirts. And the women! Oh, the women! They were wearing skirts and under-skirts in a riot of colors printed by rotogravure, made to delight the eyes as they twirled.

Departures and arrivals at railroad stations were social happenings in my country. Put simply, they served the same purpose as shopping malls for today's youth. The gents dressed fit to kill, and the women paraded about in one-piece, color-riotous dresses. They eyeballed the newcomers, tittered about fashion miscues, and gossiped, gossiped, gossiped.

Brilliant sunshine filtered through the branches of the ma-ture oak tree as a light breeze danced through its leaves. Apat-falva on a warm, blue-on-blue summer's day!

I walked up the aisle, descended the platform and negoti-ated my way across an intervening track so I could look around in the station's crushed-stone courtyard. Once there, my eyes searched the crazy-quilt social groups, looking for once-familiar faces. Instinctively, I looked toward the oak tree and its reas-suring trunk.

Rosie was there!

Even though she was only half-Gypsy, Rosie was completely filled with magic. Her shoulder-length black hair reflected the brilliant sunlight. Her eyes still flashed like stray lightning, piercing my heart when I least expected it, and she knew how to make me smile.

As I stared at Rosie in her flower-print cotton dress, memo-ries of high school days flooded my brain. While I was away, her girlish figure and finely honed features kept me alive for more nights than I ever expected.

She glanced at me, and time stood still. Her jaw dropped, her eyes opened wider than I thought eyes could open, and I watched the fixed glance in her eyes become glazed. She uttered, "Ahhhhhh," and crumpled to the ground as she fainted.

I rushed to her side as did another woman whose face I never saw. The woman moved back, so that I could hold onto Rosie as I tried to awaken her from this unexpected slumber.

I pulled her into my arms, called her name repeatedly and raised her body slightly. Her eyes fluttered open, tears streamed into them and she cried, "You died! You're dead!"

"Oh no!" I laughed. "You see me, don't you?"

Rosie's eyes were glazed as she stared into mine, and she pinched my arm. "I see you, and I feel you. What brings you here? Are you Paul?"

"Rosie, it's me," I said. "I just came back from Siberia!"

"Ohhhhhhhhh!" A look of recognition washed over her disbelief.

"Yeah, I survived!" I said. "I just came back two weeks ago!"

Rosie began to relax. Slowly she sank into my arms as I broke the "conspiracy of silence" that prisoners-of-war were supposed to maintain. I looked around stealthily to make sure our conversation could not be overheard as I related the lost, wasted years of my life.

Part I

Mako's and adjacent Places Area Map.

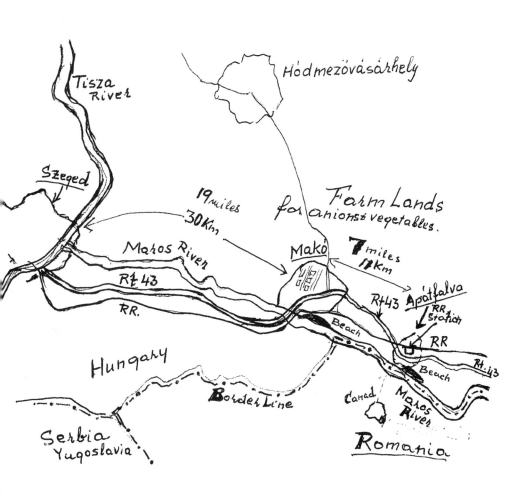

Tisza River

Hódmezövásárhely

Szeged

Farm Lands for onions & vegetables.

19 miles 30 Km

Matos River

Rt 43

RR.

Makó

7 miles 11 Km

Rt 43

Apátfalva

RR Station

RR

Rt. 43

Beach

Hungary

Border Line

Canad

Beach

Matos River

Serbia Yugoslavia

Romania

Csanad Palota

Road

RR.

Road

Nagylak Lands

Hungary.

Farming

Border Line

Hun- gary

R.Road

Road

Romania

Pasture.

Industrial Rail

1·5 miles (2.4 Km)

School

Workers Houses

Hemp & Linen Storage Soak the Hemps

Land

Switch Station

Factory

Canal

Workers & Apartment Houses

Old Oil Reistand Road

Owner's & Administration Housings

Tennis Court

Canal

R.R.

Sport field

Custom office

Canal

Gate Border Gards custom office

R.17.

RR. Station Nagylak

Keller Birth

Rt43

Nagylak

Arad

RR.

Rt43

Beach

Canal

Maros River

Farm Operat. Land

Beach

Romania

island

Maros River

Szentmiklos

Temesvar

Chapter 1
CHILDHOOD IN NAGYLAK

I was born into this world on America's Flag Day (June 14), 1922, in my grandmother's house in Apatfalva.
I grew up in a railway station. Most of my early years were spent there, because my father was the railroad stationmaster for Nagylak, Hungary. The government furnished living quarters to all its stationmasters to ensure they would see to the responsibilities of their posts. Therefore, my house was a part of the railroad station.
Our vegetable garden and land belonged to the railroad, which provided vegetable gardens to its employees. One other employee lived at the station. He sold tickets to ride the train, but I had no interest in knowing him.
My life in Nagylak was romantic, picturesque, imaginary, fanciful and idealistic, with enough rough-and-tough savvy to take care of myself.
During boyhood, I was extremely active. If I wasn't in elementary school, then I was helping my family with chores in the vegetable garden. Hungary is blessed with rich, fertile soil, one of the best in Europe, and during those years everyone in my town grew plentiful fields of parsley, wheat, carrots, new potatoes, onions, corn, tomatoes, green peppers, squash, turnips, sugar beets, peas and string beans.
If I wasn't in school or helping my family, I was playing with my classmates. We never slept during the daytime nor thought about being tired.
Even though Nagylak had a population of approximately 6,000 people, for Hungarians it amounted to less than a thousand. The remaining 5,000 people might as well have lived on another planet since the Romanian border separated them from my part of town.
Nagylak had been split up because of the 1920 Trianon Treaty that reduced Hungary's geographical area by two thirds and its population by one third. The treaty, signed in Trianon, France, near Versailles, doled out portions of Hungary to Romania, Yugoslavia, Czechoslovakia and Austria. The treaty

officially ended World War I, but now, three times a day, armed Romanian soldiers patrolled the recently redrawn border in Nagylak.

On the Hungarian side, less than a mile from the border, was the railroad station and a major hemp-processing factory. Around the railroad station were 200 houses whose families tended their respective gardens.

I am an only child. My father's name was Louis and my mother was named after my grandmother, Hermina. Mama had been a kindergarten teacher before she married Papa; then she became a housewife. Mama was blonde, and for a woman she had a good build — chubby without being fat.

Papa was 6 feet tall and slim. When he wore his railroad uniform and cap, he was stern, and there was no fooling around with him. Papa's best friend was Joseph Novak, who, being two years older than Papa, prided himself on cycling to and from Apatfalva several times a week.

Mama took care of our farm's small animals — 30 turkeys, 30 geese, 30 ducks and 50 chickens. We also owned a milker cow, her calves, a workhorse and four pigs. The ducks ate more than the other farm animals.

Our animals could run loose without being fenced in, but I had to watch the geese carefully to make sure they didn't get into our neighbor's garden and eat his corn. Sometimes I would feed an egg to the small calves to make their coats shiny. They enjoyed the taste of eggs, and it was fun seeing them beg for eggs by stopping in front of me and opening their mouths.

My schoolteacher and the Catholic priest were disciplinarians. They spanked us when they believed we needed it to ensure we learned our subjects well and always told the truth. I was taught to love my fellow man, to revere honesty, to respect authority and to honor my elders.

Apatfalva and Nagylak are eight miles apart. The Catholic Church, which accommodated 500 people, in Apatfalva was the only place to worship; therefore, parishioners would walk, while some would bicycle and others would travel by train.

My family went to church in Apatfalva every Sunday with few exceptions. My mother was religious, and one of her responsibilities was to ensure I went to school and attended each Sunday mass.

My grandma was a delightful, beautiful woman in high-heeled shoes who would sing at the top of her voice whenever she could. Her posture was picture-perfect, so her body remained straight all her life, and she enjoyed good health.

Grandma owned the general store in Apatfalva, and on most occasions I would climb up to the top shelf where the cone-shaped, foot-high block of sugar was kept. I would hand the crystal block down to Thomas, my first cousin with whom I loved to play, crawl back down to the ground, and the two of us would hit the sugar with our hands and break away some chunks.

My grandma learned how to survive by becoming a good businesswoman. When my grandfather died from stomach cancer, I was only 2 years old and my grandmother was 53. From that moment on, she had to run the family businesses — a general store and a distillery that manufactured schnapps — without a husband.

The family became prosperous, because she had a head for business. It amazed me to see what she could accomplish, and she entertained my family every Sunday. My father would arrange to have someone fill in for him on Sundays at the railway station, and then we would go visit my grandma.

In September 1926, when I was 4 years old, Grandma's coachman prepared her horse and buggy for her regular monthly trip to the "big city" — Szeged, Hungary's third largest city located 30 miles west of Apatfalva on the Tisza River — to pick up all kinds of merchandise to re-sell: southern fruit, pasta, sugar, flour, drinks, chocolate, seeds and even the lashing whip for the horse and buggy.

At 2 a.m., Grandma asked me if I wanted to go, and I nodded yes. The murmurings of fall were in the air, and moonlight reflected across the road ahead. Once we reached the Tisza River, the sun had risen and we negotiated our way through the park filled with leaf-adorned trees in an ever-changing collage of reds, yellows and oranges. Beyond the park, a vista of tall, stately, red-brick-and-stucco buildings rose above our buggy on both sides of the cobblestone street.

Railway tracks appeared in the middle of the street, and a streetcar whisked alongside us with passengers waving through open windows and a conductor who warned away horses and buggies with a golden clanging bell. "Oh, Grandma, I want to ride on it!" I cried.

"Not right now," she said, "but I will take you in an hour. Will you help me with my chores?"

"You bet!" I said, jumping up and down on the buckboard.

The coachman steered the wagon onward into the center of Szeged, stopped in front of the store to let us out and then parked the horse and buggy (a unique form of valet parking during those days).

We walked into a warehouse-size store, and Grandma handed the list of merchandise she intended to buy to a clerk wearing a neatly tailored suit. "We'll be back," she said.

She led me outside as an approaching streetcar came into view and began to slow down. I had to run while Grandma walked, because she took long strides. Once we reached the waiting streetcar, Grandma hoisted me up the steps.

I smiled at the uniformed conductor. "May I ring the bell?" I asked. "Papa is a stationmaster, and I live on the railroad!"

"Oh sure!" his thick eyebrows winked at me. "Do you need me to tell you how to ring it?"

"Not at all!" I laughed, and I clanged the bell mercilessly until the conductor decided that I enjoyed myself enough for one day.

We rode on the streetcar beyond three stations. Then we got off and waited for another from the opposite direction. We arrived at the store, and Grandma went to check on her order.

She and her driver picked up the merchandise — with chocolate and dates for me — loaded up the carriage, stopped for a quick lunch and got home during mid-afternoon.

After that first trip, I would not let her leave for the "big city" without me. If they did not take me, I raised a crying fit and threw a tantrum, so they had no choice but to take me on these monthly buckboard rides.

At Christmas time, we were able to make the same trip, even though the temperature was below zero, because we bundled ourselves up with fur overcoats and heavy woolen blankets. I enjoyed the feeling of braving the elements alongside Grandma, and these memories were to serve me well in later years.

Thomas' father was my Uncle Tamas. Everybody loved him. He became mayor of Apatfalva when I was 6 years old and served the townspeople for 10 years. As mayor, he imported red potato seeds from Switzerland and showed people how to grow new potatoes. He imported silkworms from China, and created a new industry.

He also began a distillery business by putting overripe fruit into large vats to undergo fermentation, and this distillery made 80-proof schnapps in flavors of cherry apricot, pear and plum. Nobody went hungry in Apatfalva, and no one ever had to beg. My uncle believed that everyone should be taken care of.

Even though my father had a wonderful job, he could not afford to buy me a ball or a pair of skates. So at age 6, I learned how to make use of the supplies and material around me. With my playmates' help, we made a ball from rags that we tied together with strings.

Our brand of football, known as soccer, is popular across Hungary, and we would kick the improvised ball around the pasture while maneuvering around the cows grazing upon the grass. The ball dampened from the morning dew and grew wetter and heavier as it absorbed the water and swelled up. Sometimes I kicked the heavy ball so hard with my bare feet that it was a miracle that my toes didn't break.

During wintertime, train travel occasionally was difficult, because trains would be delayed when major snowstorms caused snow to drift onto the tracks. The temperature would vary from 30° to -20° F. Because temperatures remained below freezing in January, the snow and ice did not melt. Consequently, roads were distinguishable only by footprints or bicycle tracks.

To protect our feet from the snow, the boys wore high-top shoes or boots made of leather. Instead of socks, we would take a square rag and wrap it around our feet tightly so it wouldn't get wrinkled. The winter ensemble also consisted of mittens, gloves and a makeshift muffler for our ears. With this amount of clothing, we had to get up close to our playmates' faces to be able to recognize them.

Across from the railroad station was a big pasture measuring approximately 1,000 acres. Heavy rains would collect in a low-lying section about 500 yards wide and two miles long. As temperatures fell with the onslaught of winter, the water would freeze, and the children could skate across it.

Papa took his axe and cut a piece of wood for me into a triangle shape. At the bottom of the pointed surface he inserted a wire. He then drilled a hole through the wood, ran the wire underneath it and, using a pair of pliers, tied the wood into my right shoe. Then he repeated the process on the other shoe, creating a homemade pair of skates to use on the ice.

The skates put a strain on my feet, but I was able to skate rather well. Oh, yes, I did fall and knocked out a couple of teeth, but I kept on skating. After all, I didn't want my friends to think I wasn't a tough guy.

When I was 8 years old, my father told me about the danger of going near the borderline, which was about a mile from my house. A small nine-foot-wide manmade canal served as the demarcation line for the Hungarian-Romanian border.

When it was warm, Thomas and I loved to sit on the canal bank, dangle our feet and soak them in the flowing water while looking at the guards, but we didn't dare cross the water. From the mill, the canal continued to the railway station about a mile northeast, and then fed into the Maros River three miles away.

This canal had been excavated at the turn of the 20th century to provide a water supply for Nagylak's hemp mill, which employed 500 of Nagylak's Hungarians. Romania's government did not permit its citizens to work at the hemp mill, believing that it would contribute to the Hungarian economy.

The hemp mill, a two-story building with a glass solarium on part of its roof, was the focus of life in Nagylak. Our neighbors worked at the mill while Papa took care of the railway station. The railroad worked on a timetable, and Papa made sure that everything, including me, operated on time.

Canal water flowed into the mill and was used to thoroughly soak the hemp brought into the mill 30-40 railway cars at a time.

The "noble hemp," as I call it, is grown for its fiber, and must be as straight as a corncob without any branches and a thickness close to that of a man's finger, about half an inch in diameter.

Marijuana is the weed of the hemp plant family and has branches that rob the hemp of its fine-quality fiber. Noble hemp is planted in rows similar to corn, because it grows to a height of 5 feet. Hemp plants are sown six inches apart from one another, creating a thick field. Besides my country, India is the world's other major hemp producer.

Hemp was grown all over Hungary; however, vegetable farmers, with plots of 3 to 10 acres in my area of Hungary, didn't have fields large enough to make hemp cultivation worthwhile. Those who grew hemp usually owned 100-acre-or-larger plots of land. The farther west in Hungary a person went, the more likely he would see fields of hemp. In eastern Hungary, vegetable farming was the main source for family income.

Once it reaches a height of 5 feet, hemp is mature enough to be harvested. The harvested hemp is sent to the mill to be soaked in water, which removes the pasty glue from the hemp, and the exposed woody parts are then broken away. The long fibers thereby revealed are then woven.

While soaking in water, hemp gives off methane gas, and we were always aware of which way the wind was blowing, especially when I attended the elementary school in Nagylak.

A fringe benefit of working in the hemp factory was taking home its wooden remnants. The wood was excellent for kindling, and many winter fires were started because of the hemp's wood byproduct.

Mr. Benedict, the hemp mill's director, owned the only automobile in town. He didn't drive it, though. He was driven to and from the railway station by a spiffily dressed chauffeur in a shiny black Model-T Ford — complete with leather seats and running boards, which served as a platform to enter the automobile.

When this automobile carried Mr. Benedict from the railroad station to the hemp mill, a switchman from the railroad would stop the scheduled freight train bringing in raw hemp, and both men would supervise the loading and unloading of freight at a special substation built exclusively for the mill.

When the director wasn't in the car, we would stop the chauffeur and ask him for a ride. That was a treat.

Every few weeks, he would motion us over to the car and give us a ride home from school on the running board. Then he would slow down so we could jump from the car. He didn't let us kids inside the car, because we were dirty and scruffy.

Most of my clothes were made from cotton or linen. One of my summer suits was woven from hemp, and it was cool and light, but it wasn't made in Nagylak. Our hemp mill only manufactured yarn, rope and twine.

Nagylak's elementary school, a mile-long energetic walk from my railway-station home, was separated from the hemp mill by a grassy field that we used for soccer and to watch older kids play.

Classes lasted from 8 a.m. to 2 p.m., and after-school activities sometimes kept me until 3 p.m. My school years lasted from the beginning of September until the last week of June.

Summer days were spent in the vegetable field to help my family weed the garden and pick potatoes. Whole families played and worked together most of the time. The family next door even took their baby with them in a little wicker basket and made him comfortable in the shade of an oak tree.

One night during the middle of July, with a twinkle in his eye, Papa told me that I should tend to my errands earlier than usual, because he was coming home early the next day with a surprise.

I wondered what the surprise could be, and I didn't sleep well that night. I woke up early in the morning before my parents did, rushed outside, grabbed a hoe and frantically dispatched any growth that even looked like a weed.

Before I got very far into my work, I heard the jangle of a bell and my father's raised voice behind me: "Well, Paul, this is a little big for you right now, but you will grow into it. This is for you."

I spun around, and my father was guiding an indigo blue and silver chrome bicycle in my direction. My very own bike! Half of the people traveled on the dirt roads of Hungary by bicycle. Papa had a full-sized adult bicycle, and mine was man-sized, almost as big as his. I tried to sit on the bicycle seat, but I immediately discovered my feet didn't reach the pedals.

Over the next week, I learned how to balance myself by putting my right foot in the opening under the triangular frame.

The frame felt like I was sitting on a metal pipe when I placed my full weight on top of it, so it was necessary to use the frame in an innovative way.

I fell off the bike more than I stayed on it until I mastered a technique my schoolmates showed me. Because a child can't sit on a bicycle frame and reach the pedals, I needed to pedal it without sitting down and get the bike moving that way. Then I could try to balance myself.

Well, I managed to skin both my knees and elbows, and I became bloodied from the abrasions of subsequent falls. But I learned how to ride my bicycle in one week. Within a year I grew enough that I could sit on the bicycle and feel my feet touch the pedals.

Chapter 2

THOSE YOUNG HALCYON DAYS

During the 1930s, Hungary administered a three-tiered educational system. Regardless of which program a child enrolled in, everyone attended an elementary school until fifth grade.

Children who were destined to work in the mills, on farms or in factories stayed in elementary school during the fifth and sixth grades. This working class also included shoemakers, woodworkers, forestry workers and farm workers. Most women stayed in elementary school also, because they aspired to become good partners for their future mates and to be good mothers. The subjects taught these children consisted of reading, writing, arithmetic, geometry and world history.

Children who hoped to become machinists, electricians, administrators, bookkeepers and other technical vocations transferred to a middle school for grades five through eight, where, in Mako, they encountered a general area of business-related study, consisting of such diverse subjects as basket weaving, agriculture and business administration.

After graduation, students who wanted to pursue a specialty undertook four years of vocational school, a type of high school (grades nine through 12) that taught business preparatory courses such as sales, business letter composition and calculus. Students were required to learn German and, of course, world history. Vocational school was followed by two years in a trade school, where a certificate in one's specialty was received.

Students who chose the technical path were not allowed to determine their particular specialty. Hungary's government mandated each student's specific courses and area of specialization. High quality of instruction but a lack of choice delineated the Hungarian school system from its counterpart in America.

My parents guided me toward the third tier of Hungary's education system, earmarked for engineers, doctors, lawyers and technical specialists. This educational path demanded that students master a vast pool of material. For example, the language curriculum, in addition to my native Magyar, mandated Latin, German and English.

The eight-year course of study in this high school, from grades five through 12, is known as gymnasium. I went to such a school in Mako with my cousin, Thomas. (A gymnasium in America is an indoor sports facility, but in Hungary the word is all-inclusive for the entire school.) So, at age 10, I began to obtain an excellent education and developed into a good athlete — playing soccer, swimming and rowing competitively. For someone who grew up as a farm boy, I was becoming a tough guy!

Meanwhile, Thomas constantly talked about how he wanted to become a veterinarian, and we shared dreams of how our future lives would turn out.

No matter where kids went to school, Hungary demanded one hour of religious education from its students. This educational hour was intended to instill moral values and ethics in us at an early age. Each of the three major religions was represented. Catholics were taught by priests, Protestants and the Reform Church services were led by ministers and Jews were administered to by rabbis. Even if you were an atheist or agnostic, you were required to make a choice.

Mako had a population of approximately 50,000 and served as the county seat for the towns of Apatfalva and Nagylak. I was familiar with the city, because at age 14 I accompanied my parents while they purchased a house, which they subsequently rented to another family.

I got onto the train at Nagylak, and eight miles farther when it reached Apatfalva, Thomas greeted me with some friends of ours. The train rolled on for another eight miles until the buildings of Mako loomed beyond the railroad tracks. After four years in a one-room schoolhouse in Nagylak, I was awestruck by the three-story, beige-colored gymnasium in Mako that filled an entire city block.

The gymnasium contained approximately 20 different classrooms for its eight grades (5-12). Each grade was administered in a separate classroom, and the only times we commuted to a different room was when special equipment was needed.

These rooms included a chemistry room with Bunsen burn-
ers, chemical agents and measuring utensils, and a biology
room for viewing stuffed creatures and dissecting animals. In
the exercise room, I played basketball, lifted weights, learned
gymnastics, fenced and wrestled Greco-Roman style.

On my first day of school, I became friends with Sujo, a
strong well-mannered boy of good character who lived in Mako.
Because we were fifth graders, we gathered in groups to protect
ourselves from the "wise guys" in higher grades. Sujo and I
competed in various sports, especially soccer, and graduated
together. When school let out for the summer, we experienced
many good times fishing for snapper, carp and *harcsa* (a large
river fish resembling a catfish) in the Maros River.

Zoli was another classmate who became a close friend. He
commuted to school by train at a distance greater than any of
us. His town was north of Nagylak, and he was the first one of
us to get on the train and the last one to leave it.

Because my father was a railroad stationmaster, I was able
to ride the railroad unlimited times free of charge. Mako is
eight miles west of Apatfalva, so I rode the train from Nagylak
with Zoli, Thomas would get on in Apatfalva, and when we
reached Mako the three of us would stride off happily together.

In Nagylak, my friends and I had been completely oblivious
of the mind-altering nature of the fields of marijuana. Sometimes kids would take leaves from a plant, wrap them in
cigarette paper, and smoke them. But marijuana had a pungent odor that was not as appealing as something much
sweeter.

The fibrous material at the end of an ear of corn was far
tastier, actually sweet, compared to the taste of marijuana.
Before we learned how to smoke tobacco, we boys enjoyed our
share of cigarettes made from corn.

Tobacco was preferred by the boys at the gymnasium, and I
began smoking it when I was 10 years old. The boys' bathroom
at my gymnasium constantly reeked from the telltale smell of
clouds of tobacco smoke.

Meanwhile, back at home, Thomas and I played with a
bunch of other children on the wide sandy shore of the Maros
River. Papa had taught me how to swim when I was a toddler,
and I never could get enough of playing in the water. Usually,

10 boys and an equal number of girls found this area an ideal spot to goof off and play.

One day, Thomas and I bicycled to the river to recruit a team for handball, and a cute half-blooded Gypsy girl, Rose, introduced herself to the rest of our crowd. She spoke Magyar, which was unusual for a Gypsy. Other Gypsies only talked in their native dialect, and Rosie (as everyone called her) became a talkative and affectionate companion.

Thomas and I became altar boys for the church, too. We were part of a group of four boys, sometimes six, who were given responsibilities in the altar area during mass. We were responsible for delivering the bread and wine to our priest, Father Kelemen, by placing it on the altar table prior to the serving of communion. Before each ceremony, we were given specific instructions when to kneel in church and ring a bell.

By the age of 12, I developed a taste for the sacramental wine. The "celebration" wine provided by the Catholic Church was deliciously mellow, and all the altar boys bragged about its semisweet muscatel taste. Unfortunately, the occasions that Thomas and I sampled the church wine became numerous enough that the priest determined that the wine supply became noticeably depleted.

While Thomas and I were playing outside, Father Kelemen confided his suspicions to my father. "You know how much your son and Thomas enjoy being altar boys," he said, "but I'm afraid they enjoy the altar wine much more!"

Minutes later, I was being spanked for my moments of indulgence, but the priest and my father laughed about my dalliance with altar wine whenever they thought I could not hear them.

Because my father was the railroad stationmaster, I grew up playing on the railroad cars with the boys of Nagylak. We would jump from one car to another, then run across its roof. Once, I misjudged the timing of my jump, and I fell. I landed awkwardly, resulting in some ugly discolored bruises, but luckily, I suffered no broken bones.

I usually played with John, the switchman's son, who was a year older than me, and George, a stocky boy with whom I played soccer.

One afternoon John, George and I "borrowed" the railway line's service car from its usual location — a remote piece of railroad track — for a joyride, because we enjoyed the exertion of pushing its wide two-man lever with our feet. This vehicle is built on four railroad wheels with a flatbed surface and is intended to transport the rail line's repair people.

Tools, such as shovels, pickaxes and spades, are loaded at the front of the car. At the back is a U-shaped kneeling pad where the worker balances himself with his left knee while pushing with all his might against the lever with the right foot.

John and I merrily pushed against the lever faster and faster to see how rapidly the service car could travel. We had gotten a few miles along the track when George called out, "A train!"

We stood up and, to our dismay, observed a train heading toward us on the track from the opposite direction. At the same time we saw the locomotive, the engineer and brakeman noticed us, and they began to wave their arms desperately.

George yelled, "Get off the car! There's a train coming!"

The three of us managed to stop the car, lift the 400-pound behemoth off the track and move it to the edge of the railroad bed.

But that wasn't far enough. The 30-car freight train struck a corner of the service car, cartwheeling it wildly away from the track while creating a sizable dent on the front left corner of the locomotive. We ran off, but it was too late. We had already been recognized.

That night my father spanked me so hard I couldn't sit down the rest of the night. Then he made me kneel on corn for an hour. I was righteously punished, but so were the other boys.

My childhood was tough, and romantic as well. We played together in groups of boys and girls. I rowed competitively in regattas up and down the Maros to where the Tisza River flows southward and won some awards too. These days of carefree competition provided romantic memories, and a worry-free child's life.

Sujo, Thomas and I were gifted athletically, and it was natural that our competitive nature and sense of good sportsmanship caused us to become best of friends. Our physical education instructor encouraged us, because we quickly mastered each athletic movement that he taught.

Swimming was one sport that all of us could enjoy equally, especially during the summer when I turned 15. School had let out for the summer, and my shoes flew off as I went swimming for miles and miles at a time in the romantic Maros River. Many days, I would get off the train in Apatfalva with Thomas so we could swim together, and Rosie would wait for us.

The silt-filled Maros River flows in a 100-yard-wide riverbed (the full length of a football field), and the banks of the silky-smooth flowing river look like a yellowish white beach.

Rosie had become a regular part of the group who played in the river. She was maturing as a young woman; I was becoming a young man. One thing led to another, and we became romantically involved. We would meet secretly after school, because our parents would have objected if they knew about the extent of our relationship.

My mother had a girlfriend named Lola, who was 36 years old, divorced and Jewish. Lola had curly black hair that flowed to her shoulders, and she was good looking. She also had a boyfriend who worked in the customs department.

I was swimming with Lola and her boyfriend on a warm, sunny June afternoon, and we took turns splashing one another. We played with a ball, throwing it back and forth beneath the willow trees lining the banks, when suddenly a whirlpool captured my mother's friend. The Maros has a fine sandy bottom, but in places the current erodes away the sand, creating dangerous whirlpools.

Her boyfriend looked on aghast as she was pulled underwater. I jumped in and swam toward the vanishing image of her dark-green bathing suit. I grabbed hold of her long hair, and began pulling her away from the five-foot-wide angry swirl. She grabbed hold of me and tried to pull me under, so I raised my fist and struck her arm hard. She stopped fighting me, and I began to maneuver the two of us toward shore. About this time, I felt her boyfriend in back of me trying to assist in the rescue.

On the riverbank, I placed her face down and administered artificial respiration. Lola regained consciousness, and with a start she began to cough up the water she had swallowed.

When she realized where she was, she looked up at her boy-friend and screamed at the top of her voice, "You blockhead! Where were you?"

Then she kissed me once, twice, three times, and then once again to show her gratitude. I turned several shades of red, but I loved the attention. Later, she presented me with a seven-layer chocolate cake as a reward.

The next year, I saved a 10-year-old boy who was caught in the same whirlpool, and eventually the number of swimmers rescued amounted to 10 people.

The silt from the Maros River provided an opportunity for me to make money. I had a 25-foot-long boat propelled by foot pedals. Into that boat, Thomas and I dredged sand from the bottom of the river.

We took a metal bucket with many holes punched into it, placed it onto a long rod and dropped it six to eight feet deep to the bottom of the river. The current caused the sand to settle into the bucket.

After the bucket became filled with sand, we would hoist up the bucket and the water would pour out from the holes. We dumped the sand into the boat, and dropped the bucket back onto the bottom.

After we collected a full cubic yard of sand, we pedaled the boat to shore, shoveled the sand into a wheelbarrow and piled it up by the riverbank.

We then sold the sand for mortar. Sometimes we would transport our sand to the railroad station by horse and carriage, then unload it for later transport by railroad car to cities where our sand was purchased for construction.

After I sold a load of sand, I brought the money home to my father, who kept track of my earnings. Papa owned a 12-gauge shotgun and, as a reward for my thrift and industriousness, he bought me a Hungarian '22 rifle so I could go hunting.

Sujo and I spent our weekends picnicking by the riverbank and hunted wild geese, mallard ducks, rabbits and deer in the pasture across from the Nagylak railroad station. Often the two of us would visit an old man named John, whose gristmill had been destroyed by melting ice on the river. He had subsequently moved to a wooden shack on the riverbank and achieved stature in our eyes for catching a 200-pound *harcsa*.

During the summer of 1939, Thomas, Beco (a friend of mine for three years), Sujo and I went to the river. I carried my '22 rifle to shoot fish in the river, because on sunny days, large *harcsa* would lie on top of the Maros River as if they were sunbathing. This trait made them vulnerable to my marksmanship. On the opposite side of the river, armed Romanian soldiers were patrolling.

Sujo was always worried that Thomas and I would get into trouble, and he worried aloud, "Paul, put that gun away! If the Romanian soldiers see it, they will shoot us!"

Before I got a chance to respond, Beco looked at Sujo and smiled, "Don't worry, Sujo. Paul is such a good shot than he will shoot the gun from the hand of any Romanian who raises his gun at us."

All of us smiled, but I lowered the gun. Even though we felt invincible, we were not in a mood to tempt fate.

On school days, I took the train to Mako, arriving at 7:00 a.m. But before breakfast, I had to milk — by hand — the cows to help my parents.

The trips on the train were full of practical jokes, mischief, and teasing and flirting with the girls. Many of the girls acted that way, too, and we became fond of them.

After classes were over, I played sports. I became a good 100-meter and 200-meter sprint runner, long jumper, soccer player, swimmer, rower, and even wrestled. During my last year of high school, I played on Mako's professional soccer team as goal kicker on the left wing. Once I kicked a goal into the left upper corner of the net, and a photograph of my kick appeared in the local newspaper.

At 4 p.m., I would take the train home to eat a quick meal, study, milk the cow again, study some more, eat a big supper and go to bed. In 1939, when I was in 11th grade, electric power came to Nagylak. Nevertheless, I studied by kerosene lamp, and in wintertime my family kept the fireplace filled with wood or a coal stove burning to keep our rooms warm.

Rosie had already taught me about the kind of electricity a woman can wield, but our relationship was coming to an end. Rosie had been dating a few other guys and refused to stop seeing them. We knew that our relationship could never be made public, and so we agreed to stop seeing each other clandestinely.

Louis, the son of my father's long-time friend, and I began dating two girls. On weekends we took them out to the Maros River to walk in the woods along the river, picking violets, laughing, running, kissing and playing.

My new girlfriend was named Yolanda; she was tall, blonde and beautiful; and we could date in public. We walked together along the river under the supervision of her mother's designated chaperone. During these days, we had to find an occasion when the chaperone could not see us or had walked away to steal a kiss. Chaperones even attended the dance halls.

Louis and I wanted to see our girlfriends more often, and so we devised a way to deceive our parents on sunny, warm spring mornings. While Louis' father, Lajos, and Papa played cards in Nagylak, we were sneaking out the railroad station in Mako, making sure that no one could see us.

We then joined our girlfriends at the riverbank where we would enjoy a picnic.

The next day at school, we would tell the teacher that we had been sick. We carried out this scheme cautiously, because it would look suspicious if we were sick every week.

This conspiratorial plan worked beautifully until a catastrophe occurred. I was sitting in class when I saw Louis' father walk over to the teacher's office to ask about his son's progress at school. When the teacher told him that Louis was sick often, Lajos gulped and left the school quickly.

Lajos stood by the railway station door in Mako waiting for his son. Sure enough, Louis did not see his father and showed up with his girlfriend. The moment Louis walked through the door, his father slapped him so hard that he fell backwards on his rump.

Louis' girl ran away, and on that day our secret romances came to an end. Luckily, I was in school and wasn't punished. Nevertheless, my grades were down because of our frequent outings, and I made a commitment to improve my study habits.

When I was 17, my grandmother sold her general store and moved to Nagylak to live with my family. When my mother was busy with farm work, Grandma would cook. Grandma was the finest cook I ever knew.

On days when I didn't have school, around 11 a.m., I would catch one of our chickens, lay its head on a chopping block and cut off its head. Grandma would then clean off the feathers, make a fire in the wood stove, and by noon, she would have dinner on the table. Besides her cooking skills, she baked the best gourmet cakes and cookies I have known.

She never studied cooking, but Grandma became known as the best baker in a town where women were culinary artists in the kitchen and interior artists on the walls of their homes. Her famous Hungarian *dobos torta* (dobos tart), invented in 1887 by Joseph Dabos, consisted of seven layers of thin sponge-like breading filled with sweet chocolate cream, topped with a caramel glaze. Best of all was her walnut cream cake.

Throughout my childhood days, my cousin, Thomas, was like a brother to me. Each summer, we rowed a small boat along the silky Maros River. We went fishing, hunting and trapping together. And, of course, we graduated together.

In school, I became a boy scout and learned how to organize a camping expedition and took part in competitive shooting exhibitions. Even with all our youthful shenanigans, I strived to become an honest, religious, non-bigoted person of good character.

One way I learned how to improve my character was to help weaker boys compete against me. Once I dedicated myself to helping others, my grades steadily improved.

Before my senior year, my parents made arrangements with Zoli's parents to allow us to stay in Mako, thereby providing us with two more hours of study time that we had lost while traveling by train.

At 18, I lived on my own in a small room that our parents rented for us in the city. The first year on my own was not easy, because the house lady skimped on wood and didn't keep the stove fired up at night when it was cold.

After 9 or 10 p.m. when the fire died out, Zoli and I studied while changing seats on top of the stove every 30 minutes. Finally, the stove turned cool, the room became too cold, and, before midnight, we collapsed into our beds and wrapped warm blankets around ourselves.

Zoli and I learned plenty of life's lessons in this room during our last year in gymnasium. However, these years were prosperous ones when the horror of World War II came to Hungary.

Chapter 3

ROMANCE ON THE MAROS RIVER

Graduation from gymnasium was cause for celebration. All the days, weeks, months and years of high school were finally at an end. I was proud of how I had managed my rigorous studies, but this summer was meant for me to relax and empty my mind.

Two days after graduation, Thomas, Beco and I were rowing a canoe along the Maros River. A strong wind blew from the east, which shortened the distance between each stroke of the oars.

We had not reached our intended destination by early afternoon, so we decided to beach the boat and fish where we were. We back-paddled slightly to retard the canoe's drift with the current as we searched for a fishing spot. Suddenly, we heard the faint sound of voices laughing and people splashing ahead of us.

I moored the line from the canoe to a willow tree on the riverbank, crept off the canoe and signaled my friends to follow me surreptitiously.

Each time we slipped around another tree, the louder the voices became. To our relief, we heard everyone laughing, cavorting and splashing about in the river. Whoever these people were, at least they sounded friendly!

Emboldened by the happy sounds, I stepped out into a clearing and looked across the river. On the opposite side, in Romanian territory, about 20 people were swimming in the water, and another 10 people were lying on towels on the riverbank.

Some of the words I had heard were in Magyar, so I inquired, "*Szervusztok* (hello)!!! Are there any Hungarians over there?"

A huge roar of laughter echoed across the water, and a deep voice shouted back, "We are all Hungarians!"

Other voices joined in, "Yeah!"

"I'm Hungarian!"

"So am I!"

"Me too!"

The rest of the group, young and old, men and women, applauded and laughed in glee. The echo effect from the river water made it sound like heaven itself was awash with renewed happiness.

Beco and Thomas emerged from behind a tree. Excitedly, I looked at them and hollered back to the group, "We'd like to join you. Are there any guards around?"

"No guards here!" a slender white-haired gent called out from where he lay on the riverbank. "They marched back toward Nagylak an hour ago."

"Okay then, let's have some fun!" I yelled.

I stepped down to the sandy riverbank, waded into the water until it covered my shoulders, and dogpaddled my way to the Romanian side with Beco and Thomas following each stroke of mine with one of theirs.

The water was cool and inviting. When I waded into the midst of these jovial companions, I laid eyes upon a girl two inches shorter than me. The sun's reflection glistened in her eyes, whereupon she smiled invitingly and dove under the water.

I blushed a bit, and turned my head toward the rest of my newfound company. Thomas, Beco and I introduced ourselves, members of their group reciprocated and plenty of hearty handshakes were passed in between.

Our new friends lived in Szentmiklos, an agricultural town of about 6,000 in Romania. I bragged about my recent graduation, and Beco and Thomas looked around for female distractions as pleasing as mine.

Water bubbled up in front of me, and the girl I just observed broke the surface and touched my arm. "I'm Maria, by the way," she said, and she sank underwater and swam away.

When she came up for air, I yelled out to her, "Do you have a boyfriend?"

"Of course not, silly!" She laughed and dove back into the water.

Who was this creature with yellowish-brown shoulder-length hair? Her eyes were as blue as a Hungarian sky, and her skin was as warm as the sun in June.

She moved through the water like people skate on ice: clean, efficient and strong! Her breasts were firm, not too big, and her body rippled in the water like an otter.

I tried to make conversation with everyone else. I swear I did. But I couldn't concentrate on anything except Maria. She said she doesn't have a boyfriend!

I couldn't get enough of her company, and fortunately, Maria consented to rendezvous with me the next day at the river. As I went to sleep that night, I could hear Papa playing our wind-up Victrola, as the words of a Hungarian song popular since 1939 counseled me:

Tomorrow!
Who knows if you will see me again?
Tomorrow!
Will it break your heart to think of yesterday?
I am happy for tonight; don't tell me about tomorrow!
Tomorrow!
Who knows if you will see me again?"

The winds of war were breathing heavily against Hungary, and waves of humanity were crashing against other waves. We didn't like the German imperialists, but we couldn't abide the communists either.

To avoid the guards, Maria and I agreed the next day that we would meet on a small island in the middle of the river. As we swam from our respective countries across the smooth silky water to ensure that the border patrols did not see us, our eyes caught sight of the wild red roses that grew on the island. Appropriately, we agreed to name this piece of real estate, *Senki Sziget* (Nobody's Island).

Meanwhile, finding a job became important because World War II had begun, and many Hungarian men were being conscripted into the army.

I had planned to study forestry engineering, but Thomas' half-brother, Geza, who was eight years older than me, visited our family. The purpose of his visit: to talk me out of going to the university. Instead, Geza asked me to manage his newly acquired sawmill and forestry business in Borsa, Transylvania.

This area of Romania, 50% populated by Hungarians, had been taken away from Hungary as a result of the Trianon

Treaty. Now Hitler, Chamberlain and France revised the treaty in August 1940, giving this area back to Hungary.

The southern part where Maria lived was unaffected, however, so I wasn't able to see Maria. I was in a quandary. If I applied for a visa, my father would find out about our relationship. And if Papa found out, he would have forbidden me to see her again.

And so I confided in my mother whose admonition was crystal-clear: for me, marriage would come much later.

Maria and I wrote to one another occasionally, but we agreed that our situation was hopeless. How could I take responsibility for her without our parents' permission when we lived on opposite sides of an unforgiving border?

At night, Papa took out the gramophone and I reflected discreetly on the words of the song I loved:

The world is here for only one day,
Our lives are here for only one minute,
Tomorrow,
Who knows what we can expect?
Tomorrow,
Who knows where we will wake up?
The world is here for only one day.

Guys don't cry, but I could swear that a tear hit my pillow as I forced myself to sleep that night.

At age 19, I left home with Geza to manage the start-up of his forestry business in Borsa. We rented an office with its own living quarters on Main Street. The pine-log building served its purpose well, and I settled in to my new accommodations. Geza spent a month demonstrating what was expected from me; then he went back to Budapest.

At an elevation of 1,000 feet, Borsa is a town of approximately 4,000 people located at the base of Mount Pietros. The mountain is nearly 8,000 feet high, higher than any other peak in Hungary and Romania. When I laid eyes on the snow-covered peak, I was enthralled by its majesty.

I was a lowland boy who grew up on flat farmland, so the forests and mountains were a challenge for me. The small mountain town was populated with poor, hard-working folks, and I had no doubt that I would be working hard too.

I got up at 4:00 a.m. each morning, poured two deciliters of schnapps — sometimes plum, sometimes apricot brandy — into a flat bottle, and cut off a piece of salt pork or sausage and a half loaf of bread.

Then I set off on my daily walk of four miles and a thousand feet up to a logging area on the mountainside. During the hour-and-a-half walk, I had a couple shots of the schnapps while keeping an eye out for black bear and deer.

I arrived at the site around 6 a.m. to greet the workers who had gathered together to cut timber with large handsaws and axes. Each of the workers had brought refreshments similar to mine. We enjoyed another shot of schnapps and made breakfast, roasting the salt pork and sausages on an open campfire so we could gobble down these tangy treats with some Romanian blended cornmeal.

Then we started work. The forest sang as axes slammed and saws moaned. After I gave instructions to the workers as to what stand of timber to cut, I walked down to the sawmill where I planned out what kind of lumber was to be produced that day. I left instructions with the foreman and sawmill operator and headed back down to the office.

I figured out the amount of cubic feet of lumber and rough beam wood that could be shipped in each of the one or two railroad cars we packed each day. We had time to rest each week, because we didn't work on Saturdays or Sundays. Weekdays were busy, though, and some days I worked to midnight calculating used and available volume in cubic feet.

While I was in Borsa, my father was busy too. He helped two men on the Romanian side of Nagylak who owned businesses in Hungary. They bicycled legally across the border, and my father exchanged money for them and helped them fill out governmental paperwork.

On weekends I enjoyed good hikes during the summertime, and during the winter I indulged in the challenge of skiing the countryside. Because many tourists visited the Borsa area during February, March and April, and because I developed a friendship with the nearby resort's ski lodge manager, a sizable number of vacationing girls from Budapest, Vienna, Berlin and Paris were referred to me for ski instruction.

One of my favorite students was a young sloe-eyed postal worker from Budapest, who had yellowish blonde hair, blue eyes and a body as white as bond paper. She was a city girl of modest means with no athletic aptitude and physique. When she tried to stand up on the ski boards, one ski would cross over the other ski, jamming her feet in an awkward position.

She fell every 20 to 30 feet, but I was always there to help her up. Her beautiful white body became loaded with bruises from the constant falls, and I made it a point to nurse her sore muscles with loving care on a regular basis.

One night, the lodge manager called me to say he did not have any more room in his lodge and wanted to know if I would agree to rent out my guestroom to a couple of well-dressed, jeweled girls from Paris.

Well, it was late at night — 11:00 p.m. — on Monday, my busiest night of the week, when I figure out the weekly payroll. But I said okay.

When the girls came in, they were half frozen. The temperature outside was 12 below zero, and the guestroom had become unbearably cold. So I told the girls they could stay with me in the office where I was working (which was the warmest place), as long as they were quiet and kept the fire going.

The girls made tea for all of us, and I added plenty of rum to keep us warm. The girls were well educated, well traveled and from a well-to-do family. All of us got along well, and they fully enjoyed the hospitality at my cabin. These girls didn't need any ski instruction, and so the three of us enjoyed two glorious weeks skiing together.

In summertime, a different breed of people came to visit. Many of these tourists were out of shape, yet they came to Borsa to hike the mountain.

The view from the sawmill looking out toward the mountain was spectacular. The mountainside was covered in a forest of green pine and at its peak blanketed with brilliant white snow.

Geza, his wife and one of my long-time school friends from Mako visited during the summer and asked me to guide them up the mountain. At 4 a.m., we set off on a vigorous climb to the top of Mount Pietros. When we reached the summit nine hours later, we lay down in the snow to get a little sun.

At 2 p.m., we started to walk down. By the time we reached the storefront office at 9 p.m., we were ravenous. We feasted on a late supper accompanied by a couple of glasses of premium-grade Hungarian wine. Then we went to our rooms and fell fast asleep.

The smooth nature of Geza's visit contrasted sharply with the visit of Tibor, a 40ish, friendly, short, chubby distant relative of mine. Tibor was an engineer and the long-time Sunday substitute for my father at the Nagylak railroad station. His reliability enabled my family to visit Grandma when I was young.

Tibor was excited about climbing up the peak. I picked him up at the railroad station, which was about five miles from my house, in a *fiacre* (a small hackney coach).

We shared a good conversation during the trip on the horse-drawn carriage. We talked about the girls at my hometown and exactly how I would lead him to the snow-covered peak of Mount Pietros.

Once we reached the log cabin, we prepared a gourmet dinner, along with some *Tokaji asszu* wine. At 10:30 p.m., I advised him to go to bed, because we had to awaken at 3 a.m. to start our climb.

"Oh, not yet," he complained. "This wine is too good; we have to drink another bottle."

So we did.

The next morning at 3 a.m., I tried to wake him up. He snored, snorted and when I shook him further, he mumbled incoherently. Well, I figured, we wouldn't be able to climb today, because we must start no later than 4 a.m. to make the trip during daylight. Weather conditions on the mountain frequently were unpredictable, and at night we might not be able to find our way back.

Finally, Tibor awakened at 8 a.m. The routine of mountain life in Hungary was to start the day with a shot of schnapps, so I offered him a shot of apricot brandy as an eye-opener.

After Tibor came to his senses, we washed ourselves in the rapidly running brook in my backyard. The water was guaranteed to wake anyone up, because its temperature never rose over 50 degrees, even on the hottest summer day. After our robust chilly bath, he fully woke up, and we ate breakfast.

After breakfast, I showed him the little mountain village of Borsa and the surrounding area. I took him to the sawmill, and he was amazed at the amount of lumber and long beams we were able to produce. At the mill we used axes to cut and shave raw white-pine timber into precise sizes measuring 4" x 8", 8" x 14" and any other specialty rough-beam size that was needed.

Well, Tibor enjoyed the food, drink and scenery so much that he never woke up early enough to climb to the peak with me. And after five days, he left for home. He enjoyed the view from my backyard, and he said he preferred drinking the apricot brandy and the Tokaji wine to the strain of hiking the mountain anyhow.

The quality of the local food was inspirational. The mountainous pasture's clean aromatic hay and grass gave a superior taste to the milk, cheese and butter. Pastries made with Alpine butter were so scrumptious that each taste whetted my appetite for more.

One of my neighbors was a pastry baker who came from Budapest so that the mountain air could help clear up some lung problems. Using locally produced butter, he baked delicious Napoleons and other tasty pastry, such as cheese Danish, and his shop was always filled with eager customers.

The year 1942 drew to a close and we entered 1943. A new round of ski tourists gave us details about how Hungary had been forced by the Germans to enter World War II and fight the Russians.

I developed a friendship with a guy named Pop, about my size but of slight build, who worked for the Hungarian Forestry Department in an office five houses away. The two of us were hard-drinking guys and became inseparable as we flirted with the girls in town.

Often we would visit the ski lodge and listen to music there. As the band played, the words to one of their songs reminded me of Maria and our days in the Maros River.

I'll only remember the lovely days,
And our first joyful summer,
Two stars shimmer in your eyes,
And today is our night,
The summer arrives on the aged island,

But it does not find us together,
I will think about you when lilacs bloom,
Did you love me, and should I ask?
The early summer revealed your kisses,
I will remember the beauty as long as I live.

In the summer of 1943, I met Ica, who taught the 40 children of grades 1-6 in the local schoolhouse in a picturesque valley surrounded by emerald-green pastures and tall bluish-green pines. Ica was the daughter of a Hungarian woodworking cooper who made first-rate wine barrels, and she was devoted to helping anyone in trouble.

She lived five miles from town, and we ascended the forests in the valley to several waterfalls where we could look out at the view. The water was crystal clear, and we always felt refreshed after we drank of it.

Our walks were idyllic: the sun danced between the tree trunks in the clean air of the sweet-smelling pine forest prompting thoughts of bold adventure. We chased the morning mist while picking alpine horns and wildflowers up and down the dew-soaked pastures, while listening to the bleating of goats' calling one another.

Not too far from the little wooden schoolhouse was the town church. It rested under a small hill, and everyone went there on Sundays when the ringing bell echoed across the valley, calling people to pray.

People who lived in the valley tended sheep, walked the pastures with the cows they tended, cut the timber, and taught their children to aspire to have good character.

Ica and I enjoyed our curious romance because of the uncertain future. As the song went, *What will tomorrow bring?*

We soon found out. *Tomorrow* brought the horror of war, barbarian acts and cruelty of unparalleled nature. Jews were being deported and taken to unknown places.

Ica rescued a couple of Jewish girls who were due to be railroaded to a place called Auschwitz. The two of us led them to a farmer's barn away from prying eyes and supplied them with plenty of food — 300 pounds of barley, salt and flour.

As news came that the Russian army was proceeding toward the Carpathian Mountains in Hungary, I was called into the army. I had been working for Geza for a year and a half; now I had to join the army too.

Although my intentions toward Maria were for us to marry some day, our future — and the future of Hungary — was uncertain. The thorn that constantly throbbed in my side was that at any day, I must join the armed service. Now that day had arrived. I was 21.

Maria and I met for the last time on "Nobody's Island" in the Maros River in July 1943. We knew that it would be difficult to meet again, because Romanian and Hungarian border patrols had become strict and mean. Any violation resulted in death, so we parted with a promise that I would look for her after the war was over. With a heavy heart, I asked her not to wait for me, because ...

Tomorrow,
Who knows what we can expect?
Tomorrow,
Who knows where we will wake up?
The world is here for only one day.

Part II

Chapter 4

FIVE SHOTS IN CEGLED

"Greetings!"

My draft notice was one of thousands in a general mobilization of civilians, and I was ordered to report to the seventh battalion's boot camp at Kecskemét on October 1, 1943.

Weeks ago, the Hungarian Army had suffered huge casualties — 200,000 men were killed at the Don River west of the Volga River. And now I was assigned to an anti-tank gun battalion. I am going to war.

I dutifully traveled by train and reported to the seventh battalion duty officer at Kecskemét, 100 miles southeast of Budapest, where I was told that the gunners were being quartered on private property outside the army barracks.

Kecskemét is a clean rural city with a population of approximately 70,000 people who grow, produce and sell fruit and fruit products to Germany, Austria and Switzerland. One of Hungary's largest distilleries is also located there.

Our commander during boot camp was a lieutenant, and under him was a sergeant. Like everyone else, I was given the rank of private. A quartermaster billeted the 80 men of my unit — one lieutenant, two sergeants, himself and 76 recruits — into three large homes.

Two houses were set aside to give shelter to 20 men each; one house was large enough to hold 40. Our unit's armament was allocated eight 75-millimeter guns, designed for disabling and destroying tanks, but we received only four of them.

The long-barreled guns were supported on one end by two wheels, and it took all the strength of 10 men to turn the gun around and aim it accurately.

Because we were billeted on private property, we were able to mix with the general population, and the people's affection for us was overwhelming. The army regulation canteen that I carried around the city hardly ever saw water, because the citizenry filled it to the brim with the region's abundant wine.

Food was plentiful and delicious, and we topped off the goulash dishes served us during the evening with the wine in our canteens, bolstering our courage for battles yet to be fought. Needless to say, our battalion broke into song at the slightest provocation.

Our exercise field consisted of sandy soil where a farmer planted wheat, but oat seeds from an adjacent parcel of land had invaded his wheat field, turning the harvest into an oat-and-wheat mix. Now nothing remained on the field except sand and patches of malnourished grass.

After breakfast at 6 am, our daily routine consisted of strict rigorous exercise from 7 am to 1 pm, with a break for lunch, followed by weapons instruction classes until 5 pm. After supper was served, we showered and cleaned our personal living area.

Every soldier was issued a folded shovel and gas mask. Many soldiers, however, threw these away later because they regarded the items to be too heavy. In combat, they would regret this decision.

After three weeks of boot camp, we received occasional permits to leave the barracks between 7-9 p.m. Evenings in town were spent flirting with the neighborhood girls, and drinking and singing with the local folk at the numerous bars in town. The joy we felt during these moments was unforgettable, and it buoyed our morale.

One night, one of the recruits and I sneaked out without a permit to patronize a bar where the night before we met a couple of good-looking girls. While sipping my first drink, I looked up and saw a squad of military police march inside.

Anxiously, I looked around for an avenue of escape and noticed there were no screens on the windows of this drinking establishment. I whispered to my fellow recruit, and we dashed to the open windows next to the bathrooms and jumped through them. Oh sure, the police ran after us as fast as they could, but we were in superior physical condition and outran them. For the rest of our training, we stayed in the barracks unless we held a pass in our eager young hands.

We had no drills or classes on Sundays and, after mass, we became bored while lying around the barracks. On one such day, I led a dozen recruits out into the front yard where one of our 75-millimeter guns was positioned. I installed a makeshift conversion mechanism into the giant barrel that would allow us to fire off rifle-sized .22 bullets.

Then I took aim at we called "farmer's birds," scavenging blackbirds that sat on the roof of the hay barn. I brought one down with my first shot. The rest of the recruits got excited and took their turn with the artillery gun-turned-rifle.

It didn't take long before someone suggested that we compete for money. Each man was allowed 20 shots, and the person who killed the most birds won a hastily assembled jackpot of $10. To shoot a "farmer's bird" with a long-barreled gun required superior skill, aim and coordination — and a perfect eye. Our competition was repeated four more times and provided terrific practical experience for combat. Also, it didn't hurt that I won $30 to use as drinking money.

After boot camp, I was transferred 15 miles north to Cegled for four weeks of reserve officer training. The training regimen was tough; we were constantly jumping, climbing, running, practicing hand-to-hand combat and fighting.

Instructors taught us how to kill with a bayonet, use a gas mask and survive in any climate. At the end of these four weeks, I was promoted to sergeant.

Conditions in Hungary grew progressively worse during 1944. On March 19, we received word that Germany had occupied Hungary and was conscripting Hungarian men to fight with them against the Russians.

Germany declared itself to be Hungary's ally, pointing to the land they gave back to Hungary that the Trianon Treaty took away. Meanwhile, B-17s from the United States, known to us as American "liberators," flew over the country and bombarded Budapest and its suburbs. Many innocent civilians were killed and buildings destroyed.

We were concerned about Hungary's future. Many of the soldiers had no doubt that Germany was fighting a losing war. Consequently, we figured that we needed to resist the oncoming German occupation.

As German tanks rolled into Cegled, the colonel who commanded my battalion gave orders to resist "at all costs." Subsequently, we positioned ourselves so we could use the anti-tank gun in front of our barracks in anticipation of the tanks' arrival.

When one of the German tanks revolved its gun turret in our direction, I gave the order to fire. We scored a direct hit, disabling the tank, and the 10 of us who manned the gun disappeared into the civilian population.

The Germans began scouring the city looking for us. We probably would have been caught and executed, but the colonel covered our tracks by transferring us to another battalion at Székesfehérvár, 40 miles southwest of Budapest.

I reported for duty early, but my enthusiasm was jolted. I joined ranks with approximately 1,000 Hungarian soldiers for a field inspection by a high-ranking officer. The officer strode by our group on his high-stepping horse, and the commanding officer of our battalion gave him an informal salute.

The inspecting officer stopped his horse angrily, and shouted a reproach to our commanding officer in full earshot of all the men: "What can I expect from these men when you show such a lackadaisical attitude? What's wrong with you?"

A silence fell across the field, and the inspecting officer repeated his question, "What's wrong with you?"

As our CO's face turned beet red in shame, the officer persisted, "Well?

"Well?

"Well?"

I felt embarrassed for my "CO" and later thought to myself, "Gee, because one officer is ranked higher than another one, that's no reason to publicly humiliate him in front of so many men! If he can talk to my commanding officer like that, what can I expect?"

At the end of August, I was granted four days leave from the service, and I went home to Nagylak to stay with my parents. The first night I was there, my mother desperately asked me not to go back, saying that she would hide me.

I knew I couldn't disappear, because the country's borders were being monitored closely. The military police would search for me, and if I were found, I would be executed. If I were not found, reprisals might be visited upon my family.

When my leave was up, I got onto the train to return to Székesfehérvár. Between Kecskemét and Cegled, our train came to a brake-screeching stop in the middle of a cornfield.

A frantic conductor ran down the aisle, yelling "We're being attacked! Take cover outside!"

A few seconds later, several English and Russian airplanes flew over the train at low altitude, strafing it with machine-gun fire. Everybody screamed in panic and ran out into the field to hide among the dense cornstalks.

As I got up to join the others, a pregnant woman grabbed hold of my arm. "Help me!" she cried. "Save my baby!"

I grabbed hold of her hand and pulled her out the open passenger door, down the steps and across the railroad bed while gunfire rattled behind us in staccato-like fashion.

As soon as the corn plants surrounded us, I set her down on the fertile earth and covered her body with my own. The planes made several more passes, spraying the train with bullets each time they passed over. Finally, they flew away and the shaken group of passengers made its way back to the train.

We counted up the toll, and we considered ourselves extremely lucky: two wounded, nobody killed. The locomotive had been shot up badly though, and we sat around nervously waiting for it to be repaired. A couple of hours later, we were moving again and soon arrived in Cegled, where I had attended training camp — and where I had disabled a German tank.

Once the train stopped, we received some bad news. The railroad tracks to Budapest were damaged by the B-17s, eliminating the possibility of any further rail travel. Other soldiers on the train took the news with a grain of salt, and a lieutenant and another sergeant suggested that I stay at the railroad station with them and play cards.

"Look behind the station," the lieutenant said. "The bunker you see over there is completely bomb-safe."

The invitation was inviting, but I declined. During boot camp, I dated a girl who lived on a side street in Cegled, and the attack by the B-17s on the train had frazzled my nerves. "No thanks," I said. "There's a girl I want to see who lives in the center of town."

I bade them farewell and walked through town looking out for unfriendly Germans. I found her house and knocked on the door. No one answered.

Since I had become buddy-buddy with the owner of a bar near where she lived, I figured I could enjoy a couple of drinks while waiting for her.

As I sipped on my first drink, the town's air raid sirens began to wail and echo through the streets to announce a pending bombing attack. I was disgusted, angry and too nervous to care anymore. More B-17s were bombing Hungary!

"Let's go down to the cellar," the bar owner offered. "There's lots to drink down there!"

"Lead the way!" I replied.

And so the two of us climbed down into the bar's cellar, and I drank five more full-sized shots of cognac while the B-17s bombed. The thunderous sound of constant explosions never seemed to end.

Finally, the explosions stopped and we pondered what was going on in the world outside until we couldn't stand the suspense any longer. We staggered to our feet and flung open the cellar door. Through our intoxicated eyes, we gazed at what looked like the end of the world.

Choking black smoke enveloped us. Was this Cegled or Pompeii after Mount Vesuvius erupted? My watch said it was 2:00 p.m., but the world had turned dark! Looking back at the railroad station, the blackness turned sullen red. Around us, buildings were burning, and crackling red flames licked at their collapsing structures.

At least 100 B-17 bombers took part in the raid. The railroad station, the rails, the train and several buildings, including apartment buildings near the station, were barely recognizable.

A cacophony of sirens from fire trucks and ambulances screamed about the city. I left my impromptu bomb shelter, and I rushed forward to join the emergency vehicles at the railroad station. Once there, I waved down one of the ambulances and directed it to the bunker where the lieutenant and sergeant invited me to play cards.

I ran toward the door and instead found a large crater. My drunkenness kept me from fainting.

Eighty dead bodies were strewn haphazardly all over the crater. I immediately recognized the lieutenant's face, and I gagged when I saw that his stomach had been blown apart.

Blood and body parts were scattered around the bunker. We heard moaning and screaming underneath the bodies, and we lifted them up to discover a few people still alive mingled with body parts from the dead.

Someone handed a stretcher down to us, and we took turns lifting up the injured men, women and children into the ambulance so they could be rushed to the hospital.

A "chain bomb," consisting of approximately 10 bombs chained together, had tumbled its way thousands of feet onto the top of the "bomb-proof" bunker. If I hadn't gone to see the girl I once dated, and if I hadn't decided to enjoy six shots of cognac after she didn't answer the door, I would have been in the bunker!

I dropped to my knees, clasped my two hands together, looked heavenward and murmured, "Thank you, God," with no regard for who could hear me.

Chapter 5

THE RING OF FEAR

In the fall of 1944, the handwriting was on the wall; Germany had lost the war.

Two independent-minded groups of Hungarians made separate serious efforts to win peace for their country. In late September, some high-ranking military officers and political leaders went to Moscow to make a peace with the Russians and on Oct. 11 reached a similar agreement to the one that Romania successfully brokered earlier.

In retaliation, the Germans kidnapped the son of Hungarian governor Miklos Horthy and threatened to kill him unless Horthy complied with Hitler's commands. Hitler then placed Ferenc Szálasi, a devoted Nazi, into a decision-making position in the Hungarian cabinet, who vetoed the Hungarian-Russian pact.

An era of deportations and chaos thus began. And the stupid war went on.

Members of Szálasi's Arrow-Cross Party began collecting Jews and transporting them to Auschwitz and other concentration camps. One month later, Horthy and his family were arrested and sent to Germany.

Meanwhile, Russian troops approached the Carpathian Mountains, occupied Romania and started their offensive against Hungary.

Fear of communism and the unknown horrors it would bring soon supplemented Hungarian revulsion of the Germans' master-race policies. Stories were told of how Russian soldiers were fanatical drunks and barbarians. Whispers were uttered of how they stole watches and jewelry, and how they raped teenagers and old women.

We heard warnings that the Russians collected men in good health and transported them to forced labor camps. All sorts of rumors were flying around, and we began to think that our new enemy would be worse than the old one.

In November, my battalion was ordered to the Hungarian front to defend Budapest from the Russian invaders. In effect, we had been chosen to replace the blood spilled by 200,000 soldiers now washing down the Don River.

We knew that any defense against the Soviet Union would be a hopeless maneuver. A small country with a population of 10 million and an army of 500,000 could not stop a well-equipped Russian army of 20 million soldiers.

Nevertheless, we followed orders and marched to Csepel Island, a 25-mile-long elevated prairie in the middle of the Danube River, where the Russians were advancing toward Budapest from the south.

Our orders were to fight the Russians and keep them from getting through, and I was honor-bound to look after my men and disable as many tanks as possible. Our company comprised four anti-tank guns and 40 men, and 10 men were assigned to each gun. I instructed my men, "Shoot until you can't shoot any more! Then disappear!"

The advancing Russians didn't allow time for any further strategy. After all, this was the warfront! On the morning of our third day there, we heard a rumbling noise; then the ground began to vibrate. We looked up aghast to see at least 50 Russian T-34 tanks roaring toward us.

I said a brief prayer for help. Then I asked God to turn His eyes from what we were getting ready to do.

The blast from each of our guns shook the earth violently. The shells fired by the tanks whizzed by all sides of us and overwhelmed our eardrums. The smell of smoke, oil, burning flesh and airborne earth irritated our eyes and nostrils.

Miraculously, our guns crippled 20 tanks. My gun picked off nine of them, and the rest of the guys managed to get 11. There was no time to celebrate, though.

The remaining 30-plus tanks of the Soviet blitz outflanked us on the left side and were wheeling through the breach in our perimeter. Next to our gun's "shooting trench" — a ditch dug for soldiers to hide below ground level — nine soldiers and I had prepared an underground bunker measuring 5 feet by 10 feet, which we topped with a layer of tree branches and covered with dirt. A three-foot piece of pipe protruded through the tree limbs and dirt to serve as an air hole.

One of the crews of the Russian tanks recognized the shooting trench and tried to crush us by running the tank's treads across the trench. Seven of our men ran off as I had instructed. The remaining three crawled unobserved from the trench into the underground bunker, where we huddled together in the pitch-black hiding place next to the pipe.

We stayed put until the telltale rumbling of the tanks and the sounds of feet above us gradually disappeared. As soon as we thought the coast was clear, the three of us scrambled out of our self-imposed confinement, and ran toward the riverbank in a crouching position. Although we were coated with mud and dirt, we were alive.

No moonlight shone that night, so the nighttime swallowed us up as we retreated two miles along the riverbank toward the Hungarian side of the front. The tanks had already moved ahead toward Budapest, and the remaining Hungarian troops had re-formed a new front against the Russian soldiers.

Once safe, I counted up the casualty list. Ten of my soldiers had waved a white flag and surrendered. Another 27 of the men were either killed or captured elsewhere. The three of us were the only ones from our company to escape.

Our anti-tank guns were now held by the Russians, so in late November, I was transferred to infantry duty in a different battalion. My mission: to protect Budapest's radio tower located 20 miles east of downtown by digging a succession of shooting ditches and manning them.

Across from my unit on the other side of the front was a group of 600-800 Russian foot soldiers, mostly Mongolians. All day long, we heard them drinking, laughing, cursing and yelling insults. Then it would grow quiet the next day, and the day after that a small group would mount a surprise attack. Because of the ditches and our position, we had achieved a stalemate.

In the company of these Mongolians was a Russian sharpshooter who constantly evaded us in a deadly game of cat and mouse. Several men from other companies had been shot and wounded by this sniper, and the men in my company were engaged in a battle of nerves with him.

One soldier in my company showed telltale signs of fear. He was a husky fellow and didn't speak much, but his eyes darted around continuously. As the 10 of us crouched down in the ditch, he became animated and started to shake nervously. At first, I tried to comfort him without success; then I got angry and told him to get hold of himself.

I observed the rest of my men carefully, because I could see that his fear was spreading to some of them. He began to whimper and cry, and craned his head upward. I whispered desperately to him, "Get a hold of yourself! And keep your head inside the goddamned ditch!"

He didn't listen.

He poked his head a few inches above the top of the ditch, and as I reached up toward his shoulder to pull him back down, I heard the crack of a nearby rifle. The sickening sound of a bullet penetrated his skull, and he slumped backward face up. One shot, and he was dead!

The next day, I led the men in a short prayer for our loss. Then I preached, "Whenever you feel fear, shut down your mind and rely on your instinct. Fear will kill you; instinct will save you."

From then on, every man in my company took care to avoid fear. None of us slept well, and our bloodshot eyes betrayed a growing level of exhaustion.

For the next three nights, one of our men — a poet named Maté who was tall, of medium build, about 5'7" tall and no mustache — took out some writing paper from his canvas food holder and scribbled furiously. As soon as his eyes filled with satisfaction, we leaned forward so that he could read aloud.

Some of his poems were funny; some were serious. A number of the men sat in rapt attention to his words as he read about battles won and lost. Some of us were able to relax at the sound of his reassuring voice and closed our eyes.

What was it about his work that we revered so much? Perhaps we imagined a symphony created by one of several famous Hungarian composers: Franz Liszt, Bela Bartok or Franz Schubert.

As Hungarians, we did revere art. We did revere great writing. And especially during these lonely uncertain times in the November cold, we loved to hear about great battles, fine wine and beautiful women.

For two days, Maté's poetry readings were accompanied by a steady, heavy rain. The shooting ditch, which we had created, contained a foot of bone-chilling cold water. We moved around as much as possible to prevent our legs from growing numb, but we had to stay inside the ditch.

On the morning of the fourth day, 600 Russians rose up in unison and ran toward us in a screaming horde. Our submachine gunner, whose position was to our left, killed half of them directly in front of me.

Some of the Russians had automatic rifles and were firing indiscriminately as they ran in our direction. The number of attacking soldiers was so great that some of the Mongolians managed to leap into our ditch.

None of us had bayonets, but we managed to shoot a few of them and then push them out of the trench. As our submachine gunner sprayed more bullets, the survivors ran back to their original position.

With the battle temporarily over, I noticed that 10 of our guys had been captured and were being led away toward a bushy area. One familiar shape caught the eye: our poet, Maté!

"They've got Maté!" I yelled. "Let's free him!"

Six of us jumped from the trench, and rushed the soldiers. The captured Hungarian soldiers saw us advance toward them, and they broke free from their guards and ran back toward us.

The two Russians holding Maté wouldn't let him go, however. They wrapped their arms around him and started to run. One of my soldiers kneeled, aimed, shot and killed one of the Russians. As soon as his comrade fell, the remaining Mongolian released Maté and fled.

Our rescue of Maté inspired him to recover the food canvass bag containing his poetry. We hugged one another and Maté, too! "He's back!" we cried in glee. We shared a marvelous moment of kinship on the battlefield of carnage around us.

As we looked to see who was alive and dead, we discovered a Russian who had been wounded in the onslaught. We covered his wounds with first-aid bandages and notified the Red Cross to take him away.

The remaining Russian soldiers were not able to initiate another offensive, because they had taken too many casualties. While we resumed our positions in the trenches, they dug in.

That night we heard them getting drunk on vodka and denatured alcohol. Our guns had taken a heavy toll on them.

After standing for days in more than a foot of icy rainwater, we were ordered to retreat from the coldest, most relentless bath that any of us ever wanted to endure again. The commander thanked us for our successful stand and told us we were being replaced.

We marched north for eight miles and arrived at Csepel, the island's namesake town that served as headquarters for Hungary's steel industry. A middle school served as a makeshift barracks, and we gratefully washed up with hot water to remove the one-inch-thick caked mud from our legs.

A bath and change of uniform refreshed us. In recognition of our bravery, we attended a USO-type show at the school held in our honor that featured Zita Szelecki, a popular, tall, good-looking woman with a soothing, soft voice, who sang patriotic tunes accompanied by an accordion and a violin.

On December 5, I was transferred to a company approximately 30 miles north of Budapest. My mission: to train new recruits to defend a new warfront being set up there. I was given a three-week deadline to accomplish this mission.

Another sergeant was assigned to assist me with the training along with a complement of 20 war-experienced soldiers. Then we found out who we were going to train: 400 boys ranging in age from 15 to 19 years old who had fled westward from the city of Marosvasarhely in Transylvania seeking refugee status.

The boys had nothing to eat and nowhere to sleep. They joined the army in a fit of panic and, in order to save themselves, had told the recruiters they were willing to fight.

When I looked at their fresh, scared faces, I knew that most of them would die when the Russians attacked. Their mission was virtually suicidal.

One boy who had volunteered to fight the Russians was 14 years old. I looked at him, and asked, "Why are you here, boy?"

He stuck out his chest and declared, "To kill Russians, Sir."

"Oh really? And how old are you, boy?"

"14!" he bragged.

"You have no business being here," I said. "Go home to your mother!"

I looked over the remaining 400 students. Those I believed to be weak or uncoordinated I sent home and told them to vanish.

Then I asked myself, "Am I supposed to deceive these boys into believing their anger could vanquish an overpowering, well-equipped army?" My conscience told me one thing; my sense of duty told me another. I decided to compromise.

I taught the boys how to handle a gun, how to dig a hole big enough to hide in, how to lie flat to protect their bodies from enemy bullets and how to survive.

Louis, the other sergeant who helped me to train these boys, was a short, chubby, Old World roly-poly version of a "couch potato," six years older than me. Before being caught up in the war as an army reservist, Louis had been teaching middle school in Győr, on the western side of Hungary. We shared good times together, and he was a good conversationalist.

One afternoon, his wife, Edith, brought him some food and invited me to join the two of them. She set out a lunch of Hungarian sausage, roast pork and lots and lots of pastries. She also brought a bottle of good Hungarian wine. We enjoyed a polite conversation as we plowed through the feast in front of us.

After filling our stomachs, Edith poured some additional wine into each glass, raised her glass and spoke. "Paul, I love my Louis. He's everything to me. Will you promise me one thing?"

"Oh sure," I laughed. "This meal has been splendid," not realizing how serious she was.

She gazed directly into my eyes, and begged, "Would you make sure that my Louis is able to return to me? He's not a tough guy, you know."

I looked at her, stared at Louis, thought about the consequences of such a promise, and said, "Your Louis will be okay with me."

"Thank you," she replied, and drank the contents of her glass.

I smiled at Louis, and we raised our glasses and followed suit. Edith returned home, and Louis and I went back to work.

Three days before Christmas, we were given half a day off to celebrate the coming holiday, beginning at noon. I thought about my cousin, Geza, who lived in Buda, the hilly section of Budapest, with his wife, Baba, and infant son. Szentendre was only 20 miles north from Budapest, and I figured I could get there and back before midnight.

The war had shut down the delivery of Christmas trees into the city, and I saw some young pine trees in a nearby field. "Hey, those would make perfect Christmas trees," I thought.

I grabbed an axe from a supply shed and selected a beautiful, nicely grown tree six feet tall. I chopped it down and tied a rope around the branches to narrow its circumference.

I caught the train and supported the tree against the wall until I reached the Budapest station 20 miles away. I knew the railroad station well (having been to Budapest more than 20 times), and ran onto a crowded Hungarian streetcar, where a stern-faced conductor approached me shaking his head back and forth.

"You can't carry *that* onto the trolley," he admonished.

"You've got to be kidding," I said, raising my voice. "I'm back from the front where I have been killing Russians trying to invade Budapest, and you're telling me that I can't carry the spirit of Christmas with me?"

The people in the streetcar glared an accusing look at the conductor, who coughed, turned bright red, and muttered something inaudible as he turned away.

When I got to their house, Geza and Baba were astonished to see me. No one had any report of my whereabouts during the last three months, because I was at the front. My parents in Nagylak did not know where I was or even if I was alive.

Geza quickly caught me up on the latest news concerning our family: Nagylak, the wonderful little town where I grew up, had been occupied by the Russian army two months ago! He told me how the war had been going throughout Hungary, and how each day became more difficult and brutal. The downtown area of Budapest had been bombed by the B-17s. Buildings had collapsed, crushing those trapped inside.

Bombs and tanks had killed children, doctors, nurses and patients inside the city's hospitals. Thousands of Budapest citizens lay dead. Food and water was scarce, although there was still plenty of wine and liquor. Eggs and meat were nonexistent. Food shortages existed. Small bakeries could not get flour to make bread. Stores had been emptied and were not being re-supplied. Food could be obtained, but only on the black market in exchange for jewelry or clothing. For those unfortunate people who were sick or wounded, there was no medicine. The future looked bleak.

I listened to Geza's horror stories for half an hour. All of a sudden, Baba said, "Geza, look what Paul has brought us!"

In the corner of the living room was the Christmas tree I had brought from Szentendre. Geza jumped up excitedly, recognized the affection embodied in pine, and said, "Let's have Christmas."

Geza and Baba improvised a meager Christmas dinner for the three of us. After we finished eating, Geza disappeared into the basement and brought out a bottle of *6 puttonos Tokaji asszu*, the king of the Hungarian wines.

After midnight, I caught the last train to Szentendre, and I rejoined my company at 2 in the morning. Waiting for me were three written orders: 1) that I had been promoted to the rank of officer, 2) that the boys sent to me for training were to leave with the commander on Christmas Day at 5 a.m. and 3) to move supplies of food and ammunition from the base.

Of the original 400 boys, about 350 remained. Once dawn broke, the boys responded quickly and alertly to my men's orders. We began to evacuate food and ammunition from the base, and the boys pitched in eagerly.

I organized a plan to fully load six trucks, and the men put it into action. The boys located all the food and ammunition, and the soldiers positioned the cargo and supervised its loading.

Before the boys left on Christmas morning, only two trucks remained to be loaded. The holiday seemed like a good choice, because the Russians surrounding Budapest would be sleeping soundly after eating heartily on Christmas Eve.

The boys marched northward with the battalion commander as the rest of us stayed to finish loading the last two trucks. Finally, at 5 a.m. the next day, the last truck was loaded and driven away. Our mission was complete, and it was time to evacuate.

The morning was cold and clear, and the soldiers and I spent the morning gathering tins of food and supplies. The sound of exploding armament shells grew closer, and I released the men.

Louis and I searched through the main brick building for some civilian clothes that would fit us, while the rest of my men grabbed cans of food and dumped them into their backpacks. Everything had grown quiet, which made us hurry even faster.

All of a sudden, we heard shouting, and we looked out the window. The army engineers in the building next to us — 150 men — had been captured.

We ran down to the basement of the brick building and began to climb out the windows, thinking that we might escape by the banks of the Danube River. A hail of bullets greeted us, and we pulled back inside.

We looked out the front windows, and to our dismay saw a troop of soldiers wearing Russian army uniforms holding over 100 prisoners. One of my men put a white shirt on top of his rifle butt. He walked out the door waving the universal flag of surrender to and fro, and the rest of us Hungarians followed behind him with our hands in the air.

Chapter 6

THE BIG LIE

Two guards ran to both sides of the doorway to monitor those of us trapped inside. One of them motioned for us to exit the barracks and stand in the middle of the road. The other guard detected the newly placed gold ensign star on the neck of my coat, and yelled, "Officer!"

The guard pulled a gun from his holster and pointed it at me as his steely eyes revealed his intention to use it. I gulped, closed my eyes and yelled, "No!"

Instead of the loud report I was expecting, I heard a commotion and opened my eyes. Behind the guard, a Russian captain appeared, grabbed the guard's firing hand and barked, "Do not shoot him!"

I was rescued in less time than it takes for a soldier to squeeze a hair trigger.

"Come with us," the other guard said, and used his rifle butt to motion me to move quickly. The captain walked into the Hungarian army office, I stumbled in behind him and the two guards followed me with their guns drawn.

The captain sat in a straight-back chair. I stepped forward, stopped in front of him and waited.

"Where is your battalion?" the captain asked.

"I don't know," I replied. "They just left us here."

The captain frowned and thought for a moment, then looked at me carefully. "How do you feel about being left behind?" he asked.

I thought quickly and responded, "Like a good soldier."

The captain got up from his chair. "Your interrogation is finished." I sighed silently in relief, knowing that this interview could have been a lot worse.

I was led outside and fell into formation with the other war prisoners who had been assembled in a long line of five-man rows. Russian soldiers moved into position to the left of our five-man rows, to the right, ahead of us and the rest fell in behind us.

"Forward, march!" a guard behind us yelled, and the entire group proceeded due south.

I looked around and began to count the number of rows. I figured we had a total of thirty rows, with five men apiece, or 150 Hungarian prisoners. The captain who interviewed me had disappeared, and 16 Russian soldiers guarded us.

We continued marching southwest of Szentendre where I had been captured, through the town of Pilisvörösvár. Once we reached the Pilis hills, we witnessed an eerie sight. On top of a small hill, 20 Russian soldiers had captured a dozen German soldiers wearing the SS insignias of the Gestapo on their collars. The Russians had lined up the Germans next to one another.

In front of the Germans, a five-man Russian squad knelt and aimed their rifles at the Germans. All of us stared, and then we heard a command shouted.

The five guns fired almost in unison.

The prisoners collapsed against one another. Our faces turned back to the road aghast. When fighting men surrender, they are not supposed to be executed, I thought. What was going on? Isn't God the referee of life and death?

Our procession moved drearily onward. Our faces were drawn and distressed. Our boots dragged across the ground instead of the high-stepping cadence with which we started.

As we walked on and on into the cold night, one question gnawed at me like a bloodthirsty rat: "Were we next?"

About 9 p.m., the Russians stopped our march in a little valley and ordered us into a large ditch. On top of the ditch, all 16 Russian soldiers aimed their guns at us. We huddled close together in fear.

Then one of them spoke. "This is where we sleep tonight. No one is allowed to leave this area. If you need to pee or shit, do it where you stand. Tomorrow morning we will go farther."

The Russians lowered their weapons and proceeded to open their backpacks. One of them glared at us, issuing a silent command not to make eye contact as they ate from their ration bags and drank from their canteens.

Our stomachs complained from the vigorous march and lack of food. Fortunately, we had been allowed to drink from animal troughs we passed along the way.

Before midnight under a bright full moon, one of the prisoners blew a plaintiff German melody into his harmonica, "Everything will vanish away sometime; every December results in a new May." As the haunting song filled the clear, cold air, one of the guards stormed down into the ditch and confiscated the harmonica.

Was this our fate then? Was this ditch to become our final resting place? Some of the men in my company knelt and prayed. We huddled close to one another to fight the cold and slipped into a restless sleep.

Dawn broke through clear skies, and at 7 a.m., the guards called us from atop the hill, and we resumed our formation of five men in continuous rows. Then we marched southward through the hilly countryside until we came to a clearing. "Stop!" one of the guards commanded.

As we stood in formation, the guards descended upon us row by row, looting whatever personal possessions they could find, including watches, cameras and rings. Married men who saw the commotion ahead tried to hide their wedding rings inside their clothing or anywhere else they could think of.

My watch was gone; now I would have to tell time by the position of the sun in the sky. Some of the guards paraded about us, profanely displaying five wristwatches on each hand.

The guards ordered us to resume marching, and we walked all day. When nightfall came, we arrived at an old farm building where each prisoner was given seven ounces of bread and told to sleep in the barn. The hay felt warm and reassuring, and we rested comfortably.

The next morning, we were given another seven ounces of bread and a teaspoon of sugar with hot tea. We munched on the bread, drank the tea and continued our southward march along the Danube River.

We marched all day west of the Danube River for about 25 miles. Other prisoners passed the word that the bridges crossing the Danube had been destroyed. When night fell, we stayed in another barn, and we were given some more bread and tea. As our fellow prisoners fell asleep, I sat next to Louis and devised a plan of escape.

Behind the barn where we were supposed to sleep, I had spotted a much smaller barn measuring 15 feet by 10 feet.

Being a farm boy, I recognized the sloping 6-foot-tall structure as a pig barn. Under cover of night, Louis and I slipped past the guards and got inside the pig barn. Fortunately, no pigs remained inside to squeal and disclose our whereabouts.

We hid in a corner of the piggery, and planned to disappear into the nearby small village after the other prisoners marched away the next morning. However, during the next morning's count of prisoners, the guards figured out that we were missing.

A thorough search of the farmyard and adjacent buildings began, and the guards found us cowering under a meager amount of straw. As we stood up with our hands in the air, the guards took turns hitting us with their gunstocks. Then they ordered us outside to join our place in the line of five-man rows. We nursed our bruised muscles during the day's long march and considered ourselves lucky that the guards did not kill us.

Our daily routine of marches continued until the second day of January 1945, when we arrived late at night at Baja, a major Hungarian city on the Danube River approximately 80 miles south of Szentendre.

We were ordered into a school building, which had been converted into a prisoner-of-war camp by a ring of barbed wire. We investigated our new surroundings and were given our first hot meal: a putrid bean soup.

Some of us kept our army rations cans, and we were able to use those to hold the soup. However, some prisoners had to borrow a container from someone else. Because our eating utensils had been confiscated, we were forced to drink the soup direct from the can.

The building was crammed beyond capacity and contained about 10,000 military and civilian prisoners. The heat had been turned off, and everyone slept on the bare floors in freezing temperatures. In addition, water was scarce.

Typhus and cholera were constant companions among the prisoners, some of whom had been held here for a few months. Medication and doctors were non-existent. The severity of stomach typhus was so acute that 50-60 people died each day.

To prevent the scourge of further disease, each morning the prisoners carted out dead bodies and threw them into a long six-feet-deep trench, which was then covered with slaked lime.

No funerals were held; no records were kept. The only thing certain was the daily sorry transport of lifeless emaciated bodies to a mass grave.

We became infested with ticks and woke up in the mornings covered with hordes of blood-sucking lice. If I had not seen it with my own eyes, I could never believe that cholera and stomach typhus could cause healthy young men to die within three to four weeks.

We grew weaker, and many of the men could hardly walk. During the day, guards would enter the main rooms of the school building and throw any men who could not stand into separate rooms with similarly afflicted prisoners.

One day, I opened the door to one of these vile-smelling rooms. The men inside lay moaning on the floor covered in urine and excrement. Some appeared to be half-dead; the stench of death permeated the air.

I pulled back in revulsion and closed the door as tight as my hands would allow. I thought that my head would explode. I imagined myself as the next victim to die in this place, an abomination to all mankind. These are the ones whose relatives would be told that their loved ones had vanished.

I committed myself to ridding myself of disease. My stomach was running like the others, and the first symptom — diarrhea — of typhus had begun to afflict me.

First, I spent all day killing the bedbugs that infested my clothes. Then, I put myself on a diet of nothing except charred bread. When I was a child, my grandmother and my parents had shown me a home remedy for diarrhea: toasting bread to the point where it becomes charred and turns black. They had taught me that blackened bread serves as a binding agent.

The guards had removed all the knives, so all we had left were forks and spoons. I constructed a homemade knife, took a few branches from one of the trees, tied them together and cooked a piece of bread over an open fire until the bread turned black.

I stopped drinking untreated water unless it had been boiled to make tea. This required every ounce of willpower that I could muster, because my thirst was never-ending. Nevertheless, I forced myself to be strong-willed, and I got well.

Before the sun came up on the first day of February, the Russian guards ran inside the barracks to awaken us and ordered us to move out. They assembled 9,000 of us into five-man rows and marched us to the railroad station where a train was waiting.

"Where are we going?" I asked one of the guards.

"To Temesvár (in southern Romania)," the Russian said.

"What?" I pressed him. "Why are we being sent there?"

"We have set up a command center for prisoners," he said. "Once you arrive, you will be given a paper to go home. Or you can join the new Hungarian army so you can help us fight the Germans. Don't worry! You will get your documents."

"This doesn't make sense," I protested. The guard pointed his rifle at me menacingly, and I looked away.

Many of the Hungarians, especially other farm boys, believed the Russians. I looked at Louis and told him, "This is a mistake. We can't get on this train!"

A young guy standing next to us overheard me and said, "Relax! We are getting out of this hellhole. Our detention is finally going to end. Once we get our papers at Temesvár, we will be free!"

"What the hell are you thinking?" I said. "Do you think that we're being removed from Hungary and sent to Romania so that we can receive papers? That's ridiculous!

"If they were going to give us papers, they would give them to us here in Hungary! Once we move east, we will keep going! This is a big lie!"

The Russians took all day to fill the railroad wagons. We had been limited to one meal all day — bean soup and bread. Freight cars, usually reserved for cargo or horses, were designed to accommodate 12 horses or 30 men. Nevertheless, the Russians squeezed 60 of us into each car.

Toilet facilities were makeshift. A 6-inch circle was cut into the floor of each freight car for prisoners to use to relieve themselves. Those who were unlucky enough to sit close to the hole had to endure the constant odor.

In our freight car, the hole had yet to be cut. One of the prisoners suffered from typhus and diarrhea, so he placed the hardhat he had been wearing upside down and went to the bathroom in it. We yelled frantically for one of the guards to help us. When we finally got someone's attention, he gave us some tools and we were finally able to cut a hole in the railway car, and the contents of the hardhat were thrown out.

We began cutting a circular hole frantically until the guard demanded his tools. He locked the door from the outside, and our train left the Baja station in the gloom of early evening. Most of the circle had been cut out, and a prisoner began using a spoon that he had taken from the school as a cutting tool.

We took turns using the spoon as a miniature spade until we broke through the remaining section of the circle. The wood finally gave way and fell with the spoon to the railroad bed whizzing away below. We breathed a contaminated sigh of relief, and the helmet's contents were emptied through the hole.

Everyone was tired and exhausted. Because we were squeezed together tightly, we had to improvise new positions in which to sit so the remaining prisoners could join us.

One man accidentally sat on the hand of the prisoner next to him. People started yelling and swearing at each other. "Dammit, don't lie on me!"

"Hey, stop pushing!"

"If you don't back away, I'll knock the shit out of you!"

We were cranky, miserable and impatient with one another. Space was at a premium while we were scrunched together. At least, we did not feel so cold.

Nevertheless, we were weak and tried to sleep. But the air was heavy and foul, and sleep that night on the constantly shifting freight car was a rare commodity.

As light seeped through the railroad car on a cloudy cold morning, we arrived in Temesvár, an agricultural, textile and tractor-manufacturing city in Romania with a population of approximately 60,000. The train stopped inside the railroad station, and we heard the guards opening up the cars ahead of ours and ordering the occupants to move.

Once the doors of our car were opened, we helped each other down and formed another line of five-man rows. We marched for two miles under the guards' close scrutiny, until we arrived at a massive barracks-style camp. The gates swung open to allow us entry, and a sense of dread overcame us as we began to talk to the prisoners held here.

I was right! The Russians lied to us! This camp had been specially built six months ago to serve as a holding facility for transport to the Soviet Union.

An old Romanian army two-story barracks stood in back of a massive expansion of hastily constructed one-story, wooden-barracks buildings, all surrounded by a barbed-wire fence.

I looked around at the number of people and my mind boggled as I began to make calculations. This facility was so big, yet so crowded, that it housed approximately 25,000 prisoners!

The Russians did not have enough railroad cars to transport all its war prisoners to the USSR or Siberia, so they were keeping us captive by building a holding camp and housing us here.

Conditions in Temesvár were horrid. Because February marked the beginning of the snowmelt in this part of Europe, the ground around us was turning into mud. Typhus, sickness and bugs became constant companions.

The toilets for these barracks consisted of nothing more than a ditch. Some of the ditches were rectangular; others were circular. The one closest to where I slept was 10 feet long and six feet wide.

A massive platform was built around each side of the ditch extending several feet above and one foot beyond the edge of the ditch. Wooden planks were nailed into place upon this one-foot-wide platform.

We were supposed to take a shit by squatting and balancing ourselves on these wooden planks. Not only is this routine humiliating, it's physically demanding. After being in this position for any length of time, the act of standing up is quite difficult.

Anyway, the fifth day in the Temesvár camp was like the fourth, and the third, and the second, until the commotion started.

Vile. Unthinkable. Unforgivable. My baptism to absolute horror began at mid-afternoon. The sky was cloudy, the wind was gusting unpredictably and the temperature was dropping rapidly. Voices of panic filled the air.

I looked around toward an older man in his late 40s and asked, "What's going on?"

"It's terrible," he said. And then he broke into tears.

I walked toward the direction of most of the noise and stopped another man, who couldn't speak either. Grown men were wringing their hands in desperation or hopelessness.

Finally, someone was able to tell me what had just happened. Cholera and typhus weaken the body, because whatever water is supposed to be present is lost to the never-ending diarrhea. Victims become dehydrated, and normal everyday tasks that are taken for granted become risky. The Russian-built toilets were a deadly reminder of this fact of life.

A weakened, overweight prisoner had perched on one of the planks to do "his business." Next to him was another man. The overweight man finished, and leaned on the able-bodied man for support to get up.

When the overweight prisoner began to rise, he leaned out his hand and missed the other guy. Finding nothing but air, he lost his balance, toppled backward and fell into the latrine. The amount of excrement in the ditch was at least 10 feet deep, and he sank into the shit as if it were quicksand.

As soon as I heard this, I slumped down with my face in my hands. Is this what they meant when someone was officially "missing"?

The horror from this tragedy didn't end here. Three days later when they pumped out the ditch, only the man's bones remained. The worms inside the excrement had eaten all his flesh during those three days.

Which was the biggest lie? The story told to us Hungarians that we were going to be given papers and set free? Or was it the way "vanished" was used to describe the end of a prisoner's life when he became so sick that he drowned in a pool of shit?

I spent a month and a half in this dreadful place, and at least a dozen men died while performing one of the most basic functions of the human body.

The death rate caused by the cholera and typhus rose to a peak of 70 people a day, and untreated water was banned. Each day, bodies were picked up and moved to a mass grave.

The grave was excavated in the form of another big ditch with a long channel. Chlorine and calcium hydroxide were spread upon it for sanitary reasons. And once a week, dirt was spread over the decaying bodies.

For those who died, no remembrances in the form of written records were permitted. Each man was given a number, and that number was his only identity. When prisoners "vanished," they were thrown into a mass grave to be remembered as "unknown."

Many nights when I tried to sleep, I stared into the eyes of an imaginary victim as he sank into that disgusting quicksand. Even when I awoke, the images from these real nightmares haunted me.

Because of the typhus, water was not allowed in the camp unless it was boiled. This created a shortage of water, and few of the men considered using any of their water rations to see to personal hygiene. Consequently, bedbugs, ticks and lice infested most of the prisoners' bodies.

Well, I needed to protect myself. After I stood in line and picked up my daily breakfast, I made a makeshift "sponge" by tearing off a piece of my shirt.

Our daily breakfast consisted of a liter of tea, seven ounces of bread, and two teaspoons of sugar. I applied half of the liter to my sponge and used it to clean my body. I could manage a complete bath with a half-liter of tea; I used the other half for drink.

In the camp was an area where visitors were permitted to approach the barbed-wire fence and ask the prisoners about loved ones. On rare occasions, family members were able to manage a reunion, and stories of such fortune gave us hope.

I gave my name and father's address to one such visitor so my parents could learn that I had survived the war and was living in the Temesvár prisoner-of-war camp. On Sundays, a crowd of about 20,000 people milled about the fence frantically looking for relatives, and the atmosphere among the visitors was chaotic and grim.

As March came and went, the food began to improve some. The bean soup was made with rice, barley and low-quality bran normally fed to the pigs. The horrors we experienced earlier began to ease, because of the extraordinary measures we had discovered to protect ourselves.

In early April, a few days before Easter, the guards told us to get ready for a "big trip." This was a moment I had feared, because all the stories I heard involved camps in Siberia.

The Russians were close-mouthed and secretive. The guards told us the same kind of story that we heard in Baja; they were going to get us documents and identification. I was unsure what could be worse: Siberia or another "holding camp."

The following morning, the guards lined us up to be inspected by a Russian doctor. A heavy-set Russian woman appeared, whose facial jowls enhanced her grotesque posture. Everyone undressed and stood naked.

Each of us stopped with our back to her, where she reached out to pinch the meaty skin of the buttocks. Upon pinching the skin, she pulled the skin outward and then released it.

I stood my place in line and finally assumed the position to be inspected. I felt her rough hands pull the skin back, then release it. My skin had sprung back to its original position, and I was declared "acceptable for transport."

Those weakened men whose skin formed a pocket remained at the camp. The looks in their forlorn faces showed they understood the nature of their fate.

After the inspection, I dressed while two guards frisked me to see what they could find. I had already lost my watch, my knife and my razor. My only remaining possession was an improvised razor knife.

One of the guards found it and took it away with glee. "Grow a beard!" he taunted.

On this morning, we had been denied our usual breakfast before the medical inspection. Finally, we were given a last breakfast of watery bean soup and seven ounces of bread.

The guards instructed us to form the familiar five-man rows. Then we were marched out to the railroad station where a train with 40 freight cars awaited us. We breathed a sign of relief to see that 40 men were being put in each car instead of the 60 men when we traveled from Baja.

Finally, the doors of the cars were locked shut by the guards, and the train screamed its whistle of departure. As the train jerked its way out of the station, an eerie calm passed among us. We were resigned to our fate.

Chapter 7

FOCSANI

The prisoners in our barren freight car were dispirited and lifeless. Louis and I maneuvered across the wooden floor toward a back corner where a wire-woven, five-inch-square window allowed air to crudely ventilate the railway car. We took turns looking out the window so we could determine in what direction the train was moving.

Some of the prisoners had enough room to lie down, but most had to sit. In the center of the wooden floor, a 6" x 6" square had been cut out for a common toilet/latrine. A large drum next to the toilet hole was intended to hold drinking water, but it was empty.

Since working as a forester in Borsa gave me valuable experience in determining cubic yards for the logs we cut, I estimated the size of the freight car to be 8 yards long, 2 yards wide and 2½ yards high. I multiplied the figures and calculated the car held exactly 40 cubic yards.

"So here we are," I thought, "40 moving prisons, each with 40 hapless souls, with only 1 cubic yard of air for each person. What kind of animals are we dealing with?"

Within a few hours, the stagnant air in our railway car was fouled from the combined human stink. Because we had marched two hours and then waited the rest of the day to be loaded into the freight cars with no water, everyone was thirsty.

As the train jostled us around, people began to yell at one another, "Don't kick me!"

"Get up! You're lying on me!"

"Hey, get your leg off my stomach!"

"You're standing on my foot!"

Our discomfort and complaints tortured one another. We didn't get anything to eat since breakfast, and the big empty drum teased us with a promise never kept. And thus ended our first day of life aboard a freight car.

On the second day, the solitude of being locked away in close confinement began to take its toll. The shoulders of the men slumped in resignation of their fate. I could see in their emotionless eyes that they had lost hope.

The train came to a halt in the middle of a field. No one moved, not the guards or the prisoners. The heat of late spring filled the car, and no breeze wafted inside.

I counted the minutes. Fifteen minutes, but nothing moved. A half-hour. An hour. Then two hours. Some of the men in the car began to yell, "We need some water! Give us some water!"

The cries were taken up by prisoners in the other cars, and the clamor of parched throats echoed from one car to another. Why were we stopped? What was the delay? The cacophony of misery continued from all the freight cars, sending shivers up and down my spine. We were locked up in the middle of nowhere, and no one was paying attention.

Eventually, a train rumbled by and some of the men looked out the 5-inch window and told the rest of us that it was filled with Russian soldiers. Our train had stopped to let a Russian troop train pass ours in the opposite direction.

We resumed its eastbound trek, and four hours later we stopped at a railroad station. As the men spotted some guards, some of the prisoners yelled at the top of their voices: "Water! We need some water!"

"You need some water?" one of the guards shouted back. "Gold! Give us your gold!"

An obscene auction began. Some of the married men who had hidden their gold wedding bands sold them for a gallon of drinking water. Those who bought some water shared some of it with the rest of us.

As the train rolled farther and farther along, sleeping in the cattle-freight cars became impossible. The odor of the air grew worse. The narrow space, lack of water and incredible hunger resulted in a terrible stomach-wrenching ache.

The more I thought about our situation, the more ridiculous it seemed. I caught myself laughing hysterically, and I concentrated on keeping my wits about me.

We stopped at another railroad station for another Russian troop train to pass us by, where we spotted some peasants standing around. Several women in the group produced packages and cans and called out to us. "Here, take these!" they said.

"Bring it to the hole!" we shouted, and guided the good Samaritans to the six-inch-diameter hole that was cut out from the bottom of the railway car. Yes, *that* hole, the hole that we prisoners had been using for two days for our bodily functions.

The civilians held their noses, and we reached our hands through the hole to bring up unexpected survival kits: canned food with liquid inside, jars of water and milk, pastries, baskets with eggs and corn meal.

The donations from the simple country folk gave us a glimmer of hope, and the train ride became more tolerable. However, a new menace soon affected us. Blood-sucking bugs multiplied in our underwear, shirts, under our arms, legs and everywhere imaginable. The itch and sting from the constant bites became unbearable.

When we were not scratching, we were arguing about where the train was taking us. A few optimists clung fast to the hope that we would be sent home, but the realists insisted that we are being exported to Siberia. The argument droned on and on, and Louis and I managed to slip into a state of semi-consciousness for a few hours.

We arrived at another station, and the uproar from the starving, thirsty prisoners echoed everywhere. The doors of our car were unlocked, and two guards appeared and ordered us out to stretch our legs.

"We need water!" I yelled at one of the guards.

"No water!" he spat back at me.

Guards ordered each car to be emptied, and we walked around in controlled circles for 10 minutes. The guards motioned us back to the railway cars, where we stumbled back inside and the doors rolled shut to be locked.

The train proceeded farther into Romania, and it became obvious to everyone that we were heading far out of Hungary. As the train climbed the Carpathian Mountains toward Ploesti, an older guy told us that Hungarians had been transported here before, but none of them came back. He seemed to know a few things about this train ride of ours, and we asked him what was happening to our women.

He said that women were being transported out of Hungary much faster than we were. When we asked him where they were being taken, he shook his head and said he didn't know.

Our heads spun with visions of gloom and doom as the train thundered through the Romanian night. A few prisoners groaned and cried involuntarily because of their hunger pangs. For most of the night, no one got any sleep.

In the morning, we came to another station, and the doors were opened again. "Food and water!" the guards said.

Two prisoners were allowed to depart each car to bring food to the others. One of the men from our car fell when he tried to get out, because he didn't realize how weak he had become.

Each car's designees were led to a separate railroad car in the middle of the train, which contained a large stove, 50-gallon kettle and an even larger drum.

Rations were poured out into large buckets and handed to each man. One bucket was filled with bean soup and a little meat, and the other one filled with boiled water.

Each man returned to his respective railway car and ladled his buckets' contents into the prisoners' rations cans. The men greedily gobbled down their rations of bean soup before being ladled a can of water. These servings were meager, but the long wait for food and water had weakened us and we were satisfied momentarily.

We learned a lot about our companions; some of them complained too much, while others remained quiet. Meanwhile, I kept a close eye on Louis to make sure he was doing all right.

The next day, we stopped at another station to wait for a train to pass ours. While there, the guards allowed us to walk around in a slow circle.

During the afternoon, we stopped in the countryside for another can of bean soup and a serving of water. We passed through Bucharest, and the train turned northward.

Prisoners who were unlucky enough to sit close to the six-inch bathroom hole began to defend themselves. If the train moved unpredictably, causing someone to make a mess on the freight car's floor, the offending prisoner was made to clean the area with his shirt or trousers. Everyone grew edgy and irritable.

Finally, after six days in these crowded, unsanitary quarters, we arrived at Focsani, 100 miles northeast of Bucharest, during the last week of April. Focsani, an agricultural trade center for grain and wine, boasted a civilian population of approximately 35,000, and is known as the capital city of Romania's Pulha province in southeastern Moldavia.

After we arrived at the railroad station, the doors were swung open and the sun's rays blinded us. We staggered around inside and outside as our eyes adjusted to the bright sunlight. The guards lined us up five people to a row, and we marched for almost an hour until we entered a large camp, whose main purpose appeared to be for transit.

Once we entered the camp, we received plenty of water and the prison food thick enough to chew. A 10-piece band welcomed us when we arrived — including a guitar, trumpet, trombone, two violins and drums — playing Hungarian *csardas* (fast dance music).

A precious few old or sick people were set free and told to find their way back to Hungary. The rest of us were feted as guests, and our spirits rose. The size of our food portions was considerably larger than the meager amounts we had received while in captivity. Things were looking up!

After dinner, we were led toward a renovated airplane hangar and into a disinfection/sterilization room, where everyone took off his clothes. For two hours, we took baths in round 10-gallon tubs and cleaned up with honest-to-goodness soap and water, while our clothes were disinfected in a separate room.

We were getting rid of the bugs that had bedeviled us! As we gathered our clothes and dressed, we were abruptly brought back to Earth as we smelled the same wretched odors that our bodies exuded an hour ago. Our clothes may have been disinfected, but they sure were not cleaned!

We walked outside to a row of wooden barracks painted gray, where the guards ordered us inside. Approximately 1,600 people had made the trip from Temesvár, and we were officially prisoners-of-war.

We went to sleep in an optimistic mood, and our dreams were bright and innocent. As we awoke, the true nature of the camp at Focsani became clear. During the early morning, two

Ruthenian guards woke us up harshly. The guards beat us with wooden batons, yelling, "*Davaj, davaj*" (Go, go, run, move).

Ruthenians, sometimes called "Little Russians," spoke Hungarian and either Russian or Ukrainian, so they were able to interpret our language and explain what we said to the Russians. For this reason, they were assigned to guard the Hungarians.

Ruthenians lived in the Carpathian region of Hungary until the Trianon Treaty ceded this area to Czechoslovakia. Under the 1938 agreement agreed to by Germany, Great Britain and France, this area went back to Hungary, and Ruthenians resented their subjugation to Hungarian rule.

The Ruthenian guards showed no patience or empathy toward us, and we regarded their behavior contemptuously. One Hungarian soldier was moving too slowly for the guards, and two of them ran up behind him and smacked wooden canes against his buttocks raising red welts on his body.

"What is this?" I asked aloud. "Last night, we were treated like heroes. Now we're being treated like trash."

"Welcome to the real Focsani," a bearded man said as he ran past my bunk. Then he yelled out, "And we call them *davajs*, because that's the only thing they say!"

We had been deceived by the presence of a band! Our welcome was nothing but a staged show! This camp had only one purpose: to house approximately 20,000 prisoners for future transport to Siberia.

The camp population was ethnically mixed with Germans, Romanians and Hungarians. Some prisoners were ranking officers, some were enlisted men and the rest were civilians, including policemen, postal workers and railroad workers. The Russians even arrested a groom at his own wedding, because he committed the sin of wearing a black suit.

The *davajs* rousted everyone from their bunks and herded us into the courtyard to line up in 20 five-man rows of 100 men. Each *davaj* was given responsibility for a group of 100 prisoners.

Even though such a lineup is easily counted, the process used at Focsani took an inordinate amount of time — an hour or even longer — while the numbers were compared to a list.

The repeated process of counting the men seemed silly and stupid, but the procedure was repeated every day.

After the prisoner count, we were served breakfast. Prisoners stood in their 100-man formations, and the cooks brought out huge drums of soup.

We held out our tin cans while a cook ladled soup containing potatoes, beans and *burizs* (wheat or barley ground up in its own husk and weeds) into them. The watery soup was devoid of nutrients and appeared to be nothing more than a few beans floating in water. This unappetizing mixture, without salt, was given to us twice a day.

We also received a little bit of bread, too, but dividing loafs of bread into seven-ounce portions caused chaos. When somebody received a bigger piece than another prisoner, a shouting match erupted or a fight ensued.

The wooden barracks where we slept and lived were crammed with two-tiered, wooden, un-cushioned "bunk beds." Two men were assigned to each rack of the narrow bed, and space was so cramped that when one person turned in his sleep, the other man had to turn the same way.

The snow at Foscani already had melted by the time we arrived, and each day became warmer than the previous one. Soon the wind picked up, and the sand on the ground was blown into our hair, into our eyes and inside our clothes.

Although we received half a gallon of hot water daily for drinking water and baths, we were limited to use of the disinfection room, where the bathtubs were located, once a week. Therefore, we made our trips to the disinfection area feel like special occasions.

During the afternoon of May 9, we were startled by the sound of gunfire from the guards. As we turned around to see what was going on, the guards were shooting rifles in the air.

"What's going on?" Louis asked me.

A guard rushed by with both arms punching the air in celebration. "*Berlin kaput, vojna kaput!*" he screamed.

"Berlin has fallen, and the war is over," I said with glee. "We'll be going home!"

"Really?" Louis said.

"Of course. They can't keep us here now!"

As we watched the building celebration, two guards took a barrel of gunpowder and attached a fuse to it. One guard lit the end of the fuse, and the two of them ran toward us.

Boom! We covered our ears as the explosion shook the camp, and all the guards cheered the work of their comrades. Guards carried a rifle in one hand and a half-full bottle of vodka in the other. Each took turns firing random bullets into the air after chugging down a sizable amount of the Russian-made liquor.

Berlin was occupied. The Germans surrendered. The war was finished. As we squeezed our way into our wooden beds that night, flares were shot into the air turning night into day, and a sense of optimism filled the camp.

When we awoke, the party was still going on. Nevertheless, we gathered in our groups of five-man rows and proceeded with the dull routine of being a prisoner-of-war in Focsani.

While the celebration of the guards continued, I explored the kitchen where our food was cooked. An entire building had been partitioned into six separate kitchens, and each kitchen cooked its own vat of soup and carried its own supply of bread.

Boiled water continued to be rationed, and we were no longer furnished soap to wash our bodies. To keep the bedbugs and lice away, I showed Louis how to make a sponge from our worn and tattered shirts, and we used some of our water rations to wash our bodies.

The camp at Focsani contained separate little shops where prisoners worked. A bakery had been built to bake each day's bread, and separate shops existed to make shoes, tools and other carpentry items.

Off to the side was a forbidding sight that warned us of the consequences of resistance: a bunker built underground to punish prisoners caught stealing or committing a crime against the state. The punishment meted out here frequently resulted in death through starvation or neglect.

Once again, the so-called toilet facilities served as a death trap for prisoners afflicted by illness. Approximately 15 latrines had been dug in ditches measuring 10 yards long, 5 yards wide, and three or four meters deep. On top of the ditch, wooden planks were placed. Between the planks were 10-15-inch openings, where prisoners had to squat.

The planks were arranged to accommodate up to 50 people at the same time. Because the planks were close to each other, a prisoner was more likely to accidentally soil another guy's socks or underwear.

No facilities existed to wash up afterward nor did any toilet paper exist. In order to clean oneself after leaving the latrine, a prisoner had to use a hand wipe himself and then immerse the hand in the camp's sand or soil.

Residue might be cleaned off, but the smell never went away. Not enough water was available to wash a soiled hand, and prisoners took care not to use the hand while eating.

If this wasn't bad enough, the ditches were closed at night. A 50-gallon black drum was placed in the back of the barracks, and a chair placed next to it so prisoners could raise their bodies to the requisite height to squat above the drum's opening.

The Ruthenian guards were eager to keep us in the barracks during the evening, so they could be free to enjoy themselves. This policy wasn't very healthy for us, because the barracks were jam-packed and permitted little movement or walking around.

Louis and I volunteered for kitchen work, because working in the bakery or unloading trucks offered the prospect of extra bread or other food from civilians. Our portions were so meager that any extra rations came in handy.

One day, Louis and I unloaded grain packaged in laminated paper bags. As we were working, Louis asked what should be done with the empty bags.

"What a great idea!" I shouted, and Louis looked at me befuddled. "Put the empty paper bags next to the door. We'll use the bags to make toilet paper!"

As soon as we finished unloading the grain, we carried the empty bags back to the barracks, tore them into 10-inch by 10-inch pieces and exchanged the bits of paper for extra bread. Finally, the prisoners were able to get a supply of toilet paper.

I remembered my promise to Louis' wife and looked after him. Louis was out of shape and undisciplined, but I made him wash every morning when we got up. Also, whenever I sold some toilet paper, I was able to give him some extra food.

A week passed since the celebration of the Russian advance into Berlin, and, at the camp commander's suggestion, the prisoners appointed a supervisor for each group of 100 prisoners. The supervisors were made responsible for the cleanliness of prisoners, their living area and the fair division of rations.

Each big loaf of bread needed to be cut into 200-gram portions. We had no scale to weigh the bread, so we had to estimate the rations carefully. Our near-starvation meant that little crumbs could affect whether a prisoner lived and died, so any errors in judgment created a major argument.

Each square loaf weighed about 4½ pounds. Ten loaves were allotted for each group's 100 prisoners, which figures out to seven ounces per man. Whoever doled out the rations had to cut identically sized portions so that equal portions of each loaf were given to 10 people.

Once all the pieces were cut, the person cutting the bread would ask two or three other guys to settle any disputes regarding equal rations. Once a consensus was reached, everyone could eat.

The soup line was another place where the fairness of rations was tested. The first prisoners who stood in line for soup received a thinner liquid than the prisoners at the end of the line. Whether a cook ladled from the top or bottom of the soup kettle caused countless numbers of disagreements and fights.

Tempers were short, and fists flew with little warning. Occasionally, each man was given two teaspoons of granulated brown sugar, and this treat helped to ease any building tensions. Nevertheless, the constant hunger caused men to act like animals, and I soon learned firsthand about the desperate measures that men take to live.

The petty nature of our arguments created a circus atmosphere; the moment one argument was settled, a different one began. I had begun a black market for toilet paper, and other black markets were created for empty tin can containers and *mahorka*, a peasant-made cigarette.

Mahorka consists only of the veins on tobacco leaves. After the smooth, clean tobacco leaf is separated from its veins to be sold as cigarettes, the veins are ground up into little pellets.

These pellets were placed in a funnel-shaped cone, of which the most popular form came from a page of the Moscow newspaper, Pravda. The larger end of the cone was ignited, and the smoker inhaled through the smaller end. After one's lungs received a burst of smoke, the smoker exhaled it and cried out "*Kurity!*" (smoke) to show his satisfaction.

It's lucky that I wasn't a heavy smoker, because most of the men were so addicted to tobacco that they gave up their bread in exchange for *mahorka*.

After we appointed supervisors for each group of 100 prisoners, the guards decided that an overall leader was needed for the camp, and a German sergeant was selected. He was strict, but his leadership helped us to survive.

Religious leaders were among the prisoners at Foscani, because the communists were strict atheists. On Sundays, fathers preached and gave mass to the Catholics while ministers held services and held impromptu communions for the Protestants.

A few men died when they fell into the latrines, but we became numb to the rising death count. Perhaps we were rationing our grief, because that was all we had left. After all, there were no records. There were no doctors, no medicines. There were no priests to oversee the burials, no messages to relatives.

When we arrived here, we were known only as a number. When someone died, he got buried in a mass grave and was covered with slaked lime.

Our time in Temesvár had lasted one and a half months, and one month had passed here in Focsani before our doom was settled.

Early one morning, while we formed our usual line of five-man rows, the guards counted us more times than was customary. Then they re-counted us at least a dozen times more and rearranged us into groups of 90 men. Each group of 90 men was assigned a supervisor, and a new count began.

Louis and I were included in the formation of 33 groups of 90 men. The remaining prisoners were sent back to their barracks. Each group marched toward the camp entrance, where guards stopped each group so their number could be counted again.

"Where is breakfast?" a prisoner yelled. "We are hungry and thirsty."

"When will we get food and water?" another prisoner called out.

One guard motioned with his rifle to the men. "You will get food and water at the railroad station. Shut up, and march!"

Through the railroad station passed two different widths of tracks. The train on which we arrived had a standard European (and Hungarian) width. Waiting for us on the other set of tracks were larger freight cars hooked up to a Russian locomotive.

Now we were certain that we were heading toward Russia and not back to Hungary. These freight cars were big enough to transport 18 cows or horses. And if transporting people, they could accommodate 60 men.

The Russians began loading each group of 90 people into each freight car. By multiplying the size of each group by the number of cars, I determined that the number of prisoners being transported amounted to approximately 3,000 men.

Seven other cars complemented the train, in which guards and cooks were housed and where food and water were stored.

Once we received our railway car assignment, we were able to fill our ration cans with a watery bean soup and 10½ ounces of bread. We drank the soup quickly, so we could replace it with a quart of water.

As soon as we finished eating, we were packed inside a freight car. The odor inside told us that we were not the first war prisoners to ride here. Each of two small windows was covered by steel rods on the outside, making escape impossible.

Furthermore, the steel rods allowed only a partial view of the outside by one person. Obviously, the windows were covered to discourage the car's occupants from looking outside.

Two guards walked toward the sliding door of the freight car, looked at us with crooked grins and rolled the doors shut.

The gloom of premature darkness enveloped us, and the sounds of locks being secured reverberated throughout the train.

Chapter 8

THE TRAIN OF DARKNESS

Light seeped into the gloomy interior from the barred windows and through the six-inch hole cut in the center of the floor. About noontime, the passenger car jerked to a start, and we left the Focsani railroad station.

The sound of the train was ominous. "Click, click, shhhh, shhhh, click, click," the rails murmured, as the railroad car shook from one side to the other. As the stale air wafted around us, the stink from our bodies became apparent.

I climbed onto an elevated wooden bed, and I pulled Louis up as he climbed its rungs. Each bed measured 2½ feet wide by 6 feet long and accommodated two men.

Twenty-five such beds were built at ground level; 20 beds were at the second level. With 90 men packed into such a small space, there was no room for us to walk around.

Bunks or beds imply softness of some sort. Not here! The beds were made of hardwood or softwood. Because I knew timber, I chose a bed made from pine planks, a softer wood, for Louis and me.

The army uniform that I slept in had not been washed in six months; it was filthy and smelled awful. I had kept my overcoat with me, and I was able to use it as a blanket.

Next to the door, a piece of sheet metal had been molded into a makeshift funnel so that we could pee through it. At least, I thought, we didn't have to stand over the foul-smelling hole in the railway car's floor, which required the user to be adroit and keep his balance.

As the day wore on and I tried to sleep, my hunger pangs returned. I cursed every inch of this heathen train with every breath of foul air I took. The train stopped inside a railway station, and two guards unlocked the door and brought us a large drum filled with watery bean soup and a drum of water.

We filled our ration cups with soup and drank hungrily. Then we filled them again with water, drank again and made way for the next man in line. Once we were fed and watered like cattle, the doors rolled shut and the endless gloom returned.

The nights were terrible. These sleeping places were pitch-black and so crowded that if one of us wanted to turn from the right side to the left, *everyone* had to turn. (I can't describe these sleeping places as beds, because I barely had enough room to sleep on one side of my body.)

Depending on which level a person slept on, 40 or 50 people had to roll over — simultaneously. As a result, we were lucky to get five hours of sleep in a night.

One person's comfort soon became another person's discomfort, and sporadic yelling and fighting punctuated our first night on the train. Only the hypnotic cacophony of the moving train helped to close my ears to my companions' distress.

In the morning, light crept through the barred windows and shithole, and we stopped again for food and water. Apparently, this was to be our day-to-day routine on this train trip of misery.

Our train occasionally stopped in a railroad station to allow another train from the opposite direction to pass, and on two of these occasions, some Russian civilians brought us some food. Once again, the only way we could retrieve food or drink was through the shithole, and every Russian civilian whose stomach was strong enough to brave the stench received our praise and gratitude.

After several nights of violent bickering, we appointed one of the guys to assume a role similar to a coxswain aboard a rowing event. He called out which side — right or left — to lie on, which side to turn toward, and we left it up to him to decide how often we should change position.

Days passed. The routine of twice-a-day stops for food and water was cut in half. We took turns looking outside the barbed wire-covered windows at the countryside in the Ukraine.

Whole regions were devastated, farmland made uncultivable, houses shattered, door and windows torn from churches. Farm animals roamed freely inside some of the churches we saw.

As the train proceeded farther through the Soviet Union, blood-sucking bugs infested our clothes. In addition, the combination of dirt, smell and untreated water took its toll, and many prisoners became gravely ill. Our bodies lacked exercise, our throats were parched and we were malnourished.

Days blended into nights and back again into days as our train continued rumbling through the Soviet Union— through Kursk, then Penza. Those of us who were able to move around saw a spectacular view of the Volga River through the barbed-wire windows, as we crossed over the wide, wide river at Kazan.

Finally, we faced the fate that we had long feared. We headed toward the Ural Mountains — and beyond those not-so-lofty peaks, Siberia.

Our need for water was extreme. We resorted to putting a tin can outside the window whenever it rained, and we gave the rainwater to those who suffered the most.

Incidents of stomach typhus and cholera were rampant. Our bodies turned bloody from where we scratched ticks off of them. Pain and suffering became trusted companions, and five of the prisoners died.

When feeding time arrived and the guards brought the large drums of soup and water, they pulled the bodies from the car and kicked them into a ditch next to the railroad tracks. Five men succumbed to the inhuman conditions in the freight cars, and the guards disposed of their bodies like unneeded garbage.

The train chugged along, and vast forests appeared on both sides of the tracks. We saw some people working along the railway, and a high school teacher in our car explained who they were. "Some gulag guys," he said. "After two or three years in the gulag, they find that life no longer matters."

We passed through Krasnoufimks, a point of no return before the Ural Mountains. The train whizzed along, slowed down as it huffed and puffed its way across the Ural Mountains, and sped up once it crossed the mountain pass.

After 30 days — and five dead from our railway car — we heard the train's brakes applied for the last time. The freight car jerked with the familiar double-jolt that accompanies a full stop, and we heard the guards running outside.

"*Davaj, davaj!*" a menacing guard yelled as our door rolled open.

We rolled from our beds toward the door and staggered around. Thirty days of lying around had caused the bones and joints in our legs to become stiff. We squinted and tried to look outside, but the sunlight was blinding.

"*Davaj, davaj!*" the guard yelled.

Our muscles ached, and we had no idea of how much strength we had left. The first prisoners crawled from the railway car onto the platform and helped the weaker ones still inside.

"*Davaj, davaj!*" the guard yelled.

We filed into five-man rows, and observed that our numbers had shrunken noticeably.

"*Davaj, davaj!*" the guard yelled, and we began marching to an unknown camp.

"*Davaj, davaj!*"

We were in another world, east of humanity. We were in Siberia.

Part III

Chapter 9

THE SIBERIAN FOREST

As I tried to walk across the uneven grassy soil, I staggered from side to side like a drunkard. The rest of the men were unsteady on their feet as well.

The people who lived and worked in the area gathered as we passed by. One boy who was no older than 10 years old ran alongside and yelled, "*Nyemci*" (Germans)!

Others in the crowd began to spit at us and yell obscene epithets in Russian. We hung our heads down so as not to invite recrimination from the guards.

How could they think we were Germans? Did the Communists lie to them? We were prisoners-of-war who were supposed to be set free! We were Hungarians!

We trudged our way through an industrial area where the railway station stood. As we talked, I told Louis about an elderly Ukrainian resident who talked with me at the railway station.

"Louis," I said, "that old guy told me he's been here for 10 years. Do you know what for?"

Louis shook his head back and forth.

"For not signing a *piszagy* (a printed document authorizing the state to confiscate a farmer's land)," I said. "Can you believe it? The guy was sent here because he owned land!"

I muttered to myself as we walked along. Two of the more-fit prisoners gathered alongside some of their comrades so the weaker ones could keep up with the demanding pace.

An hour later, we reached a virgin forest. As the parade of trees towered over our ragtag number, a symphony of birds announced our arrival to the green-carpeted world. Occasionally, the guards yelled, "*Pushli, pushli*" (go farther)!"

As the guards' commands echoed between splendid pine and white birch trees, I thought, "I would really enjoy this place if I was a tourist!" Soon we arrived at our future home: a tent camp in the middle of the forest. This gulag consisted of approximately 40 double-walled tents manufactured in the United States, each accommodating 80 prisoners.

As we arrived at our camp, we collapsed upon the soft ground from exhaustion. After being cramped in a cattle freight car for 30 days, it was a miracle that we were able to walk at all!

We begged the Russian guards for some food and drink. All of us were hungry; all of us were thirsty. Nevertheless, the guards refused to listen and split us into groups of 80 men. Each group was assigned its own tent.

Inside the tent were double-decker elevated bunk beds. I picked out one of the bunks and took the top rack, so that Louis could lie on the bottom. I closed my eyes and gritted my teeth while my stomach cramped from hunger. Finally, we were called outside to eat. I was not surprised to discover what we were being served: bean soup.

As the sun fell lower, the aurora borealis filled the northern sky. The North Pole didn't seem far from where we were, and the spectacular array of colors filled me with wonder.

That night, I lay awake wondering what challenges lay ahead of me. Eventually, I fell into a fitful but restful sleep.

Daylight brought the forest to life, and we awakened. All prisoners were assembled into one group, and we were told what we were expected to do: cut trees, clear the area of felled timber and build a railroad line.

Before we began work in the gulag, we received watery soup with seven ounces of bread. Eating this soup was worse than eating a dishwashing rag thrown into hot water. Nevertheless, I forced it down in hopes of receiving some semblance of nutrition.

Then the prisoners grabbed axes, saws, picks and shovels and went to work — eight hours and sometimes 10 hours — in the woods where we chopped and sawed timber, dug, shoveled and performed other demanding physical labor.

At noontime, we were given an hour-long break, half an ounce of an oily, greasy substance resembling lard and seven more ounces of bread.

At suppertime, we received more watery soup mixed with barley, millet, beans, peas or oats. And, of course, we received another seven ounces of bread.

Other prisoners had been housed in this camp, and each night we were reminded of this unhappy fact. Blood-sucking bedbugs, ticks and lice infested every part of our bodies. Whatever the bugs missed in the unsanitary freight cars, the tiny pests in the camp found. Frequently, we would scratch our bodies involuntarily while we slept, resulting in bloody sore spots on our skin.

Eight Hungarians died from disease caused by the bugs. The death toll would have been heavier, except for a quick medical checkup by some Russian doctors and nurses who advised the sickest prisoners not to drink raw water and to eat only charred bread.

Since the growing infestation weakened everyone's bodies, production at work fell off drastically. The commander of the camp met with the guards, and they came up with a plan on how to deal with our tormenters from the insect world.

The commander ordered the preparation of a bathing and disinfection facility. We took off all our clothes and put them into a sauna-like room whose temperature of 200° F. killed the bugs in our clothes. While we waited for our clothes to be debugged, the commander gave us a treat.

We were able to take a bath!

We took turns washing ourselves in six-gallon washtubs — with soap! What a wonderful feeling! After sponging every part of our body with soap and hot water, we felt clean!

That night, we slept soundly without the nauseous stink that had infected our bodies. I never heard so many guys snoring at one time in my life. When the Russian guards awoke us early the next morning, we felt refreshed — although the hunger never went away.

After we were able to clean up, life at this camp was okay. We had arrived in Siberia at the end of June — the beginning of summer — and the weather was pleasant and warm. Everything had turned green, flowers exploded into full bloom and the melody of birdcalls filled the air.

On the floor of the forest, the air was clean and sunshine filtered gently to the ground through a thick canopy of trees. Our guards were more professional than the ones in the camps, although we were still treated crudely.

We were fed three times a day, although the soup consisted of little more than flour or barley mixed in hot water. Sometimes, we were served millet soup. Another "specialty" on the camp menu was bran soup, consisting of a handful of pig-grade bran flour in a half liter of hot water. If times were good, we got some tea and at least one teaspoon, sometimes two, of sugar a day.

Once a week, we received some American-made cans containing Brazilian meat. This meat tasted like a mixture of ground pork and beef, and it was difficult to divide up. Each person received a cube-sized portion measuring one inch on all sides. I don't know how he did it, but the guy who divided the meat into equal portions performed magic.

Occasionally, we received a little fish oil containing flecks of fish. This was also difficult to share among all the prisoners.

Our diet was far short of what anyone needed to stay in shape. The only thing that seemed sufficient was our daily bread quota of 21 ounces — more than one pound of bread. But the quality was awful.

Russian bread was made from oats that were ground up with the husk. The bread was so damp that I could almost squeeze water from it. Sometimes I had to spit out the bread, because the taste was disgusting and my stomach had difficulty digesting it.

We complained about the lack of nutrition in our rations. We didn't want anything fancy, just a potato or anything that promised some semblance of food value. Sometimes the number of meals we were given declined to twice a day, especially on Sundays when we didn't work. Malnutrition sapped our energy, and once again we became too exhausted to work after a few minutes of exertion.

Once again, conditions improved. From their own rations, the guards began feeding us oats, meal and rice, supplied by the United States; however, the portions given were meager.

I came down with typhus. This was the first time I had caught it since my imprisonment in Baja, and our nemeses — bedbugs, lice and ticks — were once again to blame. The earlier disinfection and bath had killed the bugs on our clothes and body, but it didn't rid them from the tents.

Biweekly rounds of disinfection and bathing were ordered, and I followed the familiar regimen of eating nothing but charred bread. I boiled water for at least 10 minutes to make tea, and didn't touch any other water. Finally, I survived another bout with gulag disease and regained some of my strength.

We resorted to desperate measures to solve our continued malnutrition. We ate grass. We chewed bark from trees.

I discovered that round grass tastes a little better than flat grass. The bark of birch trees helped to kill the hunger pains, and it tasted better than bark from other trees. Pinecones added taste to our tea, and nettle leaves, which irritate the skin, provided nutritional value.

A black market began for *mahorka*, and I joined in, giving up some of my bread for a cone-shaped bag of *mahorka*. However, my physical strength ebbed, and my survival demanded that I give up smoking. Breaking the cigarette habit in favor of foul-tasting bread and so-called soup wasn't easy, but it was the only thing to do.

To build the railroad, we cut down the trees in the railroad's path. Then we hauled out the timber and removed the stumps, which was dangerous and backbreaking work under the best of conditions.

After the land was cleared, we built up the low land in the path of the railroad and raised the rail bed anywhere from three to six feet above ground level. Then we lay the rails and hammered bolts into them to hold the rails solidly in place.

Summer produced a voracious breed of mosquito. If we were not lifting or sawing timber, we were scratching our bodies from the bites of their virulent swarms.

Our work groups consisted of 100 men, with each group assigned a supervisor to overlook its work. Most of the supervisors were Russian, and we talked with them about life in Siberia and the gulag.

Our supervisor told us that most of the people in the Sverdlovsk area were deportees. Some were sent here for collaborating with the Germans, or were caught stealing from a factory.

He explained that from time to time, the Interior Secretary of the Soviet Union organized a purge, and people were sent here for no other reason than making a mistake at work. Some were sent here because a Communist Party leader took a dislike to the man, or a Party leader wanted to give a man's job to a Party family member.

The "official" reason for a prisoner's deportation was subject to Party whim. A deportee's personal file might be labeled "Fascist," "Imperialist," "Americanist," "Spy," "Enemy Agent," "Terrorist," "Saboteur" or "Member of SS."

Deported Russians were sentenced to forced-labor gulags anywhere in Siberia from five to 20 years. A large group of deportees were *kulaks* (middle-class peasants who owned farmland of more than 25 acres). Stalin had ordered them deported to Siberia so they could not disrupt his plans for a collective farm system. Most of these deportees perished in the mines, died from exposure during the severe Siberian winter or died from malnutrition in the gulags.

As we continued clearing away the forest, our Russian supervisor said that we weren't clearing enough land, and threatened to take away our food. Many of us immediately started to work harder and faster without any increase in the meager rations. Consequently, most of our group got sick, many of whom were too weak to walk.

One night, a husky farm worker warned us of the consequences for not raising our output. "If you guys refuse to work hard enough, we won't go home," he said.

I looked at him and replied, "Well, it doesn't matter how hard we work. If they don't want us to go home, we won't."

"Don't you think we should try to work as hard as we can? It's got to get better!" he argued.

"Listen," I said, "if you work like that for another month, we will be throwing you into a mass grave."

We argued through the night, but little did I know how right my prophecy was. Two months later, this laborer exceeded his physical limitations and killed himself from overwork.

Cutting timber was hard work. And steering a wheelbarrow loaded with dirt for the railroad bed wasn't easy, either. Yet in the few months since we arrived, we had cleared out an impressive, large area for the railroad bed.

One day, a Russian guard told us to stay inside an assigned area and threatened to shoot anyone who left it. The authorized perimeter did not include a white birch tree, whose bark was favored for its taste.

One of the prisoners was half-crazy with hunger, and he tried to sneak away. The Russian guard saw him, yelled, lowered his rifle and fired. The prisoner died in his tracks. Although our guards usually were reasonable, there were times when reason was supplanted by the madness of cold steel.

Three prisoners escaped from the gulag, and the spirit of the prisoners picked up thereafter. Six weeks later, though, the camp leader called a meeting and paraded the escapees before us.

"You see these men?" the camp leader said. "They got as far as the Volga River (about 250 miles away), before they were caught by the *Komsomol* (the official youth organization for aspiring Communist Party members).

"They thought they could escape!" he laughed. "What should be their fate? I'll tell you what; they will be *punished*!

"Today they are being sent to a karcer prison (a punishment prison dug underground). They will stay there through the winter and be fed only once a day! Don't try to escape, or you will end up like them!"

We could see how hopeless it was to try to get away. Any of us who thought that we should try to escape from the camp and go home, learned that such a mission was suicide.

The Russian secret service and the Communist system were created so that no man could ever be free. The collective wielded total control over every man. Civilians could travel no farther than 30 miles without a permit.

The Russian guards continued to put pressure on us. They constantly yelled "*Davaj!*" to make us work faster and harder. And our casualty count grew in number.

Prisoners became so weak that they were injured pushing a loaded wheelbarrow. The workload increased more, and the attitude of the guards was harsh. Soon, we were made to work on Sundays, too.

Until now, I never could have believed that the human body could endure so much starvation and privation. And there was no way out of this lethal spiral. We had to keep working, and the number of dead increased.

Each week, sickness and lack of food accelerated the death toll from overwork and malnutrition. At first, we made caskets for the dead, but later we couldn't get the raw material to make any more.

And so the dead were buried without clothes and laid to rest in mass graves. During the months that we spent in the tent camp — July, August and the first week of September — nearly 300 Hungarians died, about 10 percent of our group.

The gloom of our predicament started to depress the entire camp, and Louis and I tried to find a way to pick up our spirits. Sometimes we would sing a little bit. Eventually, we met a Hungarian pharmacist who understood what we were attempting to do, and the three of us met often to sing and tell jokes.

One evening, as we sat around the camp watching sun go down, a group of prisoners interrupted us.

"What do you guys think you're doing?" one asked. "Your happy mood isn't doing us any favors!"

"Yeah!" another man chimed in. "You're making the guards think that we should be working harder!"

"Look," I said, "our situation doesn't change one bit regardless of whether we cry or whether we laugh. Our situation here is terrible, but it's important to get many of our comrades to get over the reality of our situation and hope for the best!"

The men looked at me skeptically and left. Louis and I continued to pick up anyone's spirits who joined our little group. During our nightly gatherings, we imagined how wonderful it would be to eat real bran flakes. We pretended to sit down with a bucket of boiled potatoes and filling our stomachs. This thought became a favorite game to play when I was alone.

During the first week of September, news came that all men in three of the forest's 40 tents were being assigned to another camp. Louis and I were in one of the three lucky tents.

Chapter 10

THE CZAR'S SUMMER PALACE

Early in the morning, a convoy of trucks arrived to transport us to a different camp. "What kind of place are we going to?" I asked, as Louis and I climbed into the back.

"If it's in Siberia, it can't be very good," Louis said.

"You will enjoy this camp," one of the guards laughed. The truck's engine roared to life, as the other men hurried into this truck to find a place to sit.

"What makes you say that?" I asked the guard.

"You Hungarians!" he scoffed. "Tell me something. Do you like potatoes?"

"Of course! Why do you ask?"

"You will see!" He laughed again, turned around and watched the other prisoners.

Late at night, we arrived at a damp, uncomfortable barn. "Sleep in here," one guard told us. "You will eat in the morning."

Tired, starving and weak, we didn't take off our shoes or clothes. We just collapsed into the bunk beds that had been set up here.

As the next morning dawned, Russian civilian supervisors gathered us together, led us to a field and handed shovels to half the men. We were split into groups of 40, and each group was assigned an area approximating two-thirds of an acre.

"You are here to pick potatoes," a supervisor said. "You start work in one hour."

"Potatoes?" I thought. "We're here to pick potatoes?" I rubbed my eyes in disbelief, looked down at the ground and acted upon instinct.

"Grab some firewood!" one man hollered.

"Grab some potatoes!" I yelled.

Most of the men scurried around collecting anything wooden that would burn. The rest started pulling potatoes out of the field and piled them in a heap.

We dug holes in the ground where we placed the freshly picked potatoes, and dropped the firewood on top. One guy brought out a pack of matches, and in a few minutes we had a roaring fire.

Soon, the sweet aroma of baked potatoes delighted our nostrils. We extinguished the fire and kicked the half-burned wood to the side. We shoveled the potatoes out of the ground, and each man received six or seven charred, muddy, steaming, delicious potatoes.

Before I took a first bite, I crossed myself, looked up to heaven and acknowledged God's helping hand. In short order, my stomach was full.

Gratefully, we spread out across the field in pairs and began picking the potatoes diligently to show our gratitude. One man pushed his shovel into the ground, while the other took out the potatoes.

At the end of the day, we had harvested a hefty volume and proudly put them into one pile to impress the supervisor. When he appeared, the supervisor glanced quickly at the pile disapprovingly, surveyed the area where we had dug, and said, "Aw gee, you didn't meet the quota. You didn't dig a large enough area."

We were shocked.

"Well," one of the men said, "we were very diligent and did very good work. We took all the small potatoes out from the ground, too."

"Not enough!" the supervisor barked. "You should be able to pick at least half an acre!"

"We worked as hard as we could," our comrade pleaded. "We cannot do more."

"Well, you better learn how!" the supervisor said. "Go visit the Russians working in the next field, and see what they do. They meet the quota every day!"

We walked over to the next farm and watched the Russians at work. To our surprise, we observed that while one man picks the vines of the potato, his comrade uses the shovel only on the potatoes that are picked, leaving the remaining ones in the ground.

"The Russians aren't as efficient as we are," I thought, "because they get fewer potatoes and cover a larger area. But this seems to be what the supervisor wants us to do."

The next day, I told Louis to pull out the vines while I shovel. I instructed him that whatever wasn't picked needed to be shoved back into the ground.

In one day we managed to pick a half-acre of potatoes from the ground using half the effort that we had expended the day before. However, much of the potato crop was left behind.

It didn't matter; our supervisor was pleased. As a reward, the guards gave us extra bread that night. Over the next few days, we enjoyed plenty of cooked potatoes, and Louis and I regained some strength.

We finished harvesting the potatoes within a week. Two days later, when it started to snow, we found out why we were expected to work inefficiently.

The poorest of the poor people went out to the fields where we had worked, and dug up all of the potatoes and vines that we left in the soil. These peasants depended upon Russian inefficiency to eke out rations for the upcoming winter.

We rested two more days until a convoy of trucks took us to another location. During the trip, I learned that the other Hungarians on the train from Foscani had been transferred to a main camp close to Sverdlovsk. During late afternoon, a majestic round building came into view.

The truck trembled from a pothole we crossed, a Russian guard pointed to the building and announced, "Welcome to the Czar's Summer Palace."

Everyone asked questions about the unusual building. The guards answered enthusiastically and told us that Czar Nicholas II and his family used the building as a summer retreat until the Bolshevik Revolution of 1917-18. The czar's cattle used to graze on the surrounding fields, where Czarina Alexandra rode on her prized horse to hunt the abundant bears.

The Bolshevik revolutionaries tried to burn down the Summer Palace during the Russian revolution of 1917-18, but only succeeded in destroying the dome and upper floor. A new roof was erected to salvage the building's structural integrity, so that deportees and prisoners-of-war could be housed in its remains.

Approximately 700 prisoners were housed in the rotunda. A circular covered passageway served as the building's perimeter and contained entrances to six huge inner rooms with their own fireplaces. The fireplaces were used to heat the accommodations and prisoners' bodies.

Although it was late September, this was Siberia and the first snowfall had occurred. The latrines outside the rotunda were identical to the ones in Focsani. As we made our way to the racks of double-decker bunks placed inside the rooms, we were handed three items of apparel to help us survive the winter: *Valenki* boots made from compressed woolen felt, a thickly layered Russian *pufeika* (overcoat) and insulated slacks.

The felt in the boots would insulate our feet during the wintertime; however, we had to keep the boots dry at all costs. If they became wet, the material would freeze and wouldn't insulate our feet.

The *pufeika* consisted of layers of cloth insulated with cotton and wool. The slacks were manufactured the same way. After we finished dressing to protect ourselves from the harsh climate, we had problems recognizing each other. We looked like old Siberian Russians.

The rotunda camp operated as a forced-labor pool, and freight trucks arrived each morning to take the men to their assigned jobsites. My first assignment was at a rock mine, where I mined stones for roads and buildings.

Most days, I worked in this rock mine from early morning until late afternoon, but on some occasions I stayed as late as 8 p.m. The stones being mined here were going to the Sverdlovsk water turbine to build an electrical generating facility.

The Russian supervisor handed out sledgehammers, wedges and other tools to mine the stones, and told us to look for a little crack on the rocky wall. Once we located a crack, we inserted a wedge and then hit it with the sledgehammer.

This is not easy work, and we didn't fulfill the quota that the Russians expected. The supervisor at the mine yelled at us, and we told him that we needed better food, because a little watery bran soup or cabbage soup was insufficient for such heavy labor.

In response to our complaints, we were given thicker soups with a little bit of bran mush, peas or beans, but the strain and hard work resulted in more casualties. Eventually, we learned how to meet the daily quota, but we had to cheat.

First, we put the excavated rocks into a pile. The supervisor would inspect our work, and tell us, "This doesn't meet the quota. Get back to work."

We would then start a new pile. Once the supervisor moved on to check the progress of the other men, we moved the old pile of stones into the new one. This way, the supervisor thought our production had gone up, and our rations of soup increased.

By October the temperature dropped to 0° F. As the outdoor temperature plummeted, the rock mine grew colder. Our clothes were not warm enough, and many prisoners suffered frostbite not only on their nose and ears, but also on their toes.

The only way to keep myself from shivering was to work harder, which caused an unusual sensation of fatigue. My head felt light and started to spin, and I slumped down by my pile of stones to recover my equilibrium.

The forest around me turned emerald green. A well-managed path meandered its way to a small cottage where I could see smoke billowing up from the chimney.

Two schoolgirls in billowing sundresses danced in the sky and pointed their arms downward where my grandmother stood. I felt warm all over.

"Grandma," I said, "how did you get here?"

"I came with your parents," she said, and I saw Mama and Papa walking behind Grandma. "And this girl of yours, Maria, she came with us too."

Maria skied down a nearby hill and waved her arms in greeting. Running behind her was Ica.

This was unbelievable. "Ica," I said, "how did you get here?"

As I looked at Ica, a deep voice interrupted my vision.

"Paul, Paul, Paul! What are you doing?" I heard someone say.

The wakeup call from the voice disturbed me. I didn't want Maria and Ica to go away. Then I felt other hands slapping me and rubbing my face.

I rubbed my eyes and opened them wide.

I staggered to my feet, and a few of my comrades helped me up. "You fell asleep," Louis said. "Your face is numb, and you almost froze to death."

My fellow Hungarians had awakened me from the deadly dream of a frozen man. I had felt no pain, and I was tempted to go back to sleep because of how good I felt.

My blood started to circulate again, and I came back to life. I ran toward the rest of the miners, yelling, "*Davaj, davaj!*" because the human body cannot handle prolonged exposure to freezing temperatures without experiencing hypothermia.

We climbed into one of several tanker wagons with giant American-made tractor tires that transported us during the frigid Siberian winter. As we crawled into the wagon, the supervisor signaled a driver to take us back, and we rode over the snow to the round building where we slept.

Much of the snow on the roads had been packed into solidified ruts by *troikas* (one-horse sleds). However, the heavy weight of the tractors was needed to crush the constantly growing snowpack and make roads passable.

A few days later, temperatures plummeted to -10° F., and a Russian supervisor came to the rotunda with our latest work assignment. He needed us to replace some of the wooden planks beneath the tracks of the Trans-Siberian Railroad.

We trudged across fields of snow for an hour before we reached the railroad track. In order to change the railroad planks, we had to shovel two feet of snow covering the rails. Then we had to prop up the rails so we could remove the old plank and replace it with a new one.

Siberian nights started early; therefore, we could only work for six hours before we had to retreat to our barracks. As October came to an end and November began, our workdays on the snow-covered railroad grew even shorter. We welcomed the frigid weather at the end of November, because it meant we were done with railway work for the rest of the winter.

In December, we were assigned to a textile mill where the prisoners were given multifaceted tasks. Louis and I dried wool in huge dryers; we also worked in the spinning area. Each day, we were given a quota of wool to dry, totaling 200 pounds. After the bales went into the dryer, the dry wool was collected, put into a large bag and weighed.

Once again, we had a problem making the quota. This time, our supervisor warned us that if we didn't produce the daily quota, our bread rations would be taken away. As bad as the bread was, this was the only solid nourishment we could depend on. Without it, surely we would die.

The last time I had this problem, the Russians in the nearby potato fields showed us how they met the quota. Maybe the Russians at the mill could share some of their tricks, too.

We learned that the Russians put a large stone, weighing about 50 pounds, inside the wool before it went onto the scale. Once the wool was weighed and carted away, the stone was surreptitiously taken out and put away for its next use.

Well, if this is satisfactory for the communists, then it should be good for us, too. We found a similar-sized stone and did the same thing, and this measurement was recorded into the textile mill's books. Within a couple of days, we met our quota and our production was deemed satisfactory. We continued to adjust the measured weight of our wool for several months, and we dried wool in the warm mill for the rest of the winter without any problem.

One day, a guard handed a pouch to me, and said, "Hide this. After you get through the factory door, give it back to me."

Well, it seemed like the communist system encouraged everyone to steal. So I said to myself, "Alright. Why not?"

While waiting to leave the factory, I looked through the bag and discovered that the guard was stealing textile dye. Perhaps he was taking the dye to make some extra money.

Well, I was right. I got through the door with the pouch, which the guard took from me, and he sold the dye inside to ladies who wanted to add color to their yarn or sweater.

The communist system encouraged everyone to steal at the textile mill, but we had to be very careful. Communist Party leaders watched out for such things, and terrible things happened to anyone who got caught. I managed a little thievery for a few rubles and exchanged some money for precious amounts of food.

The sheer boldness of the thievery was beyond anything I could have imagined. While filing out of the textile mill one day, a guard asked us to take a large mirror measuring three feet by five feet. When we told the guard that such an object could not be hidden, he told us to push it ahead to the men who had already been counted.

His plan worked. In full view of the other guards, we passed the mirror to the prisoners who had already been checked out, and they returned the mirror to the guard. He took it to the army canteen's barbershop, where it was hung upon the wall.

In the textile mill, one day an old lady asked if I would give her the torn shirt I was wearing, which was completely worn out and dirty. Under socialism, she was able to take my old shirt to the area's storehouse and receive a new one in exchange.

Well, I only had one other shirt to wear, but she seemed desperate. So I agreed and gave her the shirt the next day.

The old woman repaid my kindness a week later with a few potatoes. We put the potatoes in one of the bags used for wool, and placed the bag on top of the steam heating pipe where we had drilled a hole. The small hole allowed steam to escape, and, a couple of hours later, Louis and I ate baked potatoes. The woman visited me several times thereafter with gifts of potatoes or bread, and Louis and I were grateful for her thoughtfulness.

The worst problem in this textile mill was an infestation of rats! They ran all over the wool pile and presented an ever-present risk of disease. We never needed to bother about cleaning the toilets though, because the vermin took care of that problem.

As time went by, I regained more strength. Although I felt optimistic about our short-term survival, my mood was as grim as a Siberian winter's night.

Christmas and New Year's Day passed, marking one full year of my captivity under the hands of the Russians. This was no time to celebrate; we were disgusted with all the lies and promises that we would be sent home. We didn't care about anything; we just wanted to survive.

Almost all of us who stayed at the czar's Summer Palace worked at the textile mill. Daily life was boring, and we constantly fought the frigid temperatures and the ever-growing snow pack, which was now five feet high.

After we came back to our barracks from the textile mill, we cut firewood for the fireplaces. During the worst of the Siberian winter, we were unable to heat the rooms in this huge, empty, broken-down palace any more than 40° F.

An empty steel drum with a little step was placed next to the front door for use during blizzards or when the temperature dropped below -40° F. This drum was essential, because many of us developed bladder or kidney problems that required us to urinate at least every half an hour.

About 15-20 times each night, I woke up and ran from the bunk to the drum. If someone else was using the drum or there was a respite from the awful weather, I dashed outside into the bitter cold to relieve myself on the front porch. The sickness caused by bedbugs swept through the camp, and one of our men set up effective disinfection facilities to kill the bugs that were bedeviling us.

Once every couple of weeks, a young woman doctor came to the camp to check the condition of our buttocks. As was done in Temesvár, she pulled the skin back to see if it would spring back. If it did, a prisoner was declared *kharrashow* (good for work); if it did not, the prisoner was declared *destrophy* (too weak to work).

The *destrophies* were transferred to a "recovery building," where most died and were classified as "vanished." Some of them died in a few months, some in a few weeks, but fewer than 10% of them recovered.

Every two or three months, our barracks were routinely searched. These searches had previously occurred in Baja, Temesvár and Focsani, and any paper or writing implements were confiscated. These systematic acts of cruelty eliminated any way for me to record our casualties.

Occasionally, I did smuggle writing paper and a pencil into the barracks, write letters to my parents using a fake Russian name and drop them into the factory mail chute, but I had no way of knowing if they were being delivered.

The only way I could keep track was by memory. At night I tried to remember the names of fallen comrades, but each day that went by in captivity, I forgot more of our fellows' names.

Five or six guys died each week, and one of the guys with whom I had become friends passed away. Louis and I took his body to a place that the Russians said was a cemetery for war prisoners.

We grabbed a shovel and carried my friend's body to the cemetery site a mile away. When we tried to bury our comrade, the ground was so frozen that we exhausted ourselves trying to break through the soil.

We were able to dig 12 inches inside the soil, so we put his body inside the foot-high hole and protected it with snow as best we could. We knew that the wolves, crows and microscopic scavengers would find the body, but his fate seemed kinder than how the remaining dead were treated.

For these unfortunate prisoners, the Russians set up an area next to the rotunda where we stacked the naked bodies one of top of another. Disease was not a concern, because at 20°, 30° or 40° below zero, the corpses were frozen *stiff*.

One night in February before bedtime, one of the guards entered our room and announced, "We need 40 people for tomorrow."

Well, I took advantage of every opportunity to volunteer for work, because any work offered the opportunity to get a little more food and stay in shape, regardless of how small the rations were.

"Okay, I volunteer," I said. "What do you need me to do?"

"The kitchen has run out of potatoes," the guard said. "We need you to go out to the *clamps* (underground structures built to store potatoes), and bring the potatoes to the factory kitchen."

"Oh, good! This is excellent volunteer work," I said to myself.

That night, we split up into 20 pairs, each of which received a *troika*. The potatoes had been picked previously, placed in a huge hill on the field and covered with oat straw. However, at -30° or -40° F., the oat straw didn't help much; all the potatoes in the hill were frozen.

We uncovered one portion of the potato hill and started to put the potatoes into bags designed to hold 100 pounds. The Siberian cold felt especially bitter, and I warned my comrades, "Hey, keep moving. Move, move, move! Don't stop for a moment, because your feet will freeze."

After I dropped some potatoes into the bag, I danced and yelled, "Dance, dance, jump, jump!" Then I put another handful of potatoes into the bag that Louis held for me.

I counseled Louis the same way: "Listen, keep moving. Dance and dance; jump and jump. Keep the blood circulating, because if your blood doesn't circulate, you will freeze right away!"

We gyrated around and finished loading the potatoes. After loading 20 bags onto the horse-drawn sled, our entourage headed to the kitchen. I noticed a few guys sitting on top of their sleds, and I yelled, "No, no! Don't sit on the sled, because you will freeze. Walk!"

When we arrived at the camp's storehouse at 4:30 a.m., I went to the wall where a thermometer was hanging. The temperature was 51 degrees below zero. Louis and I had made it back to the storehouse in decent shape, but eight of our number suffered severe frostbite, and three needed to have toes amputated.

The next night, the cooks made a nutritious potato soup for the prisoners and I received extra food for my help.

I became friends with the cooks in the kitchen and made arrangements to bring them more potatoes. Due to the difference between the snowdrifts and the ruts from earlier sleds, I was able to sneak six bags of potatoes into the kitchen without the guards spotting them.

In the kitchen, I was able to feed on chicken wings and chicken necks, the parts of chicken that Russians wouldn't eat. The bonanza of protein and other nutrition helped me to get back in shape, and I was able to work with less effort.

I volunteered for more work and utilized every opportunity to scrounge for food. One weekend, I joined a group of prisoners to work at a turf farm, where we cut turf into squares and dug it up. We put the turf into large wooden containers and loaded them onto a truck for transport to a warehouse in a nearby small town.

When I lifted one of the containers onto the truck, I lost my grip and the heavy box fell onto my knee, opening up a painful gash. The guard wouldn't let me seek medication; he told me to keep working.

I ripped a piece off my shirt, and wrapped the makeshift bandage around my knee. Once the truck left for the warehouse, I reported to the German Red Cross worker at our barracks and asked for some bandages.

The *felcher* brought out a few small cloths, which he had boiled previously. (In prison camps, the Russians rarely furnished hospital supplies or medications, although Red Cross volunteers were permitted to assist under varying restrictions.) He bound the bandage onto my knee, and the next day I went back to work.

After a while, my leg began to swell up. I tried to ignore the swelling, but it continued and soon I could barely walk. I limped back to the camp, and I showed my knee to the medic. "Oh gee," he said, "it's all swollen."

"It sure is," I said. It was obvious that the swelling now affected my leg, too.

"Stay here," the medic said. "Let's see what we can do."

The medic called the guard and told him that I could not work.

"He *has* to work," the guard replied.

"No, I can't," I protested.

We argued for a bit, and the guard consented to allow me to stay at the barracks. The swelling went away, but the following day after work, my knee and leg swelled up again.

I asked the *felcher* if I could see the doctor who visited us every other week, emphasizing that my leg had swollen so much that I was incapacitated.

"Well, you go to work," the medic said. "Try it for a couple more days."

Every day I went to work, the damned thing swelled up again. Finally, I got disgusted and insisted that I see the doctor.

The doctor arrived and saw the condition of my leg, she said, "This leg is in bad shape. I will arrange to have you taken to the hospital."

The doctor admitted me to the "hospital," which was primitive, dirty and consisted of 50 beds in unsanitary conditions. Nothing in this building qualified as civilized health care.

There, I saw another doctor. He looked at my leg for a few seconds and declared, "We have to amputate your leg."

"No!" I cried. "You won't amputate *my* leg."

"Well," he said, "we don't have much medication."

"What do you mean by *much*? You have *some* medication that might help me?"

"Not enough to do you any good," he said.

"Okay. Just let me rest here for a few days. Let's see how that works," I said.

I knew that if I let these people amputate my leg, I never would go home. After the doctor left, I asked the nurse if she could get hold of the antibiotic that Germans put on wounds: streptomycin.

"No, I cannot," she said.

I thought about the rubles I had saved after I sold some dye from the textile mill. Maybe this would help. I said, "Nurse! Here, I have 50 rubles. Give me some streptomycin and help me!"

Well, money talked, and she managed to steal some streptomycin. She changed my bandage, cleaned the wound, which was in pretty bad shape, and administered the streptomycin with some other medication.

After a few days of rest, the swelling in my leg abated. I started to walk and observed only a little swelling. I gained some strength, walked some more and it was evident that the antibiotic was healing my infection.

A week later, I was released from the hospital. Since it was late winter, there was lots of snow on the ground. I lay outside on a bench, and I pulled my pants down to allow direct sunlight to shine upon my wound. In little time, I was declared to be *kharrashow* (okay).

I volunteered again for extra work, and one day the guards pulled up in trucks to have us transport food to some factories, which housed their own cafeterias for the Russian workers. As we left on the trucks, one of the guards announced that we were going to pick up some *ribbah* (fish).

Russian fish is nutritious and delicious, because it originates in cold water. Quite often, the fish we moved were pink salmon, a true delicacy that was frozen and salted.

As we threw the fish into large burlap bags, each fish bounced off another as if they were stones. As soon as the supervisor turned his head, I broke off a piece of fish and chewed on it slowly and inconspicuously until it melted and softened. Once I consumed it, the salt preservative created a strong thirst in my throat.

I needed something to drink. Although there was no water, there was plenty of snow. So I ate the snow to quench my thirst.

This volunteer assignment turned into regular trips far from our camp, sometimes 40, 50, even 60 miles away. On these long drives, we were able to enjoy beautiful scenery from the back of the truck, and I amused myself by identifying the variety of trees that we passed by.

The Russian guards were anxious to catch us stealing the fish, and they searched our clothes regularly. Often they would find fish in prisoners' personal sacks or clothes.

Nonetheless, I discovered a good way to hide the fish and bring it back with me. Because the Valenki boots came to just below my knee, I slid broken pieces of fish inside one of the loose-fitting boots.

When we were searched and my bag was checked, I turned so that my leg obscured the portion of the boot that held the fish. I managed to get away with this deception without being caught. Every bit of nourishment — earned or unearned — helped me to survive.

Sometimes we handled fish packed in oil, which resembled sardines. These fish were too small, oily and messy to hide in our boots, but I was able to eat some of this fish by using a piece of tin to scoop it out.

Our desperation for food never ended. Outside the camp, while one of our comrades took care of a Russian supervisor's horse, we reached inside its feedbag and took two handfuls of oats. Eventually, the horse died because our hunger was relentless.

When the snow began to melt, we picked some grass and cut it into pieces with a homemade knife. After a few of us ate some of it with no ill effects, we cut a lot of grass and dumped it into the hot soup given us for lunch and dinner.

The Russian camp leader found out about this and warned us not to put the grass into our soup, saying that it would make us sick. We didn't listen to him and continued to eat the grass.

After all, we ate moldy bread in the hope that the mold contained penicillin.

A few weeks later, a Russian supervisor came to our barracks and asked for a few guys to transport some goods. I didn't know what we were moving or where, but I volunteered anyway.

The most joyous thing happened. We were taken to a bread factory to load a truck with bread, and take the bread to another Russian factory's cafeteria. We were delighted with this assignment, and we rode with high expectations to the bread factory.

After we loaded up the truck, all of us did something that we had wished to do for a long time: eat enough bread to fill up our stomachs. Well, I cut up a full loaf of bread, and I ate it (and the rest of my comrades did the same).

First, I squeezed a full loaf of bread to my chest and kissed it. Then I gorged myself. After I consumed the whole loaf, I was consumed by so much joy that I had to fight back tears.

We finished eating and hurriedly took the remaining bread to the factory. Eating the whole loaf of bread gave me a stomachache later on, and I couldn't sleep that night.

But it didn't matter. My stomach was full.

This assignment was repeated several times, and almost every other day, I went out with the same group to get more bread and deliver it to other small factories.

As spring began to warm the earth around us, we made frequent efforts to get some money. Perhaps, I thought, we could make a useful product and offer it for sale to the deportees. After all, they were classified as civilians; we were not.

During some free time, we went into the textile mill's machine shop and cut pieces of copper pipe into a one-eighth thickness. Then we used a metal file to shine up the copper and give it the luster of jewelry.

It took three to four days of free time to make one ring, but our efforts paid off. The Russians liked our work and used the shiny pieces of copper as wedding rings. We sold plenty of the rings to would-be bridegrooms, and we sold a few rings to the ladies, too.

When springtime arrived, the ice began to melt, and the dead bodies outside the rotunda started to thaw. The Russians brought in a bulldozer and dug a big ditch, ordered us to throw the bodies inside, poured in slaked lime to prevent the spread of disease, and then covered the bodies with dirt.

As the guards watched us shovel the dirt onto the faces of our fallen comrades, I cursed the communists under my breath, "You goddamned monsters, you won't kill me." I knew then that I cannot die here, and my will to survive became resolute.

Two weeks later, my willingness to volunteer backfired when the guards asked for volunteers. Our small group was taken to an occupied tract of single-family homes built next to one another.

In front of each house was a small hill. We were instructed to loosen all the hills and load their contents onto the truck for transport.

Well, we started to loosen the hills with a pickaxe, and we put the dislodged contents into a large straw container. While wielding the pickaxe, small pieces broke away toward Louis and me, and I placed a medium-sized piece close to my face.

"This smells like shit!" I said.

I paused for a moment, and then it struck me. This is shit!

These people didn't have toilets in their homes, and everyone left the house during wintertime to relieve themselves. The human waste froze in the Siberian winter, and they used us prisoners to get rid of it before any of it thawed.

At night, the prisoners gathered together in the barracks and exchanged frustrations on why we remained in captivity. One of the guys had smuggled in a copy of Pravda, the Russian daily newspaper. As we read the first few pages, it seemed that nobody in the government cared that we were still prisoners-of-war.

Inside, an article stated that the Hungarian Women's Association, a group consisting of mothers and wives from Hungary, had sent a delegation to ask Stalin to allow the Hungarian war prisoners to return home. At the end of the article, this sentence appeared: "The Hungarian Women's crying did not make any impression on Moscow or Stalin."

We knew that Stalin was a sadist who did not care how many people died or survived. We also knew that Hungary's communist president didn't want us back. We finally agreed that the secret to keeping up our morale was to use Pravda only for smoking *mahorka*.

As spring eased into summer, the lady who brought me potatoes to cook on the pipes reappeared with a basket and asked, "Would you cook some potatoes for me?"

"Of course, I will," I said. "You have helped me survive."

She smiled, and the next day I returned the potatoes to her — cooked. She leaned down, pulled the skins from the potatoes and gave those to me.

As she picked up the basket of peeled potatoes, she said, "Mister Hungarian, you are a good man. Stay strong and be safe."

Later that day, my comrades and I were taking a *mahorka* break. Even though I no longer smoked, this didn't keep me from fraternizing with my comrades. An aged, veteran worker with a scruffy beard sat down next to us. Louis enjoyed being friendly and asked, in broken Russian, "How are you, papa?"

In Hungarian, he answered, "Good."

We talked excitedly to him and found out that he fought against the Hungarian army in World War I. He had been a prisoner since those days and was now working in a Siberian beer factory.

He told us that the work he was doing was the most pleasant experience during his entire prison life. Considering our own working conditions, we considered ourselves lucky as he told us detailed stories of the terrible things he had seen.

He said that he wished he could be in a Hungarian war prison once again. As we began filing back into the textile mill, he sobbed uncontrollably and walked away.

Chapter 11

PUNISHMENT

"Davaj, davaj!"

I awoke to the sounds of our guards yelling. The August sun had not come up yet, and I could hear trucks idling outside the rotunda.

"Get ready!" a guard yelled to me. "You are going to another camp!"

"Where are we going?" one of my fellow prisoners asked him.

"Another camp," a guard answered.

Only one thing was certain: My stay at the czar's Summer Palace had come to an end.

The convoy of trucks motored west for nearly a full day until we arrived at Sverdlovsk's main camp, about 25 miles southeast of Siberia's major industrial city. This camp housed approximately 25,000 war prisoners, with a smorgasbord of nationalities: German, Hungarian, Romanian, Lithuanian, Polish, Latvian, Estonian and even Japanese.

The camp looked to be at least eight acres and was ideally constructed to keep people inside. As we approached the entrance, we saw some low-rise buildings surrounded by thousands of feet of barbed wire and numerous tall towers where guards stood watch with machineguns. Powerful spotlights were set on top of the tall towers so the guards could see any movement around the camp.

Our trucks jostled across the camp's dirt entrance leaving dust clouds in our wake, and I wondered what nasty turn of fate that life was dealing us. As we looked around, we saw buildings with tiny windows that reminded us of storage facilities for potatoes.

These buildings were to be our barracks, and Louis and I marched inside the one to which we had been assigned. Half of the building was built underground, and the other half aboveground. This type of construction was typical in Siberia, because the ground insulated the buildings during the brutal winter. We walked down a flight of stairs to a series of large rooms with smooth wooden floors.

Each room, accommodating 300 men, was filled with wooden bunk beds that were built on wooden planks. There were no pillows, blankets, sheets or anything else to offer a promise of comfort. I climbed up to the top half of a bunk, and Louis took the bottom.

In this camp were some big buildings resembling the seating area of a cafeteria where we could sit down to eat. And, thankfully, the food here was different. Some of it was better; some of it was not. However, the portions were still small and never enough.

The food consisted of oats or barley cooked in water with three seven-ounce helpings of bread daily. I heard a rumor that there was some meat in our soup, but I didn't see any. In the morning, we also got two teaspoons full of sugar. The only other addition to our food supply was some occasional pieces of fish, but that was all.

The Japanese were very brave, and we could thank them for whatever sustenance we received from the food supply. Prior to our arrival, food servings were so meager that some of the Japanese protested by committing hari-kari. Rather than lose their Japanese manpower, the Russians capitulated by making modest changes to the camp's food supply.

In this camp, I began work as a mason, and I used a wheelbarrow to transport bricks and cement blocks to construction sites. This work wasn't difficult during the warm days of August, but the freezing temperatures in October changed that.

Mortar from the heated truck always was dangerously hot, but zero-degree temperatures caused the mortar to freeze within a couple of hours. Therefore, I had to lay the bricks and blocks before the mortar became useless.

If I worked too slowly, I wouldn't meet the daily quota; if I worked too quickly, I would be completely exhausted plus the Russians would move the quota upward. I dealt with my anguish by wondering if next summer these buildings still would be standing or if they would collapse.

The amount of activity at the construction site was impressive. The foundation for a huge main building was being laid, and similar work on adjacent buildings gave me the impression that this site was going to become an industrial complex. A railroad track led to the Trans-Siberian Railway, and about 600 men worked here.

After working as a mason for a few weeks, I was transferred to a huge steel mill with blast furnaces that bellowed pungent smoke from several smokestacks. The steel mill contained large grinding and machining equipment and constantly churned out huge machined pieces of steel. Approximately 1,000 prisoners from Sverdlovsk's main camp toiled from daybreak to sundown in the mill's vast confines.

One of my early assignments required me to function as a blacksmith. I used the huge furnaces to heat large steel beams so I could bend them with a heavy hammer as soon as the steel became white-hot.

On a bitterly cold day, I saw a Russian welder 20 feet above me handling steel with his bare hands. Concerned for his welfare, I approached the Russian supervisor who was with us and asked, "Why don't you give this guy safety gloves? He's a Russian like you!"

"Well," the supervisor laughed, "we only have a couple thousand of you Hungarians, but we got plenty of Russians."

I couldn't believe my ears. How could the communists have so little regard for their own people?

We continued working at the steel mill until Christmastime, when I became so weak that I couldn't do the really hard work. All rations in this tightly run camp were carefully measured, prohibiting me from getting the needed extra food that I had scavenged from previous camps.

I turned to the Hungarian camp kitchen for help, and the cooks told me how they obtained their food supplies. I recruited seven guys like myself who were good athletes and in shape. After dinner, we made plans to break into the main supply magazine and get more food to the kitchen.

The food magazines inside the camp were earmarked for Russian people only; however the caliber of guards used to watch these magazines didn't measure up to the guards who watched prisoners. Soon we discovered an unguarded back window.

Every other day, we managed to pilfer from the food supply, taking care to avoid leaving any evidence of our hungry thievery. The cooks were delighted to receive fish, beef, chicken, rice, peas and beans, and this bounty was passed on to the kitchen and the 1,000 prisoners it served.

We found Brazilian beef packed inside 50-gallon wooden drums. If a drum had not been opened, we left it alone. If a drum was open, we took only enough to avoid the appearance of blatant theft. The cooks used this beef to make a highly edible goulash soup.

Around 4 a.m. one January morning, our group of eight men crept from the barracks toward the storehouse. As usual, we ducked around a corner next to the back window. Suddenly, three bright lights shone in our eyes, and a Russian voice commanded, "Halt!"

We froze in our tracks. The Group of Eight was caught in the act!

The next morning, the Group of Eight became the star attraction at a command performance presented by the camp leader to a captive audience of 20,000 prisoners-of-war.

"Look at these men!" the major's voice resonated through the loudspeakers. "See what they've done!

"They have stolen food that belongs to every one of you! When someone steals from the state, they steal from all of us!

"The Soviet Union is strong! Comrade Stalin warns us to be aware of traitors! Do not be deceived by these men! They dare to break the union of us all!

"They will be treated justly – and severely! They will be sentenced to the karcer (punishment prison) camp – and sent there without delay!"

Our doom was set. The karcer camps that we knew about were snow bunkers. In these places, two prisoners were incarcerated wearing only the clothes on their backs — with no blankets — and the only thing not certain was the time when the prisoners would freeze to death.

After the prisoners were dismissed and sent to work, Louis walked up to me.

"Paul," he said, "I must come with you."

"You can't, Louis, " I said. "None of us will survive in there. That is the harshest punishment anyone can receive in Siberia."

"I don't care," he said. "I don't know what I would do without you!" Even though I always shared the food I scrounged with Louis, I hadn't realized how dependent he felt toward me.

Louis walked over to the major who commanded the camp. "Let me go with them," he begged. "Please!"

The major looked at him, and hollered, "You're supposed to be at work! Get out of here!"

Two guards rushed him away and, as he was practically carried off, he looked at me sorrowfully.

Our Group of Eight was placed inside a temporary jail away from the other prisoners and given the usual meager rations. Two days later, a truck pulled up in front of the jail, and we were ordered to get in. Our hearts sank as we crawled into the uncovered back of the truck. In the back sat 10 other prisoners, and we exchanged greetings and stories about the "bad" things we did to warrant a virtual death sentence in the gulag.

When the truck left the camp, we turned back on the road heading east toward the czar's Summer Palace but turned off the road halfway there. We huddled together in our overcoats as the looks in our faces reflected the grim fate we knew waited for us.

As the sun began setting on the bitterly cold afternoon, the truck thumped to a stop inside an agricultural area with very few buildings.

"Climb down!" the guards said.

I jumped off the truck onto the snow-covered road, and the first thing I noticed about this place: no barbed wire.

As soon as the guard walked out of hearing distance, I whispered excitedly, "This isn't a karcer camp! This is a kolhoz (collective farm) camp!"

The other men looked around and clapped their hands to keep them warm. "Yeah," one of the other prisoners said. "You're right!"

Walking toward us through the snow was a man wearing a Hungarian army officer's uniform with lieutenant gold bars underneath his overcoat. The guard handed him a paper, and he signed the receipt for all of us.

"Are there any Hungarians among you?" he asked.

"Yes," I said. "There's our Group of Eight. And four of these other guys are Hungarians too. The rest are German and Polish."

The lieutenant said, "Oh? Then you guys are lucky that you were sent here."

"Don't say that!" I said. "We had plenty of lying during the past two years. That's all that we've had: lie, and lie, and lie again! So don't lie to us any more! Tell the truth!"

"You don't want to believe it?" he said. "Well, follow me and see for yourselves. You came to a nice camp."

"This can't be true!" I argued. "The major made a big speech at the main camp and told everyone that we would be punished here!"

"Well," he said, "I don't know what he meant, but here you will work for the kolhoz."

The Hungarian lieutenant led the way, and we followed him toward a building similar to the barracks at the main camp. Half of the building was built below ground, and the other half was above ground and had windows. Outside, I spotted a thermometer, which declared the temperature to be -30° F.

Guards joined our procession as we walked into our barracks, but they were easy-going. None of them were shouting, 'Davaj! Davaj!' Maybe the lieutenant was telling the truth! Maybe this is a good place to be a war prisoner!

We were tired and frozen from our trip, and each of us picked out an unoccupied bunk bed. We had barely lain down before everyone was called to a meal of bread and watery barley soup with a little casha (bran cooked into bran mush) therein.

We talked for a while with one of the guys being held here, and he told us about the work the prisoners perform in the greenhouse.

"Where is the punishment area?" I asked.

"There is no such thing in this camp," he said

The camp contained approximately 250 prisoners, mainly Hungarians, with a few Germans, Poles and Lithuanians sprinkled in. We finished eating, crawled into our bunk beds and fell sound asleep.

Although we awoke to another bitterly cold Siberian morning, we felt revived. The Hungarian lieutenant walked into the barracks toward the wall, and nailed a calendar with today's date circled onto it. "You guys are in good hands now," he said.

We cleaned up the barracks, kept ourselves busy and began to adjust to our new surroundings. The other people here, and sometimes the guards, acted quite friendly toward us. The camp was in the middle of a collective farm. Most of the people worked on the farm or supported it, including maintenance and repair of the combines and other farm equipment.

My first work assignment was to cut firewood for the Russian kitchen and bakery, which provided food for all the people of the collective farm. After I supplied them enough, I was to cut firewood for the greenhouse.

For this kind of work, I was assigned a partner: a stocky Hungarian pilot with wavy brown hair named Andy. The first day, Andy and I walked to our assigned wooded area where a two-man saw lay, and we cut the fallen timber into manageable pieces. Then we used axes to split them into firewood.

Andy was not a farm boy. He had grown up in Budapest and didn't know how to saw. I told Andy that when I pull the saw, he should let go. When he pulls, then I would release the saw.

However, no matter how often I told him, he could not get the hang of pulling when he should let go and vice versa. Therefore, our collaboration was quite uncoordinated. However, we still managed to make our production quota for the people in the kitchen, bakery and the greenhouse. The civilians were pleased with our work and production, and we cut plenty of wood.

Two men who now worked for the kitchen had cut wood before our arrival. Some days, we would switch assignments, and they would let us work for the kitchen. We also switched jobs with other people who worked in the cabbage and potato storage areas, and with the guys who performed other farmyard chores.

Other than potatoes, cabbage and onions, there were few vegetables. Cabbage was the main source of vitamin supply, and throughout western Siberia huge silos had been filled with cabbage grown in greenhouses. The greenhouse where we worked was one of the largest in the Sverdlovsk area, and green onions and regular onions were grown here after transplantation.

Unfortunately, we only got enough cabbage leaves boiled in water to make a thin soup. However, the food in the kolhoz camp did help to get me in better condition. I received bran soup and a thicker version when peas and beans were mixed in. Also, barley and oats occasionally were mixed into the soup.

Every once in a while, the kitchen would get chicken wings and legs, and the cook would boil them into the soup, giving it an immensely better flavor. This way, I received Vitamin C from the cabbage and protein from the chicken wings.

As another spring brought buds of life to the outside world, my strength returned. I had avoided the expected severe punishment, and I began to feel comfortable with the kolhoz routine.

My relationship with the Hungarian camp leader was cordial, and I appreciated his honesty and empathy. This meant a lot to the prisoners, and he helped us to relax.

One night, I awoke with a start. I had dreamt about a guy in the forest camp who did not wake up one morning. The dream was horrific as I watched disbelievingly at the guard hitting him but who still couldn't wake up. My bunk neighbor was dead!

I couldn't figure out if I was asleep or awake. I didn't dream this! But it happened a year ago! I was only now able to remember how his emaciated body was carried out of the barracks, and thrown onto the "dead men's pile" to stay frozen during the winter.

Was this civilization? Was this history? Can these casualties be explained in numbers? No! These are dead men whose dreams are frozen for eternity.

I thought about how Louis was faring at the main camp, and I was haunted by the promise I made his wife. He tried to come with me, but the camp leader wouldn't let him. I felt powerless. Was Louis sick? Was he getting enough food? Was he taking care of himself?

Anger and resentment filled my thoughts. I dwelled about the injustice of being a Hungarian prisoner-of-war in Siberia. Paper and pencils had been taken from me ever since I was captured. I wanted to write to my uncle. I wanted to write to my parents. I wanted to write to Maria!

I mulled over how precious it is to write whatever one thinks or feels. What a precious freedom to keep accurate records of death, and life!

Life? My father doesn't know I am alive! Neither does my mother!

And what about Ica?

And Maria?

How long have I been in captivity?

Oh God, over two years!

Terrible fears surfaced. I thought about my cousins, Geza and Thomas. What was going on in Budapest? In Nagylak? In Apatfalva?

I had hoped to go back to my homeland, but those hopes had faded. Over two years had come and gone — long, lonely years of shovels, pickaxes, hammers, spades and hoes for digging and wheel barrowing. Nothing mattered. The Russians could strap me down and chop wood on my back; I didn't care!

I had stayed in filthy barracks, slept in bloodstained bunk beds, wore shirts and underwear bloodied by hideous invisible bugs, ticks and mosquitoes. I miss having a hot shave and a clean room!

My senses have been assaulted by horrid-tasting soup with a gut-wrenching smell. Seven ounces of watery, barely edible bread filled with sawdust and oat husks. The body needs energy. Every day, I imagine having enough soup to eat and tasting delicious Hungarian bread!

March, march, *davaj, davaj, bistra*! I am a prisoner; I am nothing but a number. They can beat me, kick me or do anything they want with me. All the lost years of forming lines of five-man rows, always the interminable lines! I am no longer a man; I have been turned into a two-legged working animal!

These two years have forever plummeted from my life. This life in captivity never can be replaced or given back to me. My memories are not subject to rehabilitation or rebirth.

God did not invent this hell. Neither did the devil. Humans are responsible for treating one another like animals, and I have experienced this loathsome existence for over two years!

This is the twilight of my life — and I am a young man! "Let yourself go," a voice inside my head murmured. "Soon all of us will be gone. Give up. Life is over."

I shook myself, saying, "No! God, I don't want to die. I will do everything to survive."

Days dragged by and two sounds echoed over and over:

"Tick.

"Tock.

"Tick.

"Tock."

The planks on the bunk bed felt harder. The pain in my bones grew deeper and more intense. Nights became increasingly longer.

My days of inner turmoil and depression continued, and soon I faced an undeniable truth. Only two things would enable me to survive captivity: a will to live, and faith.

Spring arrived. Temperatures reached 33° F., which for Siberia was warm. The weather moderated more, and soon Andy and I were finished cutting wood. Work was available in the greenhouse, and tilling the soil helped to heal my raging heart. Days passed as I spent soothing hours transplanting root-growing bulbs of cabbage and onions into wooden pots.

The temperature extremes were astonishing. On April 27, the temperature was substantially below freezing. But by May 1, it reached 60° F. The sudden temperature spike caused a massive snowmelt, the dense snow pack receded into constantly flowing rivulets, and torrents of water flowed through the field.

The first week of May, I couldn't go outside, because there was water everywhere. The whole kolhoz appeared to be swallowed up by one huge flowing river.

The water receded, and for a week the thick, soupy mud made walking treacherous. A hot, dry wind blew constantly and the mud dried up as quickly as the snow melted. Hordes of workers descended upon the fields with plows, and the planting season had begun.

The kolhoz workers plowed the fields and made them ready for the planting of cabbage, onions and potatoes. As soon as a row was cleared, the prisoners rolled wheelbarrows into the germinating rooms and loaded them with pots of healthy-growth cabbage, onions and potatoes. Seed was used to sow fields of oats and carrots, which ripen in a short time. (Wheat, barley and corn took longer to ripen and were not grown here.)

As we worked outside, I noticed something unusual. Guards were not around much, and I felt a growing sense of freedom to our movements. None of us tried to escape though, because the Communist Party used pervasive tactics to encourage one man to report his comrade's wrongdoing.

One warm spring day, Andy and I noticed a goat grazing on a rapidly developing area of grass. I figured that one of the farmers in the collective farm had set one of his goats free to feed upon the grass.

During my captivity, I never had a drop of milk, and there was no doubt in my mind that this was the right moment to break a milk-free diet.

I said, "Andy, I've got an idea. Let's milk this goat."

"What?" he said. "How?"

"Don't worry," I assured him. "I know how to milk. I grew up on a farm."

"Where will we put the milk?" he asked.

"Hmmmmm," I wondered. "Let's see."

I thought for a moment and then looked at him. "How about in your hat?"

"No!" he protested. "You're going to ruin it."

"Don't be a spoilsport," I nagged him. "We'll wash it afterward."

Andy finally offered his hat.

"Hold onto it and get down here with me," I said, and I kneeled on the ground and leaned underneath the goat. Andy joined me, positioned the hat under her teats and milked the goat long enough to fill one-third of his hat.

"Have a taste," I said. He drank hungrily while I stood up. He then handed me the hat with the rest of the goat's bounty inside.

I looked at Andy and drank the rest of the milk in one uninterrupted series of gulps. I smiled, wiped my mouth and announced my satisfaction. "Ahhhhhhhhhh!"

We left the goat and went back to our chores. That night, after our nightly serving of bread and watery soup, the camp commander announced that a farmer had lodged a complaint.

Apparently, when the goat found her way back home, the farmer had attempted to milk it with little success.

"This animal belongs to the kolhoz," the Hungarian lieutenant announced. "Does anyone know why such a poor animal would become unproductive?"

Andy and I suppressed a chuckle and managed to look as puzzled as the camp commander did.

Later that night, the rest of the men and I gathered together to sing Hungarian songs, tell funny stories and sing the praises of goat milk in Siberia.

Chapter 12

SURVIVORS OF THE GULAG

The days of June passed by, and rumors flew around the *kolhoz* that the Soviet Union and Stalin had agreed to let Hungarians return to their homeland. At the end of June, a Russian guard sauntered into the barracks and said the words we longed to hear: "*Vengerski* (Hungarians) go home!"

We stared at one another in disbelief. Was this another lie? We didn't know whether to shout with joy, or groan with disgust.

The sound of an approaching convoy of trucks interrupted our moment of doubt. For some unknown reason, the trucks' horns sounded joyful. We began to hug one another; tears started to flow. It's true! We are going home!

Our caravan headed toward the main camp of Sverdlovsk. Because it was summer, the ride in the open-air truck was refreshing. As the trucks pulled into the main camp during the late afternoon, I looked for Louis, but couldn't see his face anywhere.

Once we departed the trucks, the guards instructed us to report to the administration building. We stepped inside and lined up behind the other Hungarians who had populated the camp.

We were being given a medical checkup prior to our departure. As I looked toward the front of the line, I spotted my faithful comrade, Louis, who was being inspected by the same doctor who inspected prisoners at the Summer Palace.

I ran to his side and saw no glimmer from his eyes. He appeared very weak, very sick, and my heart sank as I looked at him. I spoke to the doctor in crude Russian who planned to declare him unfit for transport.

"Don't do this!" I pleaded. "If he stays here, he will die. It doesn't matter where he dies, so let him go! I will take care of him! I promise: He will not die, and he will arrive in Hungary."

"Okay," she said. The doctor turned to Louis, and said, "You're very lucky to have such a good friend." And she stamped his paper, FIT TO TRAVEL.

Louis acted lethargic and his face stayed pale. He attempted to make polite conversation but was unable to complete his thoughts. I took him with me to the back of the line so I could tell him stories and cheer him up.

We talked about the illustrious Group of Eight, the Russian-American conflict, the dropping of the atomic bomb on Hiroshima and our immediate future.

While I waited for my medical checkup, I thought a lot about the major who sentenced us for stealing food. Did he commute our death sentence because we were brave and resourceful enough to survive the gulag? Did he knowingly send us to a collective farm so we could get better food and recover from the bad shape that we were in?

Perhaps I should thank him for being alive, I thought. I looked for his face, but he was nowhere to be found.

I cleared the medical exam and sat down to talk more with Louis. The constant companion I once knew as a jolly, chubby friend had turned into a frail, thin shell of a man. After a dinner of watery bran soup and the all-too-familiar seven ounces of foul-tasting bread, we went to bed.

White beech trees filled the eastern slopes of the sloping Ural Mountains as I proudly waved toward them. "You see how sweet they look?" I told my wife. "The panorama you see is perfect if you walk down to the valley to enjoy the green pines in the foreground."

A troupe of American soldiers marched behind us. I looked back at the general, who was explaining to a colonel, "This is where he was working. He helped build the railroad and the huge building here."

Around me, the building where I put down a foundation of mortar lay in absolute ruin. The bomb that hit this building must have been enormous!

I woke up with a start and opened my eyes wide.

What just happened? I realize I was having a dream, but it seemed so real! I'm married? I'm a guest of honor for the Americans? Do I live in America?

This makes no sense. I could never leave Hungary. I want to return to my parents and never leave their side.

I got down from the bunk bed and walked to the latrine, surrounded by feelings of confusion Later, I stayed awake recalling details in the dream over and over until I passed out, exhausted.

The next week was spent waiting — and waiting — and waiting. The exhilaration of learning that we were being sent back to Hungary was tempered by seven days of impatience.

Each day, we watched thousands of men leave the barracks toward a huge building complex where I once had poured mortar. The main building exceeded 10 feet in height and the entire complex encompassed 10 acres.

A few days later, we stood in line outside the barracks and were told to put our Russian boots and overcoats into a pile. We then exchanged our smelly winter clothes for lightweight summer clothing. We had lost so much weight that nothing fit — everything was baggy —but it felt comfortable.

The next morning, we were served morning rations and then lined up in five-man rows. We were counted, recounted and recounted again. And finally, the order to march was given!

We headed out of the barbed-wire perimeter. Eventually, we reached a railroad track where we were loaded onto 25 of the same cattle cars that brought us to Siberia. Instead of the 90 men per car that began our journey, the number of men in each freight car was now 65.

We climbed aboard the railroad car's bunk beds. I grabbed a space on the top, and Louis situated himself in the bottom row. Few people talked, perhaps because we couldn't comprehend that our time in captivity was really over.

I multiplied the number of men times the cattle cars being used. I figured that our number had been reduced to approximately 1,600 men — barely more than half of the Hungarians who left Focsani two years ago. A guard walked by and rolled the door shut. We held our breath waiting for him to lock it, but he never did.

Half an hour later, the train jerked into motion, and our ride to Hungary began. Besides our ration cans and the light clothes on our backs, we had nothing. All our possessions had been taken away, but we didn't mind. Everyone on this train had survived the gulag. We were on our way toward freedom!

As the locomotive chugged its way westward into the Ural Mountains, one of the men opened the sliding door about halfway. Louis and I gazed out at the city of Sverdlovsk beyond the ascending train and the vast landscape of Siberia.

"Louis, we made it!" I said.

I looked down at the bunk where Louis was lying and realized he had fallen asleep. The rest of us watched the Ural forest whisk by. We passed by places where the emaciated bodies of our comrades had been kicked off the train two years ago. Part of me wanted to rejoice on our train to freedom; the other part wanted to grieve.

Out of 3,000 men who were transported from Focsani to Sverdlovsk, only 1,600 remained. The only reason I had a little elbowroom on the return trip was because Hungarians had starved to death!

I remembered the mass graves that I had seen. I remembered how the ground was frozen when we tried to bury one of our comrades. I remembered how some bodies were left exposed for the wolves and insects to forage upon. I thought about the official term that the Communists used to describe their fate: "Vanished."

I seethed in anger until the steady rocking of the train lulled me to sleep.

A few days later, we crossed over the Volga River at Kazan, and then the train headed due west toward Moscow. We were able to open and close the door to the freight car whenever we pleased, and the guards' main function was to assure some semblance of organization when bread, soup and water were issued.

When we stopped in a train station, anyone with money could bargain with civilians for eggs or food.

I had a few rubles stashed away from the sale of fabric dye and the copper rings I manufactured at the textile mill, and I bought some eggs and strawberries.

I fed most of them to Louis, and he seemed to get better. I continued to talk with him as long as his eyes showed interest, and his spirits were raised. A sense of growing optimism convinced me that Louis was on the way to recovery.

Approximately five days passed on the train, until we reached the outskirts of Moscow, which appeared dirty compared to Budapest. We opened the doors so we could see the Russian city's big buildings, churches and the Kremlin. But the rails were too far away from downtown to see anything worth talking about.

After Moscow, the train steamed through Kiev and Lvov, and I noticed that parts of the Ukraine were being rebuilt. Then we headed south toward Munkaohevo in the Carpathian Mountains, an area called White Russia or Ruthenia.

When our train rolled through, the older people cheered us. Many of them regretted Soviet rule and longed for the old days. However, the younger people seemed to hate us, recalling incidents of the Ruthenian guards' sadistic behavior.

Three weeks of train travel to Hungary agreed with Louis. As each day passed, the joy of life grew inside of him and he seemed quite well.

After three weeks in our freight car, the train approached the Hungarian border. The journey had agreed with Louis; each day the joy of life grew inside of him.

Some of the Russian guards expressed their appreciation, saying it had been nice to know us. One guard went so far as to thank us for helping to rebuild the Soviet Union, but a couple guards spat in his direction when they overheard his words.

During the last 20 miles of my Soviet captivity, I struggled to reconcile conflicting feelings from my youthful, war-torn perspective. Russian people are all different, similar to how people in different nations have diverse philosophies.

The Russian politicians, such as Stalin, were horrid and didn't want to send us back from Siberia. But the country's people were good, and they showed us instances of kindness.

I wondered why we were kept in Siberia for so long. Perhaps the things we saw and would report might discredit the communists, because we never saw anything exemplary about their system.

The communists couldn't produce enough food for their people, and they didn't advance any new sound economic principles. The Soviet Union's agricultural economy was inferior compared to Hungary or the United States.

Production methods were inefficient, and communist technical expertise was far short of the European standard. The Soviet system was rife with cheating and encouraged the destruction of human rights. Workers and guards stole from their factories.

People were fearful of their coworkers and didn't show an inclination to do a better job. They worked only because it had to be done; there was no joy or pride in what they did.

I didn't see many well-educated engineers or designers, and people's homes were falling apart from poor construction. I didn't see concern for personal hygiene.

Russians were denied basic freedom. They couldn't own radios. They couldn't travel farther than 30 miles from one place to another without obtaining a permit from the police.

The wheels of the train squealed as it slowed its approach to a railway station. As the train stopped, a Hungarian stationmaster strolled toward the train leading a chorus of schoolgirls singing Hungarian songs. "Welcome to Zahony, Hungary!" a sign said.

People inside the station applauded, and though our legs were weary, our hearts rejoiced and 1,600 exhausted bodies crawled out of 25 railway cars.

We were home.

We were on Hungarian soil.

And we kissed the ground.

One of our comrades, after kissing the soil, suddenly collapsed. Everyone rushed to his side.

"Stand back. Give him air," yelled a doctor wearing a beige suit.

The crowd eased back and held its collective breath.

After a few minutes of leaning over the prisoner, the doctor held a stethoscope to the man's chest for one minute.

He looked up at the crowd mournfully. "I'm sorry, everyone," he said. "This man has died." Apparently, he suffered a heart attack.

A frightful sound of wailing came from across the station. His wife and children had been waiting for him, and their misery put tears in everyone's eyes.

As we stood around our fallen comrade, some Hungarian townspeople holding photographs of loved ones approached us and passed us some bread, the first Hungarian white bread that I had seen in almost three years.

I grabbed one slice and took a bite, swirled the disintegrating contents around my mouth, closed my eyes and asked myself, "Is this true, or am I only dreaming?"

Then reality set in again, as we quietly filed away from our newly fallen comrade and his grieving family. We changed trains here and were put into comfortable Hungarian passenger cars where a familiar steam locomotive awaited. We pulled out of Zahony and headed south.

I recalled the train-station environment of my youth as the familiar designs of Hungarian signposts caught my eye. The train puffed across miles of rich soil full of life, and I felt a sense of peace from the ready-to-pick produce and harvested wheat fields. Hungarian land was as bountiful as the day when I left.

Three hours later, our train pulled into Debrecen, an agricultural and cultural city of approximately 80,000 people whose railway station had been set up as a temporary Hungarian debriefing area. Eye-popping baskets of rich Hungarian breads, cheese, ham and sausage were presented to us. We sat on comfortable cushioned chairs where silverware and napkins awaited us on picnic tables adorned with pitchers of fresh, cool milk.

"Louis, be careful of what you eat," I warned. "This food smells wonderful, but it might disagree with our bodies."

The two of us ignored my common-sense warning, pushed aside the forks and spoons, and used our hands to satiate the long-held hunger of our first meal in the cradle of freedom.

After we finished, we were shepherded into a dormitory building with single-bunk beds piled with baskets of Hungarian army and civilian clothing. I quickly grabbed underwear, socks, a pair of size 9 shoes, an army shirt and belted pants that looked long enough. Then I threw away the old Russian suit that was the object of some unexpected laughter at the station.

We walked into a large bathroom filled with tubs and sinks and honest-to-goodness hot water. I filled up one of the tubs and luxuriated inside it for half an hour with what seemed like an endless supply of fragrant soap.

I stepped out of the tub, put on some clean underwear and looked at myself in the mirror. "Look at that beard! Oh, this will never do," I said to no one in particular.

Louis and I picked out two adjacent cots. As I sat down, I almost jumped out of my skin. On top of the cot were a real mattress, real sheets and a warm blanket. "I am going to sleep like I never slept before," I bragged and curled up contentedly.

With such ideal conditions, I hardly slept at all; the excitement was too powerful.

After dawn broke, we cleaned up again and went back to the cafeteria for breakfast. Tables were filled with sausages and fried eggs. Baskets were stuffed with Hungarian breakfast rolls. Steaming pots of coffee scented the Hungarian air.

After this culinary delight, we were ushered into a two-story building where experienced barbers gave us haircuts-to-order — and hot lather-rich shaves. We spent the rest of the day in an administration building where each man was interrogated thoroughly. Some of the men were detained in a holding area for transfer to jail.

"What did these guys do?" I asked one of the members of my Group of Eight (who participated in filching food from the Russian storehouse at the main camp).

"Those guys collaborated with the Germans," he said, "They are guilty of anti-Semitism." I looked at the detainees with contempt.

Fifteen minutes later, a pudgy-faced interviewer motioned for me to stand up, shook my hand and handed some official documents to me. "You are free to go," he smiled. He turned to the lineup of men where I had stood, calling out, "Next!"

I walked outside into brilliant sunlight where a butterfly grazed my cheek, and realization overwhelmed me. "I'm free. I am able to move about freely. I can get on a train to go see Papa and Mama!"

I went back inside the Hungarian army building and looked at today's date on a calendar: July 30, 1947. I had been in captivity for two years, seven months and four days.

In front of me, the Red Cross and Hungarian social services had set up hospitality tables. I filled out a paper, and I was handed a bag with toiletries and $5 in spending money.

The girls from the Red Cross helped me to get the telephone number for the principal of the gymnasium where I had gone to school. He lived next door to the house my parents were renting out, and I knew he had a telephone. (My folks didn't have one.)

"Would you like to use *our* telephone?" the Red Cross worker offered.

"You bet!" I said. The worker got hold of the principal, who expressed surprise and delight at my return. I asked him about Papa and Mama, and he told me that they lived next door to him — in Mako.

"Tell them I am coming home," I said. "I will call again and let them know when to expect me."

"That's wonderful news," he said. "I'll tell them as soon as we hang up."

I handed the phone back to the Red Cross girl, who asked, "Do you need a railway ticket?"

"Oh yes!" I said. "That would be wonderful."

In a few minutes my ticket was ready, and I waited for Louis. Once he cleared processing, we discussed our itineraries and decided to take the train early next morning.

Again, we couldn't sleep very well, even in comfortable hospitable surroundings, and we awakened before the sun arose to take one more bath and use our shaving kits and toothbrushes.

We enjoyed another breakfast buffet and headed back to the train station where we boarded one of the frequent trains to Budapest. The train huffed and puffed due west for approximately 70 miles until we reached the city of Szolnok. I needed to transfer to a different train here, and Louis followed me off the train to bid me goodbye.

"We've been through a lot, old friend," I said, "and I must ask you a big favor. Be careful of what you eat. You were very sick when I found you. Please don't eat very much; your body needs to adjust. Follow a good diet, watch the size of your portions and avoid greasy food!"

"Of course!" Louis said.

"Is that a promise?" I asked.

"Of course," he said. "Stop worrying! We'll both soon be home! Nothing can hurt us now."

I shook his hand; then I hugged him. And I watched him happily head back to his seat aboard the Budapest train.

I found a train schedule, and I telephoned the principal at Mako from the stationmaster's office with my arrival time. I thanked everyone for their help and climbed aboard the train to Mako. I felt conspicuous, though, because the other passengers were staring at me.

"Excuse me," a stout woman asked, "but were you in a Russian war prison?"

"Certainly," I said. "You can see from my shape and clothing."

The train to Mako jerked to life as the passengers in the car surrounded me with questions of where I had been during the last three years.

"Stop talking, everyone," yelled the conductor. "Give him a chance to speak!"

I answered as many questions as I could, and time flew by. At one station, a middle-aged farmer handed me a small package as he disembarked. "Please take this and eat it," he said.

I opened the package to discover a pastry delicacy: poppy seed challah. I yelled, "Thank you!"

While everyone watched, I closed my eyes, crossed myself and said a silent prayer. Then I feasted on his generous gift of food.

Early in the afternoon, the train arrived at Mako. As I stepped onto the ground, I saw my father for the first time in three years.

His eyes opened wide. His eyes filled with tears. He tried to blink them away, but this action only caused the tears to splash onto his chiseled face.

I choked up, and as our uncontrollable sobbing continued, we hugged each other with all the devotion that fathers and sons could share. Papa fought back his sobs long enough to utter, "Your face looks different. I hardly recognize you."

"Oh, it's me, Papa," I said. "It's me."

A shadow of a disembarking passenger passed over me. Subconsciously, I glanced over my shoulder to see if a guard with a submachine gun was lurking nearby.

"False alarm," I grimaced to myself. "There are no angry looks. Everyone has a kind look. Nobody is speaking Russian; everyone speaks Hungarian!"

And with my father at my side, hugging me, sometimes laughing, sometimes crying, we walked through the streets of Mako on a warm, sun-drenched day.

I was home.

Part IV

Chapter 13

THE AFTERMATH OF WAR

Papa and I walked across the cobblestone streets as the sound of our shoes echoed from building to building. Soon, we arrived at the elegant house that my parents once rented out.

Through the window, I saw my mother drying her hands on a familiar apron. She burst through the front door, tears filled her eyes, and her arms opened wide. The rest of the world disappeared, and I walked into her waiting embrace.

"Oh, how you have changed in three years!" she cried. "You're nothing but skin and bones!"

"Oh, Mama! I cried. "I'm so glad to be home!"

Mama held me with one arm, crossed herself with the other hand, looked up above and said, "Thank you, God!"

"Let him breathe, Mama," Papa said happily. "Let him breathe!"

Mama released me, and I stepped back to look at her and Papa. "There's so much we want to know!" Papa said, as his eyes twinkled like a jolly elf. "When did you get into Hungary? What trains did you take?"

"Oh, hush, Papa!" said Mama. "Let's let our boy eat and rest!"

"That's okay, Mama," I said. "There are some things I need to know. Did you get any of my letters?"

"Letters?" said Papa. "We never heard a word."

"Oh no," I said, and put my hands to my face. "I wrote more than 50 letters to you!"

"Well, none of your letters made it here or to Nagylak," Papa said. "I went to Temesvár to try to find you."

"You did?" I said. "What happened?" A sudden thought occurred to me, interrupting my train of thought. "Where's Grandma?"

Papa hung his head for a moment and looked up. "She's dead, Paul," said Papa. "She passed away three months ago."

"Grandma was never sick!" I said. She's one tough woman! What happened to her?"

"She died in her sleep, Paul," Mama said, placing her hand on my shoulder. "She didn't suffer."

I fell silent for a moment. "Was there any warning that she might have been ill?" I asked.

"She wasn't sick, Paul," my father said. "When we woke up in the morning, she appeared to be sound asleep. She just stopped breathing. It was very peaceful."

I sat down at the kitchen table with a look of dismay on my face. I couldn't imagine life without Grandma.

"Take it easy, Paul," Mama said. "You're home, and that's all that matters." She leaned over my right shoulder and placed a hot bowl of veal paprikash under my chin. "Eat some stew," Mama said, "and try to relax. You're home — home where you belong."

"Oh, how I dreamt about this moment!" I said, and delicately stabbed a sauce-laden midget dumpling with the tines of my fork. "I just wish that Grandma was here."

My mother and father didn't eat; instead, they admired the way I devoured each tasty morsel of Mama's home cooking.

"Would you like a slice of homemade Hungarian bread?" Mama asked.

"Homemade Hungarian bread?" I said. "You bet!"

I picked up a bread slice, and held it to my mouth. I closed my eyes and slowly inserted the bread until a goodly sized portion was stuffed inside.

I severed one piece from the rest of the bread, and slowly moved my mouth just enough to encourage the fresh ingredients to dissolve inside my mouth.

"Ahhhhh!" I sighed, and began to munch ravenously on the rest of the slice. "This is heaven — Hungarian style!" I said. "I'm so glad to be home!"

My mother told me that a returning prisoner-of-war told them that I might have died in Focsani. "But your father wouldn't hear of it," she said. "His only words were: 'Paul will survive. Some day he will arrive.' And here you are!"

With these words, Mama started to cry and ran off to dry her tears. While I continued eating, Papa told me that he visited Temesvár two years ago, because he received a letter from one of the visitors that I was being held there.

"I brought some food," he said, "but I couldn't find you. And the guards were nasty; they didn't let me get within 300 yards of the barbed wire."

I realized all of us had many stories to tell each other. I needed to know what happened to them during the war, and I wanted to let them know what happened to me.

"Paul, darling," Mama said, "have some more." She took my bowl to the kitchen, refilled it and set a second serving in front of me.

"Mama," I said, "as good as this tastes, I must stop. I have to be careful with greasy food."

I pushed the newly filled plate away, looked longingly at it and changed my mind. "Maybe tomorrow I can diet," I said. "This is too good to pass up!"

I pulled the plate back toward me and ate greedily. "Tell me," I said, "how is everything in Budapest? How are Geza and Baba?"

Mama's countenance dropped. "Paul, I have some more bad news. Your cousin was hit by a piece of shrapnel. He died instantly."

I dropped my silverware on the floor. "Geza, dead?" I said disbelievingly.

"Baba told me to thank you for bringing them the Christmas tree," she said. "That was their last Christmas together.

"You see, two weeks after you went to see them, a bomb exploded two blocks from their house. Geza was chopping wood in the backyard. Pieces of metal hurtled through the air, and Geza was hit in the head. Seconds later, he was dead."

I stopped eating and hung my head. Mama cried again. I stood up, and we formed a circle to hug and hold one another. "We will eat later," Papa said. "I'm going to take Paul outside to see the garden."

I carried my plate into the kitchen, and then followed my father into the backyard. In Nagylak, my parents grew vegetables, but here in Mako, tall trees abundant with fruit surrounded me. Papa picked some ripe cherries and apricots, and handed them to me.

My stomach rumbled as it began to digest the hearty goulash, but I sampled the delicacies from Papa's hand and from the trees. Each taste inspired another one.

"Tell me what happened to you and Mama," I said eagerly.

"That can wait until tomorrow," Papa said. For now, let's enjoy each other's company."

As late afternoon waned into evening, Mama served supper for Papa and herself, and she set aside another small plate for me. As we sat together, I had to pinch myself to make sure I wasn't dreaming.

Finally, as Mama cleared the supper dishes away, she noticed I was suppressing a yawn. "Paul," she said, "it's time for you to go to sleep in your own bed."

I looked into the guest bedroom and saw an old friend: the ornate walnut bed of my childhood. My parents had rescued it from the station! I looked disbelievingly at the soft mattress adorned by a feather comforter.

A luxurious hot bath later, I crawled into the bed of my youth, pulled the covers around me and closed my eyes. I listened to my parents talking softly in the other bedroom. I listened to crickets serenading each other outside. But I could not sleep.

Memories of good times and bad times filled my head, and I listened to the clock in the hall toll midnight. My eyes stared wide onto the ceiling, and I still couldn't fall asleep.

Finally, I decided that the soft mattress was interfering with my sleep. I got out of bed, grabbed a blanket and lay down on top of the hard oak floor. In a few minutes, I fell into a sound, restful sleep.

I slept so well that when the clock chimed 8 a.m., I didn't awake. My mother opened the bedroom door to check on me, and saw me asleep on the floor.

I was suddenly awakened by her excited voice calling my father, "Papa, come here! Our son fell off the bed!"

I leaned forward and rubbed my eyes. I opened them in time to see Papa rush to my mother's side by the open door.

"Oh no, no, Mama," I said. "I didn't fall off the bed. I had to sleep on the hard floor, because the mattress and the comforter were so soft that I couldn't sleep."

My parents looked at each other and began to laugh at my impromptu sleeping arrangements. "That's alright, Paul," my father said. "It will take some time, but you will adjust. You're home; that's all that counts. Sleep where you want."

After a hearty breakfast, the three of us sat in the kitchen and caught up with our years of separation. Papa said he had retired from position as stationmaster, and he and Mama had chosen to enjoy retirement here in Mako.

"So the Russians left you alone?" I asked.

"Not really," he said. "Since you have had a good night's rest, I can tell you our story."

My father began to tell his tale, and I listened intently as he told me what happened at the Nagylak railroad station.

"I was inside the railroad station," Papa said. "Your mother came to my office yelling about a lot of shooting. We looked outside the front window, where the rails are.

"Partially hidden by a ditch, some Hungarian soldiers had taken a position to protect the station. The rest of the unit ran through the front door and took up defensive positions next to it.

"I looked toward the rear of the station and saw a full-sized Russian battalion advancing from that direction. Some of their troops had begun to occupy the station.

"Then bullets began flying through the windows. I told the Hungarian commanding officer to evacuate the building and retreat, or surrender, because his group was badly outnumbered.

"Bullets continued to fly, and your mother hid underneath the bed. Meanwhile, I relayed the information about the ongoing battle and Russian troop movements to Budapest and Mako by the telegraph line.

"The Hungarian commander eventually took my advice and ordered his troops to retreat, leaving the railway station empty. I went back to the rear of the station and hung out a white bed sheet through the kitchen window.

"Bullets continued to fly, so I made my body as small as I could against the kitchen wall. Finally, Russian soldiers burst through the kitchen door. I stood up, hands in the air, smiled and gave them the friendliest greeting that I knew, '*Drusztutye!*'

"Boy, were those young soldiers surprised! I told them that all the Hungarian soldiers had left the building. I guess they didn't believe me, because they took me room to room to make sure that no one was hiding inside.

"I yelled to Mama to come out from her hiding place. Very soon, at least 30 Russian soldiers were milling about the station. An officer came up and demanded that we give the soldiers 15 chickens and have your mother clean and cook them.

"Soon, all the excitement was over. A few days later, the main Russian occupation force arrived. They took the cash box, your Leika photo camera, my watch and anything they thought was of value.

"From our yard, they took the rest of the chickens, ducks and geese. Then, they killed and cooked them.

"They even took an old clock and a brand-new pair of dress shoes. I never got a chance to wear the damn things!"

"What about Thomas?" I asked. "Where is he?"

"We're not sure," my father said. "We heard rumors that he is in a gulag somewhere."

"Oh no," I said. "That's awful!"

"Maybe not," Papa said. "After all, you're back. Maybe he's coming back, too!"

I stood up. "I've got to visit Auntie Margit. She might know something."

"Not today, young man," Mama said. "Not until you've got some meat on you and a few weeks rest!"

I looked at Papa, and he nodded his head. "Okay, Mama," I said.

Papa and I spent several days walking through his garden and comparing notes about the Soviet Union and its communist regime. Papa had become treasurer for the Farmers Party in Mako and was afraid that abuses similar to what I described were going to happen in Hungary.

Free elections were scheduled on the last day of August, and he feared that the Communist Party would make enough of a strong showing to take over the government.

After our conversation, my father took a nap, and I asked my mother about Ica. Mama told me that she received a letter from Ica, and that she wrote back that I was in a Russian war prison.

Then Mama handed me a second letter that Ica wrote before Christmastime, 1946. The town of Borsa, where she lived, was under Romanian government control. Ica asked my mother if

she had heard anything more about me, because some returning war prisoners told her that I had "vanished" in one of the
gulags.

"Aw, gee," I said. "She thinks I am dead."

Mama put one arm around me and held me tight.

* * *

Rosie's fainting spell in the railway station appeared to be
over. As I had related the story of my life in the war prison,
she gradually came to her senses. Now she was alert and fully
conscious.

"During my first two weeks home," I said, "many of my old
school friends came by to visit once they heard that I was back.
They are doing their best to cheer me up and help me start a
normal life.

"I'm back on my feet again. I shave every morning. I got a
fresh haircut, and I'm starting to look like a man."

"Well, you need plenty of good Hungarian cooking to put
some meat on those skin and bones," Rosie said. "Let's go to
your aunt's house and see if Margit and I can fix you something
special."

Apatfalva looked untouched by sorrow, but as we walked
along I saw a hint of fear in the faces of the people. Untrue
rumors often flew around small towns, because of the huge
number of war prisoners in the gulags and the growing suspi-
cion that Communist Party spies may be among us.

Most of the people I knew, including my parents, thought I
had died. Rosie dashed ahead of me with an ebullient smile
and a swirl of her skirts.

A familiar flower garden dotted with sunflowers caught my
eye, and I looked around to see Auntie Margit shedding tears of
joy and hope.

She hugged me tight and remarked how thin I looked. "I
don't know what's going on with Thomas," she said. "There are
so many different rumors going around." She confirmed that
Thomas had been taken prisoner and put in an unknown camp.

"Rosie, would you like to come in?" Auntie said.

"I would love to, but I've got things I must do," Rosie said.

"No!" I objected. "Rosie, you said you were going to join us!"

"You will always be dear to me," Rosie said, "but spend this time with your Auntie. I'll see you plenty of times!"

And with that remark, Rosie skipped out the door, and out of my life.

As I talked with Auntie Margit, she told me how Thomas became a surgeon in the hospital at Pécs, and that the occupying Russian army captured him there in February 1945 because they were in need of a doctor.

I spent the night in the extra bed that was used for my overnight visits with Thomas. I woke up several times, staring at the empty bed where Thomas used to sleep. I felt uneasy and worried about the constant companion of my childhood.

Early the next morning, I took the train back to Mako. Over the next few days, I began to undergo periods of depression, but my parents and former school friends helped me get over them.

My parents told me they had plenty of food in the pantry and I should take plenty of time to recover. I returned to the shores of the Maros River to soak up the sun and swim during the remainder of summer. Slowly, I started to put on some weight and get into better shape.

One Sunday evening two friends from school, Imre and Pista, invited me downtown for a night of drinking and dancing to Misi Fatyol and his happy band of musicians at the Korona Restaurant. Misi's band consisted of three violinists and a cellist, and they played tangos, foxtrots and *csardas*, a Hungarian double-step, two-movement dance.

I had fond memories of the Korona because after I graduated from high school, I had spent many nights there flirting with the girls who joined in the good times we had at the restaurant.

Back then, after the restaurant's 1 a.m. closing, my buddies and I would convince the band members to go with us so we could serenade the girls we liked under their windows. This approach worked so well that our serenades had been the talk of the town.

Anyway, one particular girl I favored lived a mile and a half from the restaurant, but the cellist had complained that the distance was too great to carry his cello.

I had asked, "If you didn't have to carry it, would you join us?"

"Of course," he had said, whereupon I picked up his cello and didn't relinquish it until we reached the girl's house. The band then played, we sang and my girl squealed in delight.

Well, that was in the past. I dressed up in my finest clothes, and Imre, Pista and I walked to the Korona. As we stepped through the door into the restaurant, the band was playing a tango and people were dancing. All of a sudden, Misi looked my way and signaled the other musicians to an abrupt halt.

He started singing, "As I love you, nobody else does," and the band joined in. The people in the restaurant applauded, because they realized that a special moment was taking place.

Misi remembered me, and what started out as a night of celebration between three friends turned into a night of memorable music.

As other old memories started to come back, I began to wonder what happened to Maria. I asked my mother, but she didn't know. So I decided to write a letter to Maria, take it to Nagylak and find someone to deliver it in Romania.

As soon as I arrived by train, I espied a fellow riding a bicycle who used to visit my father at the stationhouse regularly. I remembered that he owned some land in Nadlac (the Romanian side of Nagylak) and had free access over there. I shouted at him, he stopped the bicycle and I walked up to him.

"I'm so glad to see you alive and well," he said cordially.

"Would you deliver this letter for me?" I asked.

He took the envelope from me and looked at the address. "Nagyszentmiklos is five miles away from here," he said. "We're old friends, your father and me. Meet me at the railway station in seven hours. I'll let you know what happens."

I spent the day visiting my former neighbors around the railway station while keeping an eye out for my father's friend. Eventually, I saw him riding toward the station.

"I'm very sorry, Paul," he said, "but I've got some bad news."

"What is it?" I asked. "Is she okay?"

"Paul, listen to me," he said. "Many people with Germanic names have lived in this region since the 16th and 17th centuries. But the Russians didn't show mercy to any of them when they came through here.

"The Russians 'collected' most of them and treated them as German prisoners-of-war, with a particular preference for young girls. Female prisoners who resisted the Russians' sexual advances were killed or ended in Siberia. I'm sorry, Paul."

The man pedaled away as I stood in the road staring at his fading image. Like so many others, Maria "vanished," but I needed to give meaning to her life and death. Imaginary thoughts of her capture and death came to mind, and I decided that Maria fought for her honor.

Maria was brave, a good swimmer and athletically built. I imagined that before she was shot, Maria probably punched a Russian in the nose for his unwelcome moves. This is what must have happened to Maria.

Election day in Hungary held the promise of a brighter future for my country, and the citizenry turned out *en masse* to vote on August 31, 1947. Louis Dinnyes spoke eloquently to that promise, the Farmers Party received 51% of all votes cast and Dinnyes became President-Elect.

In order to make peace, the Communist Party, which realized less than a quarter of the popular vote, demanded that it handle the duties of the Interior Minister, thereby controlling the police and Hungary's security forces. Through this political maneuver, the communists had managed a *fait accompli*: a *coup*.

A week after the elections, my father told me that a former prisoner-of-war in Apatfalva had looked up Auntie Margit to tell her that Thomas was dead.

"How much more suffering must I endure?" I thought. I told my father that I would visit this prisoner-of-war, and Papa told me how to find the man's house.

The train ride to Apatfalva was gloomy, the railroad cars shook annoyingly and I held my head down almost the entire way. I trudged from the station to a peasant-owned small farm on the outskirts of Apatfalva. Tilling the soil with little purpose was the unmistakably drawn, emaciated face of a recently released prisoner-of-war.

"Hello," I said, extending my right hand. "I am Thomas Vereb's cousin, Paul."

"Hello, Paul," he said mournfully. "I knew your cousin well. Come in."

He led the way into the modest house, took two chairs from the dining table to face one another and motioned for me to sit down.

"I hope you don't mind me asking this question," I said, "but how old are you?" The grim look inside his hollow eyes gave him the appearance of being 50, but I figured he was younger.

"I'm 28, Paul."

Surely, this couldn't be. I was shocked. "You're joking, right?" I asked.

"What I have been through is no joke," he said. "You look like you have been through a lot, too."

My eyes briefly watered, I choked a little and said, "I've had a few rough times, yes. I was in the Sverdlovsk area."

The farmer nodded to show his compassion and the depth of his comprehension. "I'm glad you visited me, Paul," he said. "Unmarked graves are inhuman. Thomas deserves a few words said on his behalf. I'm not much of a talker, but it helps me to deal with how we were treated by telling you how he died."

"Thank you," I said. "I suppose we are the lucky ones — to survive, that is — and yet the news I have been getting makes me wonder who is lucky and who isn't."

"Don't think that way, Paul," he said. "Captivity is all about staying strong — in mind as well as body. Hungary is still in captivity. We must not lose hope."

"Yes, you're right," I acknowledged.

"Thomas and I were near Tigyina in the southern part of the Ukraine," he said. "Thomas was working as a doctor in a hospital, and the Russians decided his medical skills should be used in the gulag.

"Conditions in the camp were horrendous, because this part of the Ukraine is plagued by hordes of mosquitoes. Thomas helped sick people who came down with typhus and malaria.

"As you know, every prisoner is restricted to seven grams of bread. The rations are so ridiculous that we had to improvise, and Thomas managed to get hold of some meat.

"Unfortunately, the meat was contaminated with bacteria, and Thomas came down with malaria. Eventually, he succumbed to the fever and died. The next morning, they threw his body in a mass grave with the rest of those who died over-night and poured slaked lime over them.

"That's no way to treat a good doctor. Thomas was a hero!" he shouted. "How many people came back home in your group?"

"We came in with 3,000; we left with 1,600," I said.

"Our death rate was 70%," he declared. "All of them rest in an unknown place where human bodies become nothing but a number and 'vanish!'

"I know," I said, holding his hand. "I know."

"Thank you for coming, Paul," he said. "Now if you don't mind, I'd like to be alone for awhile."

"Certainly," I said. "Thank you for telling me about Thomas."

When I walked outside, clouds filled the sky and rain fell. I didn't have an umbrella with me, and for once, I was glad.

I took the train home in stony silence that night. The next day, the sun came up as it always does, and I went back to Apatfalva to share the story of Thomas' demise with Auntie Margit.

I began to stay at home more frequently, and I could see that my parents were worried about me. My left leg had developed rheumatism since the days of standing in foot-deep frigid water during the battles on Csepel Island. In addition, the prison conditions I experienced had damaged my kidneys and bladder, and my freedom of movement was limited to places where I could relieve myself frequently.

A month after I learned about Thomas' death, I received a letter from the wife of my gulag comrade, Louis. I tore open the letter and read it carefully.

"Dear Paul, please forgive the delay in writing this letter. I couldn't find your address for a long time. While moving some of Louis' papers around, I finally came across it.

"Louis has been gravely ill. I'm sorry to let you know that last week, he succumbed to his illness and passed away. I wish I could tell you what the cause of his illness was, but no one seems to know.

"I can tell you that he had been sneaking extra sausage and bacon from the pantry whenever I was away from the house. One day when I came home, Louis complained about severe cramps in his stomach, and I rushed him to the hospital. He kept getting worse, and the doctors couldn't figure out what was wrong.

"I thank you for taking care of him. Louis had to die, I guess, but you don't know what it meant for me that he could die here and not in Siberia.

"Thank you, Paul, for keeping your promise."

I put the letter back inside the envelope, closed it, placed it under my pillow and cried myself to sleep. I stayed in my room — grieving — for the next week.

Chapter 14

THE HEALING MUD OF HEVIZ

"Hey, Paul! Are you going to sleep all day?"

I yawned and looked at the alarm clock. Eight o'clock in the morning! Who could be yelling at me from outside?

I dressed quickly and ran outside to encounter my cousin, Steve!

"Good heavens," I said. "Look what the cat dragged in! What brings you here?"

"The end of the war, Paul," he said. "I just got back from a prisoner-of-war camp."

I was thrilled. At last, here was someone with whom I could share good and bad times.

Steve was a year older than me, as tall as me and strong as an ox. He lived over 20 miles away — beyond Nagylak —with his parents and grandmother in the town of Csanadpalota. After breakfast, we socialized in the living room, and I noticed that his left hand had shrunk and a stainless steel rod inserted into it.

Because he was Hungarian, Steve had fought on the German side against the Russians near the Carpathian Mountains in 1943. While there, he stepped on a landmine. Steve was fortunate, because he had triggered the explosion with his left leg before the rest of his body caught up to the leg. Fragments from the mine embedded throughout his left leg, but the leg was the only part of his body affected by the mine.

Toward the end of the war, Hitler pushed the Hungarian government to conscript more soldiers. Therefore, doctors removed half of the shrapnel from Steve's leg and declared him fit for duty six months later.

Steve was ordered west into Austria and fought against the Russians again. Then he was sent to the Austrian side of the German border where he fought against the Americans.

During one of the battles, he was shot three times through the left arm and once in the back. Two of the bullets that passed through his arm landed inside his stomach. The bullet in his back pierced his left lung. He lay there until a German medical unit picked him up and took him to a hospital.

At the hospital, a surgeon removed the bullets from his stomach and lung, put a stainless steel rod into his left arm and sewed him up. The German doctor worked a miracle with his surgery, and after a year Steve was released from the hospital.

Steve said he arrived in Hungary a few months before I did. We compared experiences all day and into the night.

We talked about how we were not welcome by the communists in Hungary, and how we had been labeled as Americanists, reactionaries and imperialists. The labels were convenient for the communists, because we owned a small farm of 17 acres and believed in free enterprise.

Before he left, we discussed the growing intrusion of Russian communists into the country and the confiscation of private property. Steve took the last train home, and we agreed to spend plenty of time together.

I continued to get better, and my mother's cooking restored 30 of the pounds that I lost in Siberia. Because both my parents took care of me, I also began to feel stronger in mind. However, the rheumatism in my leg and the constant need to pee bothered me.

One day, I received a mailing addressed to all former prisoners-of-war. The pamphlet promoted a Hungarian resort that had been reserved for prisoners with untreated injuries. Doctors, hospital care and a regimen of physical therapy were being made available in the resort town of Heviz, approximately 150 miles west northwest of Mako. I reserved space for myself and filled out papers describing the condition of my leg.

After arriving by train in mid-October, I was taken to the hospital where a surgeon removed pieces of shrapnel from my leg. The procedure went well, and I was allowed three weeks to convalesce — from the last week of October until the middle of November — at the spa.

The town of Heviz is built around a 60-acre thermal lake of the same name near Lake Balaton on Hungary's western side. In the middle of the lake, a structural foundation accommodates the natural lake formation where large underwater wooden platforms are connected to wooden posts. This engineering feat allows hundreds, even thousands, of people to use the lake at a time.

While I was recuperating from the surgery, one of my new-found buddies handed me a flyer advertising an outdoor music festival that night. The festival's main attraction was to be a performance by the Holeczi Orchestra, a well-known big-band jazz ensemble composed of about 15 musicians.

Even though we wore civilian clothes and were devoid of anything resembling the army, we were still required to obtain written permission before leaving the spa.

Well, it was too late in the day to follow the exact proce-dures. And Hungarian guys will go to extremes whenever passion strikes us. So because Hungary was enjoying the prolonged October warm spell known as an "old woman's summer," we agreed that no fence was going to keep us con-tained!

Half an hour after the sun went down, two of my buddies and I climbed over seven feet of strong wire encircling the spa and walked into town. Our cooperative success in thwarting the spa's restraints put us in a cocky mood, and we sprawled out on three adjoining chairs at a hastily set-up café.

We sang lustily and drank heartily while waiting for the orchestra to begin. Not too far away was a group of two older guys and two well-put-together women.

"Hey, guys!" a dark-haired woman called out. "Come here. The seats on the other side of our table have an unobstructed view of the stage!"

She licked her lips deliberately as she smiled at her blonde companion conspiratorially.

"Hell, yeah," one of my buddies said. "We don't need a sec-ond invitation!"

I grabbed my drink and napkin, managing to stay in the front of our group, and I introduced myself.

"Who are your friends?" said a blonde. "Don't you think you should introduce them?"

"Oh, of course," I said, "but we met only a couple of days ago, and ..."

My buddies interrupted me to introduce themselves, and the blonde clapped her hands with glee. "Now this is more like it!"

An onstage fanfare introducing the Holeczi Orchestra interrupted the conversation. The two women whispered to one another. Then the blonde announced, "Well, we're going to run off for a bit.

"Would you boys keep an eye out for us later on?"

One of my buddies took off his cap, performed a gesture of chivalry by sweeping it toward her feet, and answered, "It would, indeed, be our honor."

We never got a chance to learn the identities of our new companions before they wandered off into the audience, clapping and laughing. The stage lights of the outdoor amphitheater went up, and the show began. We danced and used hip jargon to show each other how really cool we were.

Hours flew by; dance partners came and went. None of us had much of a chance to rest before another enthusiastic dancer swept us off our feet.

After midnight, the multitude of vogue men and women began to pair off and leave. Once the applause from the orchestra's finalé echoed from the stage, we prepared to go back to the spa.

"Hey, mind if we take a load off our feet?" laughed a stocky middle-aged man in a tailored linen suit accompanied by the dark-haired woman we had met earlier. The man pulled out the vacant wicker chair next to me, and she plopped into it immediately.

The sound of a record with a smooth ballad filled the air, and a waiter wearing white gloves and a white towel over his lower left arm appeared. Beckoning to the dark-haired woman, he asked, "Madame, what can I get for you?"

"Well, she said, "it looks like these boys are having some of our best wine. How about bringing us another liter or two?"

"Of course," replied the waiter as he bowed and backed away.

"Excuse me for asking," I said, "but the music started before you could introduce yourselves. Do you mind?"

"Not at all!" she said delightedly. "I am Elizabeth. And these two wonderful married people are George and Magda. George is responsible for everything concerning the rehabilitation of POWs. And Magda," she winked mischievously, "is responsible for lots and lots of other things."

Elizabeth and Magda both laughed at an inside joke known only to the two of them.

"And Paul ..."

"Yes?" I said.

"No, not you," she laughed. "I wanted you to meet Paul. He's the pharmacist of Heviz and simply delightful!"

I stood up and shook hands with Paul and George and kissed the outstretched palm of the blonde, Magda. I then leaned over to kiss the hand of the dark-haired Elizabeth, whereupon Magda leaned next to me and whispered in my ear, "Be on your best behavior, Paul. Elizabeth is the [provincial] governor's wife."

I kissed Elizabeth's hand uncertainly, and both women laughed again among themselves.

"So, Paul," said George, "how do you like life here in Heviz?"

"Well, so far, it's been ..."

"Oh, George, don't be a bore," Magda interrupted. "Paul is new here. What do you expect him to say?"

Turning to me, she said, "Paul, tell us what it was like being in Siberia."

"Oh yes, please," Elizabeth concurred.

"Well, I suppose one of the things that most impressed me — and depressed me — was the czar's Summer Palace."

"Summer Palace?" Elizabeth repeated.

"Oh yes," I said, and I launched into a series of tales about my life in captivity there. Eventually, my soliloquy turned to the difficulty of killing bedbugs in Siberia.

"The Russians created a fireplace in a 60-foot-by-120-foot stucco-and-wood building," I said, "and it was used by prisoners and Russians alike. Fifty of us guys were able to take a bath every 10 minutes. But the other 250 had to stand bare-ass naked in the 40-degree corridor."

"Hmmmm," said Elizabeth.

"One of the prisoners there was called 'Stove-maker Frank,'" I continued. "In civilian life, he made ceramic fireplaces. Anyhow, he figured out how to modify the fireplace and make the room hot enough to kill the bedbugs. But he never could figure out how to keep 250 naked Hungarians from waiting in line!"

"What a delicious sight!" Magda exclaimed. Both women giggled deviously. Leaning toward Elizabeth, she added, "I think Paul is dying to dance some more. Don't you think so, Elizabeth?"

"You are so good at reading my mind!" Elizabeth howled.

"C'mon, Paul," she said, pulling me up with her hand. "Let's see if you can dance!"

I took Elizabeth into my arms at a polite distance and matched the rhythm of a sultry samba record. She flared her skirt, stomped one foot and cried out, "Oh yeah!"

The next tune was a slow one, and although I began holding her at a conservative distance, halfway through the song she pressed tightly toward me.

"Paul," she murmured dreamily. "Do you know about the slightly sulfurous waters that push their way up into the lake? They come from more than 20 cracks on top of a volcanic crater, which makes the water really — *hot*." Elizabeth moved closer to add a delightful discomfort to the word, "hot."

"In the middle of the lake," she continued, "a structural foundation accommodates the natural lake formation where large underwater wooden platforms are connected to wooden posts. This engineering feat allows hundreds, even thousands, of people to use the lake at a time. Because everyone loves it — *hot*."

Elizabeth leaned back to stare in my eyes as she licked her lips deliberately.

"Around the shallow rim of the lake are areas of warm radioactive mud," she said, "which serve to cure diseases of the joints and nervous disorders. This mud oozes into every single little nook and cranny of one's body, and it feels so good, because it's so — *hot*."

She leaned her head back, exposing the exquisite curves from her slender neck to her partially exposed bodice to my nervous view.

Her knee pressed against my inside thigh, and I gritted my teeth.

"Three years without women!" I thought.

"So, Paul," she asked with pretensions of naiveté, "do you like it — *hot*?"

"Oh yeah," I muttered, with my mind in a blur.

"That's so sweet, Paul," she answered. "How *hot* do you like it?"

As she gazed intently into my eyes, I felt skyrockets go off, my body momentarily convulsed, and my face turned ripe-cherry-red.

Elizabeth immediately turned to the table, grabbed a glass of wine and threw it on my pants.

"Oh dear!" She said. "I'm sorry. I spilled my wine. Do you forgive me, Paul, dear?"

"Of course!" I answered. "Anything you say!" And I rushed to the nearest bathroom to thoroughly clean the wine from my pants.

When I returned to the table, one of my buddies said, "Elizabeth apologized, but they had to leave. She thanked all of us for an entertaining evening and said goodnight."

I glanced at my watch and saw the time: 4:00. "I can see why," I said. "We better get back to the spa before the sun comes up!"

We crawled over the wire, walked quietly to the barracks and crept stealthily toward our beds. The occupant of the bed next to mine leaned up and said, "You guys are in big trouble! The supervising doctor paid us a surprise inspection — with the president of the resort — while you were gone. They found stuffed pajamas in your beds!"

A few of the other former POWs awoke and laughed quietly.

Two of us had stuffed our pajamas with rags, towels, sheets and blankets to give the appearance of real bodies. However, the third guy did not bother to carry out his end of the ruse, exposing the group to intensive inspection.

We spent a short night of fitful sleep in anticipation of the next day's consequences. Sure enough, the three of us were confined to quarters and told to report for "sentencing" in three days.

On the afternoon of our "sentencing," an ambulance pulled up in front of the spa, and the attendants told us to get inside.

We shrugged our shoulders and got into the back. The vehicle flew across the road toward town and dropped us in front of a nightclub. The driver opened the back door, and we rose to our feet in front of the two delightful women and their companions we met three days earlier.

"You are hereby sentenced," Elizabeth said, "to stay here for an additional three weeks. You will be staying here through the first week of December. Enjoy yourselves!"

We all laughed and hugged one another until George signaled the driver. "I'm sorry to say this, boys," George said, "but Elizabeth must be on her way."

We shook hands, exchanged kisses on the cheek and were led back into the ambulance. Once we got inside, the three of us celebrated our favorable impression on the spa's management and VIPs.

Days went by, and I amused myself with thoughts of Elizabeth while submersed in the squishy-warm gurgling mud. The first days of November were chilly and blustery, so I would stay in the water each time for an hour or two. Moments of reverie caused me to lapse into flights of fancy and be unaware of my surroundings.

That's how I met Lola. I was engrossed in the warm feelings from the mud until she waded toward me and introduced herself. Lola's brown eyes sparkled, she had the right equipment in the right places, and she matched my height perfectly. Furthermore, she was good-looking, worked for the postal service and liked to party, party, party.

My moments of reverie turned into days and nights of ecstasy, and I lost track of time while her name rolled across my tongue over and over, "Lola, Lola, Lola."

One night, Lola and I went to the local winery on top of a lofty hill. The winery had hosted a winemaking contest, and Lola drank so much of the competing wines that she had difficulty managing her equilibrium.

"I've got a solution," I offered, noticing a nearby wheelbarrow. "To get back to the resort, we must complete a tricky descent. Climb in the wheelbarrow and let me wheel you down!"

"What a good idea!" she said, and she fastened the white sweater securely to protect her body from the chilly gusts of wind coming up the hill. She lay down in the wheelbarrow with her head dangling over the front and her legs dangling toward me. I grasped the farmer's implement tightly and guided the makeshift vehicle downhill.

When we arrived at the street below, an onrushing crowd of fun seekers ran past us proclaiming the imminent start of a cotillion. And we hollered, "Wait for us!"

We entered the lobby of an exclusive resort and followed the crowd through a long, well-lit hallway until we reached a formally appointed ballroom where a well-rehearsed ensemble was playing.

Lola smiled like a pleasantly awakened child, and we started to dance. As we circled the other dancers, I noticed that everyone was laughing — at us.

Every move I made with Lola caused dancers near us to step back, stare and then double-up with laughter. "What the hell are these people laughing at?" I said to myself.

"Lola," I said, "turn around."

My beautiful partner spun around slowly as if caught in a slow-motion whirlwind. She raised both arms dreamily into the air. As the back of her white sweater came into view, I saw uneven lines of brown residue. The breeze from her slow twirling circle carried the telltale odor of cow manure.

"Lola, let's get the hell out of here!" I said.

"Why?" she asked. "What's the matter?"

"Because," I said, "your sweater is covered with manure!"

"Oh, that's just fine!" she screamed. "It never fails! I always have to put up with shit from somewhere!"

The crowd of merry-makers roared its approval of Lola's sentiments. We discarded the sweater outside, and then came back in to dance some more.

That night, when Lola and I returned to the two-story resort reserved for Hungary's postal workers, we went to sleep by counting sheep, all of whom were wearing diapers.

Chapter 15

RHAPSODY

My six weeks of recovery and bliss were complete, and I returned to Mako invigorated. My parents wanted me to rest in my room, but I was restless and filled with robust energy.

"Papa," I asked, "why don't I get a job and try to support myself?"

"Paul," he explained, "things have changed since you left for Heviz. There are no jobs available unless you work for the Communist Party."

"That's hard to believe," I said. "I'll get hold of Steve, and we'll figure out a way to make some money!"

While I was a prisoner-of-war, the communists had exploited Hungarian farm workers' frustrations by portraying owners of large farms as enemies of the people. Their land was confiscated and placed into a collective farm system to be apportioned to the disgruntled workers.

The system didn't work. Agricultural production plummeted, because most farm workers lacked the sophistication and experience to implement efficient harvesting methods that worked. Shortages began to appear for previously plentiful staples of food.

Governmental price controls were put into place to compensate for items in short supply. The price controls created a perfect environment for a "black market" where farm crops could be sold at substantially higher prices.

When Steve appeared at the house two days later, we hatched a plan to sell — at the Austrian border — onions, garlic and other vegetables grown by his parents and mine. The size of Steve's parents' farm was 60 acres; my father's farm consisted of 16 acres. Even though the growing season was over, much of our harvest normally was stored in the cellar for sale during the winter months. Therefore, we had plenty of produce to sell.

Papa and Steve's father agreed to our plan, and they sold off some acreage to purchase the three-ton, heavy-duty truck needed to transport crops to the Austrian border.

I didn't have a driver's license; Steve did, so he did all the driving. We sold some of our produce in Budapest; then we drove westward to sell our remaining goods in the border city of Sopron, where every tenth house manufactured its own fine-quality red wine.

Sometimes we drove into Szombathely or traversed the roads northwest of Lake Balaton, where vineyards faced southeast, traditionally the best wine-growing direction to situate a field in Hungary. Here, we picked up wine, grapes, schnapps and cognac to bring back to Mako.

Most of the highways on the route we charted were four-lane, and we easily chalked up 600 miles on the truck's odometer each roundtrip. However, we experienced problems replacing worn tires at black-market prices.

Steve and I built up a solid camaraderie during our first entrepreneurial experiences. During the long drives to and from market, we talked about politics and what the future might bring.

The communist regime grew stronger, and it established penalties for anyone who owned or managed a private business. Big factories were confiscated and turned into state-owned properties.

Communist literature proclaimed that a factory belonged to its workers; therefore, workers should receive its profits. Once the state took possession of a business though, lack of management experience caused the business to become unprofitable, and no profits remained to go to the workers.

As these problems became evident, anyone who tried to point them out was castigated as a troublemaker or, worse yet, a traitor to the country. Voices of dissent were silenced.

In January, I finally learned where Ica lived. She had moved from Borsa to the northern part of Hungary, and I talked to her briefly on the telephone. She was delighted to hear from me, because she had heard that I was dead. She told me she had married a Hungarian guy last year, and she sounded happy.

We talked awhile, briefly recalling some of the wonderful times we shared together. "What happened to those two Jewish girls?" I asked.

"Oh, they're fine," Ica said. "I kept them hidden in the barn and brought everything they needed. Once the Russians invaded, the Germans fled."

Ica murmured something to her husband, and I figured this was a good place to end our conversation. I wished her happiness in the rest of her life. Then we said Godspeed to one another, and we disappeared from each other's lives.

Steve and I made about a dozen runs on our truck, and we began to expand our operation by buying vegetables in Mako's open-air market. At the end of January, we loaded the truck over half-full and were negotiating a deal for some parsley when two of Hungary's dreaded AVO (secret police) asked us what we planned to do with the vegetables. I took one look at the unsmiling men in their dark-gray suits, and I knew we were in trouble.

I gulped and looked downward. "We're planning to take this to our parents," I said.

"Oh really?" said the taller policeman as he kneaded the right side of his mustache thoughtfully. "Your parents must eat a lot. You two guys follow our car to the station. We need you to fill out a statement."

Steve and I got into the truck and followed the unmarked black passenger sedan to the Mako police station. As we walked into the station, a couple of policeman I knew waved at me in recognition, and I waved back.

"Do you know these troublemakers?" asked the taller AVO policeman, holding up a 10-pound bag of onions.

"Certainly," said one policeman who waved at me. "He's a good boy and popular here in town."

"We'll see about that," said the AVO man with a scowl on his face.

An hour after signing typed statements, Steve and I were released, but our truck and its contents were confiscated. As we emerged from the station, I recognized a neatly dressed man with mostly gray hair who was one of the town's Farmers Party officials.

"Hey boys," he said, glancing at our truck. "Did you have a little trouble?"

"We sure did," I complained. "The AVO took our truck and all our vegetables."

"They're starting to crack down on all of us," he said. "The Communist Party wants to expand the collective farm system. That's why they outlawed your experiment with private enterprise. Did you hear what they plan to do with the pigs that we farmers raise?"

"No!" I answered. "What in the world ..."

"You will love this!" he interrupted. "As you know, the Communist Party is establishing quotas for everything, but most of their leaders are not experienced around the farm.

"One of them was checking the inventory of animals at a nearby farm and reached the line on his list where a female pig was listed. He asked the farmer, 'I see you have a female pig. Tell me: After she mates, how many piglets will she produce?'

"The farmer looked astonished and said, 'How would I know?'

"The party leader kept his head down, ignoring the farmer's answer and routinely scribbled while talking aloud, 'Oh, maybe 12 or 14. Can I write that amount into my book?'

"The perturbed farmer responded, 'Hey, did you talk this over with the pig, too?'"

Steve and I doubled up in laughter, and our merriment drew reproachful stares from the AVO policemen as they walked out of the police station.

"Be careful, boys," the old man cautioned. "The communists don't enjoy our sense of humor." He walked away as Steve and I contemplated what to tell our parents.

We walked to my parents' house; Papa was waiting for us. "I heard the news," he said. "The police called me from the station. I'm glad to see both of you safe and sound!"

He ushered us into the house as if we were being watched. "Steve," he said, "you should sleep in the guest room tonight. Paul, we need to have a serious talk after supper."

After dinner, my father explained what he knew about the quota rules set by the Communist Party in the new government administration.

Basically, small farmers agreed to set aside 80% of crops and farm animals we raised to the *kolhoz*, and the government determined the price we were paid. Anything smaller than a pig was designated to be a household or domestic animal and exempt from the rule.

The government established a two-year plan that established a quota of crops and animals to be raised by a farmer based upon the amount of land he owned. Since my father owned 17 acres of land, he was given a quota of five pigs, and he was expected to sell four of them to the collective farm.

"But Papa," I said, "this system can't work. You have five pigs outside in the piggery, and you usually slaughter two of them to provide meat for us during the whole year. According to this logic, you would need 10 pigs in order to hold onto two of them. What are other farmers doing?"

Papa said, "I don't know. No one seems to know."

"Well," I said, "I know what *we* should do. We need to build a fake wall close to the edge of the barn and hide two of our pigs there. This way, even if the communists take the remaining three pigs, we'll have enough meat."

"That's pretty dangerous," my father said. "These rules are being strictly enforced. Make no mistake about it: A party leader will come to this house to inspect our barn. Gulags are being built throughout Hungary, and any farmer caught cheating the government can be sent away."

"Papa," I said, "while Steve and I were making our deliveries, I could see that many of the farmers were hungry and didn't have enough food. The Communist Party had taken away most of the agricultural products that they grew. We could starve to death trying to make this stupid system work."

My father finally agreed to hide two pigs, and the next day I went out scouting for wood to make a false wall. In the meantime, my father sold six of our seven cows to the collective farm.

During the next week, my father asked me what direction I wanted to choose for my future. I told him how much I enjoyed working in the timber mill, but this career didn't seem practical after the Hungarian forests were ceded to Romania.

I told Papa that I was interested in getting more experience in the textile industry, because of the mill where I worked during captivity in Siberia. We talked in depth about this type of work, and gradually we decided that I could earn a good living as a chemist in the textile industry.

Papa talked to a few of his friends, and in February, due to my experience with textile dyes, I landed an entry-level position as a stock clerk in the paint and chemical division of the Hungarian National Agricultural Association Center (Moszk).

Moszk was a huge governmental monopoly created in Hungary to collect and warehouse farmers' crops into the collective farm system. Everything produced for the collective farms — wheat, corn and other vegetables — was warehoused in Moszk's branch offices.

The company's main office was located in Budapest, and the Mako branch was close to the center of town. One week after I started work, my supervisor provided a guided tour of the company's office and introduced me to many of its 30-plus employees.

A short girl with dark-brown hair was working intently on the company's books, and she looked up and smiled. "Paul," my supervisor said, "I'd like you to meet Margit Alexa. Margit, this is Paul Tarko. He is helping us in the paint department."

I sized her up and down. She was short, not like the tall girls with whom I spent most of my time. The supervisor led me toward the warehouse area where I was instructed how to perform my duties.

My social life in town was quite active, thanks to my attractive next-door neighbor, Irene, whose parents had died during the Russian invasion. Irene's girlfriends gave me plenty of attention during the summer, and I became very popular due to my single status.

The workload at Moszk picked up dramatically during September, and we put in equal amounts of overtime regularly. One afternoon as the clock struck five o'clock, our work was finished on time, and the large building echoed with the sounds of people scurrying to leave.

Lately, I had been admiring Margit's fluency at working with numbers. I observed that she could add up a mountain of figures accurately and do it without using pencil and paper. It was no wonder that Moszk hired her as an accountant.

As I bolted outside into the bright sunlight, I noticed Margit next to Elizabeth, a slightly taller girl who worked and roomed with her. The two of them shared an animated conversation while walking home.

"Hi, Margit," I interrupted. "Hello, Elizabeth. Do you think you can keep up with me if I walk the two of you girls home?"

"Hello, Paul," Margit said as Elizabeth showed her disapproval of my smart-alecky question. Elizabeth was a couple of inches taller than Margit but still a full four inches shorter than my 5'9" frame.

The girls set a rapid pace toward the house where they roomed, which was located two blocks before mine. I lengthened my stride to keep up with their rapid gait. Margit was well proportioned, but short and skinny, with dark brown, shoulder-length hair.

Her brown eyes flashed at me. "Paul," Margit said, "I'm surprised such a popular ladies' man would humble himself to walk us poor working girls home. Are you turning over a new leaf?"

Elizabeth stifled a laugh, and I bristled a little. "What makes you say that?" I asked.

Both girls howled in laughter, and I stared at them quizzically. "Paul," Elizabeth said, "every time we see you, you're with a different girl."

"I'm 26 and single," I said. "I go out with a few girls. What's wrong with that?"

"A *few* girls?" she said. "A *few?*" And both girls stopped as they doubled up in laughter.

I could feel my face turning red, and my emotions ran the gambit of embarrassment to righteous anger.

"What gives you the right to talk to me this way?" I yelled, and both girls roared with laughter.

Elizabeth leaned my way and said, "Paul, can we finish this another day? Our sides hurt from laughing."

"Of course! I replied. "Very well!"

I stormed away to the sound of uncontrolled belly laughter.

A couple of days later while walking home from work, I heard the sound of running feet, and I turned around to see Margit and Elizabeth running to catch up with me.

"Hello again, Paul," Margit said. "How are you today?" Her eyes gleamed fondly at me.

"Okay, I guess," I said.

"You must be," she said. "You sounded energetic at 6 this morning."

"Six o'clock! Are you spying on me? " I asked.

"No, Paul," Margit said. "We always hear you in the morning."

My father had sold all his cows except one and kept it at the vocational school five miles out of town where students learned, among other things, how to properly milk a cow. Every morning at 5:30, I bicycled out of town to pick up the fresh milk that the cow produced and came back half an hour later.

Because the house in which Margit and Elizabeth roomed was near my parents, the girls were in perfect position to hear me come and go. Margit told me that when I ride back from the school, they get out of bed, get dressed and are never late for work.

"So I'm your alarm clock then?" I asked.

"Of course," Margit said. "You wake up all the girls in one way or another."

I blushed from the unexpected compliment, and we walked the rest of the way to their house.

During the next two months, we saw each other frequently and became good friends. I would kid them about talking too much at work. They would accuse me of being a Casanova because of my endless succession of girlfriends.

Eventually, Margit and I went out on a double date with Elizabeth and her boyfriend to the theater in Szeged. While waiting in line to buy our tickets, a pretty girl looked my way and smiled.

Margit poked my shoulder and said, "That girl is trying to catch your eye. Don't you think she's pretty?"

I looked at the girl; then I looked at Margit. "She's flirting with me. Aren't you mad?" I asked.

"Of course not, silly," she replied. "Why should I spoil your good time?"

I said silently to myself, "Why can't all women be like this?"

The rest of our date went famously. When we returned to Mako, I asked Margit if she would go out with me again. She smiled contentedly and said, "Of course."

A week later, we went out together — without a chaperone. As I walked to the house where she lived, I found myself rehearsing every word I was going to say to her.

We traveled by train to Szeged. As the train sped through the night, I told Margit about my life as a prisoner-of-war. She listened intently with willing ears and captivating eyes that encouraged me to speak on and on.

As we entered the train station at Szeged, she squeezed my hand, and we glided across streets that I recalled as a boy when I rode with Grandma in her horse and buggy. The night air smelled crisp and clean, and I felt at peace with the world.

The show at the theater went in one ear and out the other. Once the theater let out, we sat down at a café to talk more. I told her about my childhood playmate, Thomas, how he died and what a decent man he was.

"Auntie Margit had two girls from a previous marriage," I explained. "One girl was 10 years older than Thomas; the other was four years older. My aunt felt close to those girls and never spent much time with Thomas. That poor guy, he never complained about the attention they received.

"I'm not saying he was neglected, because she always treated him like her son. But somehow the two girls were always privileged in the attention they received. And the girls used to tease him because they were older and called him 'little Thomas.'

"Thomas knew his role in the family and accepted that. That's why he was always coming to my house, and to my grandma's house, too. Anytime he could get away from his house, he was with Grandma or me.

"I have never met — and I don't think I will ever meet — someone as gentle, and unselfish as Thomas was. I miss him so much."

Margit reached for a handkerchief to wipe away a tear streaming down my cheek. I realized that time had slipped away, and we had to walk quickly to catch the last train to Mako.

When we got onto the train, we sat together as Margit told me about her life. "Paul, I came to Mako from the central office in Budapest," she said, "because food is in short supply there. The branch manager in Mako had worked with me and asked me to come down here, because he remembered how much I knew about the agricultural trade."

Margit told me about her expertise with crop cultivation and grades of wheat. She could look at a farmer's crop and instantly gauge its quality and value.

"Where are your parents?" I asked.

"My mother died when I was 11," she answered softly. "My father works in Budapest. He sells weight scales to grocery stores and anyone else who can buy them. Sometimes he makes good money; other times he doesn't. But he does his best to help.

"My older sister lives in Budapest also. She has seven kids and another one on the way. Her husband has a gambling problem; he loses money at the racetrack all the time."

"Who provides for your sister then?" I asked.

" Usually, I send her one of my weekly checks or whatever spare cash I can manage," she said. "Sometimes my father has a little money to help out, but most of the responsibility falls on me."

"That must be hard on you," I said. "Do you have any other relatives who help out?"

"No one except my younger brother, Bela, but he left Hungary after the war, and he's now in France," she said. "He travels all around Europe, and I hear from him only two or three times a year."

Margit's loyalty to her family was inspiring. As the train pulled into the station, I discovered that her greatest wish was to get married and have children. Margit wasn't seeing anyone romantically, and I admired the values she espoused.

My developing relationship with Margit was much different than the one I experienced with my former girlfriend, Etta, who flew into a jealous rage at the slightest provocation and threw dishes at me. She turned me a nervous wreck by constantly asking where I was going, what I was doing and whom I was seeing. Etta's jealousy hurt me in all sorts of ways.

Whenever I took Margit dancing and she felt tired or bored, she delighted to see me sweep a pretty girl into my arms and frolic across the dance floor. Margit was spectacular; she was "a pearl of a girl" who never showed the slightest hint of jealousy.

A true romance ensued, and I bought two season tickets for the Szeged opera theater so I could share my enjoyment of the bravura performances with her.

Meanwhile, Hungary's political climate grew more oppressive. The day after Christmas, the Communist Party began an assault against organized religion. Cardinal Joseph Mindszenty, leader of Hungary's Catholic bishops, was arrested, denounced as an American spy and charged with trafficking in foreign currency.

Shortly thereafter, in 1949, a "people's tribunal" sentenced the cardinal to life in prison. Churchgoers knew he was completely innocent and were angry that the communists could win this "show trial" on trumped-up charges.

As weeks went by, church attendance began to shrink. My parents warned me that Party members went to church services and wrote down the names of people who worshipped there. Every other Sunday, I stealthily wound my way through Mako's cobblestone streets to two Catholic churches where no one knew me and worshipped there.

The "show trials" of 1949 continued, and more priests, ministers and rabbis were denounced as spies and informers. The Communist Party accused them of traitorous activities against the Hungarian Republic, and the accused religious leaders wound up in jail and concentration camps. Everyone feared they were being watched, and many churches lost so many members they had to close their doors.

My parents approved of Margit, and I spent most of my free time with her. Steve and I got together only twice a month, and he longed for our zesty bachelor days when we hauled vegetables to western Hungary.

During the height of spring, Steve and I were talking about our past adventures with capitalism while strolling among my father's fruit trees. Suddenly, Steve noticed my next-door neighbor, Irene, planting poppy seeds in her garden.

"She's a good-looking girl," he said to me. "Maybe she could use some help."

"She might," I said. "I'll introduce you."

"Good afternoon, Irene," I called out merrily. "Do you mind if Steve gives you some help? He thinks you could use it."

I introduced them to one another. Steve's eyes seemed particularly debonair this day.

"So, Irene," he said, "would you like some help?"

"I think so," she said. "Have you planted poppy seeds before?"

Steve was cocky and sometimes too sure of himself, but he meant well. "Oh, sure," he said.

Irene handed Steve the bag of seeds and pointed to the 50 hoed rows in back of her. Then she went into her house to fetch a shovel.

When she returned from the house, Steve was emptying all the seeds into the first row. "Oh no," she cried. "What do you think you're doing?"

"Hold on! Steve said. "I'm almost done."

"You are done!" Irene hollered. "Helping me, that is! Those seeds are meant for all 50 rows, not just one!"

I slipped back into my parents' house to let Steve defend himself. His *faux pas* caused both of them to laugh, and they seemed to rub each other the right way. A few weeks later, they were dating one another.

Margit and I spent lazy weekend afternoons on the beaches of the Maros River. In May, I applied for entrance into the textile program at the Technical University in Budapest. Margit had planned to return to Budapest in September, and I wanted to stay close to her.

As summer went by, I looked for a place in Budapest where I could stay when school began. But I received a form letter in August stating that my application had been rejected.

One of the fellows where I worked was a Party member. I figured if anyone might know why my application was rejected, he would. So one evening, as he was leaving work, I walked up to him.

"I applied to the Technical University in Budapest three months ago," I said, "and just found that I wasn't accepted. Can you help me find out why?"

He looked at me and sneered. "Well, maybe it's because you are an enemy of the state," he said.

"An enemy of the state?" I said. "How could that be?"

"Well, your father was treasurer for the Farmers Party," he said, "and you did go with him to two of their meetings."

"Everyone in Mako knew that," I thought, "and how could my attendance at a political organizational meeting interfere with my ability to study?" I thanked the Communist Party member for his time and wondered what I would have to do to gain admission to the school.

Even though I would not be attending school, I decided to move to Budapest and stay close to Margit. I helped move her luggage to the station and promised to join her in the capital city as soon as Moszk granted me a transfer.

Margit obtained a room close to where her sister lived, and I visited her by train twice a month. I worked hard and applied for a transfer. In January 1950, my transfer was approved; I was designated as an administrative worker assigned to the Budapest office.

Housing in Budapest was tight. The confiscation of private property drove many farmers who lost their land into the city where they lived in substandard conditions. One of my co-workers told me about a six-story apartment house where long-time residents were renting out small rooms formerly reserved for servants.

I looked around the building and found a vacancy being offered by a sweet, gentle 70ish Jewish lady. I squeezed my belongings into a modest 8' by 10' room consisting of little more than a bed and a table. The landlady looked after me like a surrogate mother, and I lovingly called her "Little Mama."

Hardliners in the Communist Party ousted the president of Moszk in March, accusing him of surrendering to capitalist dogma. In his place, Joseph Szücs, a moderate party member from Mako whose loyalty to communism dated back to World War I, was tapped to lead the 80,000-employee company.

When I took the train to Mako to see my parents on weekends, Szücs would be on the same train. The second time we met, he recognized me and asked about my parents. Papa had met Szücs while I was in the Siberian gulag, and the two of them developed a cordial relationship.

Szücs invited me to sit with him, and after a couple of hours, he reached into his pocket and pulled out his lunch: four walnuts and two apples.

"That looks like a healthy lunch, Comrade Szücs," I said.

"And that's a proper observation," he answered approvingly.

We often passed the time together in silence, which he welcomed, punctuated by brief respites of polite conversation. From then on, the president and I sat in close proximity whenever we took the same train.

This politically correct turn of events encouraged me to reapply to the university. Sure enough, Szücs gave me a glowing review, and in August the Technical University accepted me as an incoming student.

The school's curricula were divided into two shifts. This way, students could work full-time and go to school too. Because of the exodus of competent professionals after the Russians invaded Hungary, students with a proven technical aptitude were recruited to attend the university.

Tuition was free, but I had to pay for my books. My shift at work was shortened and changed to 8 a.m.-2 p.m. At 3 o'clock, the second shift at the university began, and I attended classes until as late as 9 p.m.

These hours didn't leave much time for study. While class was in session, I could see Margit only on weekends. Considering the political climate, I considered myself lucky to be accepted as a student, and I was not going to let this opportunity pass me by.

Once spring arrived, Margit and I spent weekend days on the Danube River. In the early morning, we crossed over the bridge to Margit Island, a half-mile-wide strip of land separating the cities of Buda and Pest.

Moszk provided a boathouse for its employees on the island, from which I reserved a two-man scull for our use. I paddled the boat north against the Danube current until we reached Romai Beach or Lido Beach on Szentendre Island.

Once we beached the small skiff, we sunned ourselves on the clean white sand and enjoyed a delicious meal from the picnic basket that Margit packed the night before. Around 3 o'clock, I put the boat back into the water so that Margit could drift with the current back to Budapest while I swam next to the boat.

After a few of these outings, Margit learned how to handle the long oars of the boat. She wasn't a good athlete, but in my heart she was a pearl of a girl.

Two chemistry classmates, Paul and Peter, lived in my building. The three of us studied together in my tiny room until midnight, sometimes as late as 3 a.m. Nights went by quickly, and we forced ourselves to stop studying so we could get at least four hours of sleep.

As the communists tried to operate once-prolific large farms, production dropped and rationing began. Tractors fell apart, plows were stolen, the land could not be cultivated and the workers didn't have the skill to make management decisions.

Food, especially meat, became scarce, and rationing was imposed. One morning, I got up at 3:30 a.m. to stand in the long queue to pick up my landlady's rations. Little Mama was always nice to me, and I wanted to show my appreciation by picking up some meat for the Sabbath.

At 6 a.m. as I reached the front of the line, a clerk walked outside to declare there is no more meat and locked the door. I stood in place clenching my fists as I thought about breaking the store's door. Even though Little Mama told me that it didn't matter, I felt ashamed that I couldn't obtain any meat for her Sabbath.

During the fall of 1952, Steve and Irene got married. A month after their nuptials, Margit and I went out to a jazz nightclub in Budapest where I ordered a bottle of wine. We drank a toast and declared our love for each other. We agreed to get married, and when the night was over, the only question to be answered was when.

In October 1953, I had in my senior year at the university, and my parents announced they were coming up to Budapest. Mama had been diagnosed with breast cancer and, after undergoing a mastectomy in Mako, was scheduled for follow-up procedures in Budapest.

Geza's widow, Baba, had moved into an apartment in Buda, and I met my parents at her apartment where we reminisced about my late cousin. Papa told me that he had been forced to give up all his cultivable land to the *kolhoz*.

He was disappointed with the actions taken by the communists, and we talked about the massive influx of farmers into

Budapest looking for work. During the last five years, Budapest's population had mushroomed from 1½ million to 2½ million.

Papa returned to Mako to take care of the house and fruit trees, while Mama recuperated at Baba's apartment in Buda. Occasionally, I took Mama to the nearby hospital's oncology department for radiation treatments.

In a month, she recovered completely, and I was able to bring Mama home on the weekend train as a light snow signaled the beginning of another Hungarian winter.

Chapter 16

FIGHTING FOR FREEDOM

Josef Stalin died on March 5, 1953. The Russian leader called "Commander" was gone forever, and communists used the occasion to reveal their fanaticism.

At administrative headquarters for Hungary's agricultural department where Margit and I worked, a Party member accused one of our section heads, a highly regarded consultant on the proper warehousing of various crops, of being "a baron from the capitalist regime."

Two "screening agents" from the AVO took him into a sealed office to interview him and asked what the "Pr." Title before his name meant.

The section head's answer: "Proletariat."

It turned out that the section head had whimsically written an honorary title before his name.

He was shipped off to a Hungarian gulag.

Any display of dissent, no matter how much it was camouflaged by satire, was stamped out.

I continued my regimen of work during the morning and school during the afternoon, and in June 1954, I graduated and received my bachelor's degree.

The ceremony was a huge letdown. Back when I graduated from the gymnasium to end my high school years, everyone's parents were invited and cameras flashed away. Not any more! Our graduation ceremony consisted of the graduates sitting stony-faced in a brightly lit auditorium while the dean gave a 10-minute sermon extolling the virtues of socialism. The speech was so dull that we were thankful to pick up our degrees single-file and leave.

Summer days passed as I continued working at Moszk, and when September arrived I began writing my master's thesis entitled "Impregnating Clothing With Chemicals to Make Them Water-Resistant and Waterproof." As I wrote pages in longhand, Margit typed up the document on weekends.

Now that I was working toward my master's, I figured that I could find more-skilled employment. My education was going to waste in an agricultural company, and I was determined to get into the textile business.

In the gulag's textile mill, I was thrilled about working with dyes so that I could specialize in rotogravure cloth finishing. So when I heard in February about a newly created position — fabric quality-control chemist — in the light-industry administration department, I jumped at the opportunity.

I applied immediately and, within two days, the job was mine. After work, I met Margit and told her the good news.

"We don't have to wait any longer to get married," I said. "They are making me responsible for the quality of almost every fabric produced in Hungary! This will give us much more money. We can afford to get married!"

We had already put in an application for a regular apartment from the state, but requests such as ours were doomed to remain in limbo. We looked around and found a woman named Anna who was renting half of her large apartment in a heavily populated section of Buda.

Anna was widowed with a 17-year-old son named Steven. Our third-floor rooms were separate from one another, except for the kitchen and bathroom that we shared with them and their *vizsla* (Hungarian hunting dog). Even though the building was old, its construction was solid, and the apartment offered a grand view.

Margit and I figured this was the best we could get, because the communist system couldn't build enough apartments and houses to accommodate the out-of-work farmers flooding into the city.

At the beginning of April, Anna agreed to share her apartment with us, and we applied for the earliest government-approved marriage ceremony available.

We learned the date right away: April 16, 1955.

I was elated and must have told everyone I knew, because the night before my marriage day, my next-door neighbor invited three other guys to attend a stag party being thrown for me at the local tavern.

When you have a stag party in a communist country, don't expect to see any wild women. We spent the night drinking great Hungarian wine amid intermittent taunts about giving up my male freedom. When the night was finally over and I put my head on my pillow, one more day remained until I could hold Margit close to me.

At 11 a.m. in Budapest's five-story city hall, a dour-faced, chubby uniformed woman in her 50s performed our terse marriage ceremony. I wore a dark black suit, and Margit wore a beige silk-and-cotton-blend wedding dress with a veil.

My parents attended the 10-minute ceremony along with Steve's sister, Maria, who furnished a bouquet of red roses and acted as my best lady; and Margit's older sister, Ica, who served as her maid of honor. Baba was there, too. She had married an obstetrician named Zoli, and she was happy again.

After a small celebration, Margit and I spent a private weekend in our new apartment in Buda. The following Monday, the two of us were back at work "building the socialist system."

A week later, we sneaked away to a Catholic church where nobody knew us so we could observe a brief church wedding. Ica came along to serve as our witness, and we wore casual clothes so no one would suspect what we were doing.

The days and nights of our life together were amazing. We bought some furniture for the apartment, and we talked to one another for hours of delight.

My work was interesting, so I had stories to tell when I got home. I was a young chemist, and I could make my work as challenging as I wanted it to be. I didn't have any experience in making clothes, but I had the knowledge. I had a lot to learn about yarns, their various qualities and the finishing of clothes.

When work was done, Margit was at home waiting for me, and she listened to me describe each accomplishment as if it were an achievement. Our moments together were as bright and merry as anything I had imagined, and the bliss of our lives resulted in Margit getting pregnant three months after we married.

I supervised nine workers in a quality control laboratory. The people in my group inspected different factories to determine the level of each factory's quality-control procedures and teach them how to make improvements. One guy was responsible for rotogravure prints on women's dresses. Two of my guys were responsible for cotton, and one each was assigned for wool, for linen and hemp, for silk, and for synthetics.

Laszlo, who had 20 years experience, was the carpet wizard. Often, I went with him to different factories to check the strength of their carpet compression. He showed me how to test a carpet's worth by pressing hard against it to determine its resiliency.

Laszlo was brilliant, but he was diabetic and went into comas whenever he didn't eat enough to compensate for his insulin. Back in Siberia, if a man experienced a diabetic attack, I shook him until he woke up. Therefore, I did the same with Laszlo and gave him some of the sugar cubes that he carried in his right-hand pocket.

One of the great prides in our clothing factory was the "MADE IN ENGLAND" label that we sewed inside thousands of 100% worsted-wool men's suits and Lloden water-resistant light overcoats. The companies that ordered these products from our Budapest factory knew the quality matched the original made in England.

All of the workers assigned to me had years of valuable experience, and our little group thoroughly enjoyed working with one another. They knew what to do, and collectively our department achieved one success after another.

It took a year and a half to prepare for my master's degree and write my 138-page thesis. I defended all of my formulas and proved them. And on a bitterly cold day in January 1956, I received my master's degree and hurried home to tell Margit that the examiners said my thesis was well written.

The next day I visited a Budapest bookstore to find some information about the proper care of a newborn. As I rummaged through the shelves, I discovered a book written by Maté, the poet whose work I helped save.

Excitedly, I leafed through the pages and read a couple of his poems. It seemed like he was espousing mythical virtues of communism to keep his work from being censored. After a couple of minutes, I closed the book and shook my head sadly.

On April 14, a Saturday, Margit checked herself into the hospital after working a full week. Her leg had swollen up, and the baby was due any day now. Baba's husband, Zoli, was our obstetrician, but he was out of town undergoing army reserve training.

Margit seemed to be stable, so I left the city to make a round of inspections. Of course, both Zoli's and my absence meant that Margit's labor pains could begin.

The hospital located me at a carpet factory and phoned me that she was ready to deliver. Meanwhile, a nurse got hold of Zoli by telephone, and he gave her instructions how to slow down Margit's contractions.

The doctor arrived at the hospital at 7:30 that evening, I arrived at 9, and my newborn son, Laszlo, arrived at 9:30. Although hospital regulations did not permit fathers to be in the delivery room, Zoli let me go in right after the baby was delivered.

As I held my newborn child with the greatest of care, I felt small compared to the mysterious universe around me, and I blessed every star I had ever gazed upon for this magnificent moment of birth and hope.

That night, I telephoned my parents and told them the good news. After I described what times of night that the doctor, Laszlo and I arrived, Papa told me that our timetable was better than anything the Hungarian Railway ever operated.

My mother said that because our apartment was small, Margit should stay with her and Papa, so the baby could have constant attention. Margit agreed to stay with my parents, and she stayed with them until the beginning of September when her paid maternity leave was complete.

The green leaves of summer turned orange and red as growing voices of dissension permeated the government. Hungary's workers were fed up with its present leadership; articles appeared in the newspaper saying that for the good of the country, a reform communist should be made president.

Rumors were flying about workers' demonstrations, and I phoned Paul, who used to study with me, to meet me after work in a nearby bar on Friday, the 19th of October.

Paul entered the tavern looking animated and nervous. We huddled in a corner and ordered a bottle of wine and two glasses.

"I think we're headed for an important moment in history," Paul said. "Polish workers have already demonstrated for higher wages, and Hungarians are now willing to let the world know that their government is incompetent.

"Food is still in short supply. There is no freedom, and the secret police continue to take people away without justifiable reasons."

"That's very true," I said. "I never imagined the scope of what the hard-line communists could do to us. We were supposed to have reforms under the Communist Party, but where are they? There is no free speech; there is no freedom of the press.

"From what I can see, the party leaders in the plants and factories are pushing for faster and faster output. They remind me of the Russian guards, who were always yelling *'Davaj! Davaj!'"*

"That's the way the steel workers in Csepel feel," Paul said. A big demonstration is planned for Tuesday, and the workers are going to march to the Bem monument."

"That's great!" I said. "Have they organized everything yet?"

"No!" Paul answered. "They're waiting until Monday night. Why? Are you thinking of going?"

"Oh yes," I said. "None of the five-year plans that the communists come up with make any sense! We Hungarians have suffered long enough."

On Monday night, I passed through the familiar halls of the Technical University of Budapest to find out where and when the demonstrations would start, and to volunteer my help.

Posters had been drawn up demanding free elections, for Russians to leave the country, and for the installation of Imre Nagy, a popular communist who promised reforms that students and workers requested. Other signs complained about workers' salaries, long hours without paid overtime and the critical shortage of decent housing.

The next day, Tuesday, at 1 p.m., I cleaned off my desk as I usually do when I leave. Then I walked toward Buda as other citizens of Budapest filled the streets alongside me. Two hundred thousand Hungarians marched shoulder to shoulder in solidarity toward the monument commemorating the Polish general who commanded Hungarian troops to defeat the Hapsburg, Austria dynasty in 1848.

When we reached the square, a Hungarian flag was raised and the sun shone through the section where the hammer and sickle had been removed with a pair of scissors. The crowd roared its approval and another "purified" Hungarian flag appeared. Then another.

Famed Hungarian actor Ferenc Bessenyei's voice boomed through a microphone as he recited the Hungarian *National Song* and *Appeal to the Nation*. Then Peter Veres of the Hungarian Writers' Federation jumped on top of a car that had a loudspeaker mounted on top of it. He gave a prepared speech and finished it by thrusting a fist into the air.

We yelled a roar of approval that echoed to the Danube. We chanted slogans that bounced off every building in the huge square: "Freedom, free speech, freedom, free speech!"

The unified sound of 200,000 Hungarian consciences echoed all the way to the Kremlin.

"Join us!" yelled one of the students in the square. "We're going to the Petöfi monument! Then we're going to take over the radio station!"

The leaders of the demonstration took off toward their destination six miles away where the statue of Hungary's national poet stood — only two blocks away from Radio Budapest. In the meantime, another group headed off to demonstrate at Parliament Square.

"There's going to be trouble," said a man next to me. "You think the Russians are going to stand for this?"

My eyes opened wide. "You're right!" I said.

We had openly demonstrated our feelings and gotten away with it. This was a real accomplishment. But the students' zeal for change and justice had not been assuaged. There was going to be trouble.

I walked home swiftly. As I entered the apartment, Margit flung her arms around me and asked if I was okay.

"Sure," I said. "It was an inspiring demonstration, but I decided to come home. I think there's going to be trouble."

"Oh, I know there is," she said. "At 2 o'clock, the people in daycare, two floors above my office, called me to take Laszlo home. I've been listening to the radio for news. I was worried about you."

"When I left," I said, "the students and steel workers were headed to the radio station and to Parliament Square."

"Oh, my God!" Margit said. "Ica lives only three blocks away from the square!"

I turned up the volume on our radio, because the usual humdrum fare of marching music on Radio Budapest had stopped. Ernö Gerö, Hungary's hard-line communist leader, was addressing the nation.

Gerö accused the students of spreading rumors that Hungary wants to loosen its "close and friendly ties with the glorious Soviet Union." He went on to characterize these rumors as "a barefaced lie, hostile slander without a grain of truth."

He called the demonstration a "fascist putsch" and described the students as a "fascist mob and gang of bandits." Gerö said that he ordered the secret police not to let the demonstrators present their petition. The words of his speech were as incendiary as a Molotov cocktail.

That night as I huddled in bed with Margit and Laszlo, I held them closer than usual. Although our apartment building was far removed from where the demonstrators had gone, I knew what the Russians were capable of.

The next morning, none of the streetcars were running. Banks and factories had shut down. Radio Budapest announced that a general strike was underway and that martial law had been declared. The announcer instructed everyone to stay inside and not go on the street.

"I'm worried about Ica," Margit said. "Paul, we need to find out if she's okay."

"I know we do," I said. "If we don't hear anything from her by this afternoon, I'll go over there."

Early in the afternoon, I walked downstairs to the front-door entrance. I glanced outside, and an eerie quiet filled the air. I darted along the buildings and crossed the bridge to Pest. As I got close to Ica's building, a far-away rifle shot pierced the silence and echoed through the streets. Finally, I reached Parliament Square, three blocks from her apartment building.

I was stunned. A massacre had occurred here. Lying around the square were more than 150 bodies of workers and students whose placards of protest had been drenched in blood.

The Red Cross was on the scene, and volunteers were carrying the wounded and dead away on stretchers.

I ran past the square into Ica's building and ran upstairs to her apartment. She thanked me profusely for checking on her, and she told me that she and her children were okay.

As I made my way back through the square, I looked over the scene of carnage in horror. A little girl was leaning over the body of one of the students and sobbing uncontrollably.

I made my way home and bounded up the stairs. As I opened the door to our apartment, I vowed to stay inside until the danger was past. It was difficult to tell what was going on around the city.

As I held Margit and Laszlo in my arms, I thought about the nightmare of survival in Siberia and how brutal the communists could be. Those bastards had already stolen 2½ years of my life. They were not about to take away the love of my life and our child.

I clenched my fist silently. Margit felt my body tense up and asked, "What's wrong, Paul?"

"Oh, nothing," I said. "Just a bad dream."

On the morning of Friday, the 26th, Margit was fixing breakfast when a special announcement was broadcast on the radio. Popular communist reform leader Imre Nagy was introduced as the new Secretary of the Communist Party.

Gerö was out; Nagy was in!

The familiar voice of Imre Nagy resonated throughout the surrounding buildings in our section of Buda as he announced that martial law had been repealed, that the government is under control and that the country is secure.

Nagy promised to consider the reform program contained in the 16-point Manifesto of Hungarian Youth presented October 23, 1956 and promised to reorganize the government. He called for all workers to report to their usual places of work, because everything had been "normalized."

Margit and I looked at one another in amazement. We couldn't have asked for better news! As we hurriedly dressed for work, Margit hummed a happy melody and Laszlo seemed to coo along.

When I walked into my office, everyone was engrossed in sharing together the information they knew. After Gerö denied the students permission to appear on Radio Budapest, they began to chant for freedom. The dreaded AVO ordered the demonstrators to disperse, then fired indiscriminately into the crowd.

When the rest of the demonstrators saw this, they became furious and gathered stones to fight back. A Revolution had begun. A small Hungarian army unit joined the demonstrators and handed out guns.

Soviet tanks were brought in for use against the demonstrators, but Hungarian civilians explained the situation to the Soviet troops who then refused orders to put down the rebellion violently. Radio Budapest was taken over by freedom fighters and changed its name to Radio Free Kossuth, filling the 0420 spot on the dial with credible, independently produced newscasts.

Anarchy had spread throughout the city. Meanwhile, loyal units of the Soviet Red Army fired indiscriminately at civilians and used their tanks to level civilian buildings and historic landmarks. The 2½ million people of Budapest were irate.

Finally, Imre Nagy threw his support behind the demonstrators and promised a free government. He promised the citizens of Budapest to speak with the Russians and have them take out the troops and tanks. That evening on the way home, I bought a bottle of *schlivovitz* (plum brandy) so that I could celebrate with Margit.

The weekend provided ample opportunity to celebrate as Radio Free Kossuth announced one victory after another. On Saturday, Hungary officially had a new government. On Sunday, a ceasefire became official and Paul Maleter, who defended the Kilian Barracks against Russian tanks, was named minister of defense.

Hungary was free. Residents of Budapest opened up their windows to let the cool breeze rush into their apartments. Church bells rang in celebration. People greeted one another with enthusiastic hugs, and a hint of color was apparent in everyone's wardrobe. The workers were happy; the students were happy; the writers were happy.

Farmers brought bread, meat and other food to the big city. Suddenly, there was plenty of food to eat, and babies didn't cry. The invading Russians began pulling back, and the bells of freedom resonated throughout the land.

Part V

Chapter 17

THE IRON CURTAIN

Hungary's "independence" during the end of October 1956 was a Soviet ruse: a sick, theatrical charade.

Margit and I woke up early on Sunday, November 4. The weather was chilly, and we eagerly anticipated being able to worship in an independent Hungary. Around 6 a.m., Radio Free Kossuth announced, "Attention, attention! Premier Imre Nagy will address the Hungarian people!"

Comrade Nagy then spoke. "Today at daybreak," he said, "Soviet troops attacked our capital with the obvious intent of overthrowing the legal democratic Hungarian government.

"Our troops are in combat. The government is at its post. I notify the people of our country and the entire world of this fact."

The announcement was continuously repeated in English, Russian, Hungarian and French.

"Those goddamned communists are it again!" I swore. I turned off the radio in disgust.

Anna, the woman who rented out half of her apartment to us, owned a short-wave radio, and we frequently listened to Radio Free Europe when there was nothing on the air except communist propaganda.

I asked her to turn it on, and we learned that elite Soviet paratroopers and marines had occupied Hungary's airfields, highway junctions, bridges and railway yards in a surprise massive attack. The attack was so overwhelming in force that the Hungarian Writers' Union made an all-out appeal for help from the West.

Margit and I got dressed and prepared breakfast. We wrapped Laszlo up into a blanket. Along with other devout Catholics from the Buda section, we went to church to pray for divine and Western intervention against the Soviet forces invading our country.

We arrived home at 2 o'clock, ate dinner and hunkered down to await further developments. We heard no further news. We didn't know if help was coming from the West, so we went to sleep that night with a wait-and-see attitude.

In the morning, everything seemed calm. We heard little news on the radio, and Margit asked, "Paul, what do you think we should do?"

"You stay here," I said. "I'm going to work."

About half of the men in my group showed up, which was better than I had hoped. The single-story warehouse, offices and testing laboratory in Pest were only a few blocks from the parliament building. Those who showed up to work quickly forgave our missing colleagues who stayed at home with their families.

The streets outside remained calm until shortly before noon. Suddenly, the sound of machineguns filled the air, and bullets pierced the windows of the warehouse.

Everyone in the office kneeled down onto the floor. "This is war!" someone said.

"Paul, can we go home?" another voice yelled.

"Yes!" I yelled. "Go home and be safe!"

I locked the front door after everyone left. I moved cautiously along the buildings, stuck out my head when I came to an intersection and ran like hell until I got to the other side.

The farther away I got from the testing laboratory and the nearby parliament building, the more the gunfire abated. Soon, I felt confident to walk briskly along the east side of the Danube River.

Once I crossed the bridge from Pest, I arrived at Zsigmond Moricz Square, less than a mile from my apartment in Buda. The square served as a junction of four main roads and, under orders from Paul Maleter, Hungary's new minister of defense, contained a 75-millimeter antitank gun. Sitting behind the gun was a supply of shells — live ammunition.

A dozen boys ranging in age from 15 to 18 were inspecting the gun, trying to move it around and generally figuring out how to use it. The boys had pulled up some of the street's cobblestones and piled them up around the gun to construct a barrier that was 3 feet high, 10 feet long and 1 foot thick.

"Mister, do you know anything about this antitank gun?" one of the boys asked me.

I looked at the gun and at the puzzled looks on the boys as they examined it. I remembered the boys I trained at Szentendre. How young and earnest their faces were!

"Yes," I said.

"Hey, guys," one of the boys yelled, "that's my neighbor, Paul!"

I turned around and recognized Steven, the young son of Anna whose apartment we shared.

"Steven, what are you doing here?" I asked.

Steven ignored my question and spoke to the other boys. "Paul has used these guns many times. He will show us how to use it!"

"How many tanks have you shot?" one of the boys asked me.

"Well," I blushed, "I shot a German tank, and on Csepel Island, my men brought down 18 tanks. So I've shot a few."

The boys clapped their hands in approval. "Will you show us how to use it?" the first boy asked.

I looked at Steven. "Only on one condition," I replied. "You have to make me a promise. If you are prepared to use this gun, you must be ready to defend yourselves. This isn't a game. This isn't make-believe. The Russians will shoot back. And you are not here to die. Do you promise to defend yourselves?"

The boys gathered around me, and their eyes blazed in rapt attention.

"Yes," one said.

"I will," said another.

"Me too. Me too."

The boys fell into line.

"Then you need to make these barrier walls thicker," I said. "Russian T-34 tanks shoot 75-millimeter shells, which is the same size as this gun here. Those are big bullets, you know?"

The boys nodded.

"When those tanks fire back at you — and they will — you will need three feet of these cobblestones to protect you."

I measured the cobblestones and figured that a thickness of five cobblestones would provide the requisite protection. A group of boys began piling up the stones hurriedly, while the older ones followed close behind me as I pointed out the basics of using an antitank gun.

For the next hour, I showed them how to determine trajectory based upon range, how to raise the muzzle to the desired level, how to load the shells and when to take cover.

The boys learned so fast that I was amazed. When we finished and I walked the rest of the way home, I thought to myself, "These are no longer boys. These are now men."

When I got home, Margit threw her arms around me. "Oh, Paul," she said, "I was so worried. Listen to the radio!"

A recorded speech by Janos Kádár was playing on what used to be Radio Free Kossuth. He announced that he is the rightful premier of Hungary and was handpicked by a new communist government formed Sunday in Szolnok. He also announced that Imre Nagy was arrested.

His speech continued that the only purpose of "freedom fighters" is to overthrow the Hungarian regime and spread lies about the Soviet Union. Once again, the station was Radio Budapest, and its format hard-line propaganda.

"Margit," I said, "there is going to be a big fight here. Let's try to protect ourselves as best we can."

Since anything can slow down the impact of a bullet, we used the furniture in the apartment the same way I showed the boys to use cobblestones. We moved the big couch from the living room and turned it upside down to brace the picture window. Against the couch, we leaned the coffee table and the chairs that sat next to the couch.

About 50 families lived in our apartment building, and all of them protected their families the best way they could. The streets echoed with the squeal of heavy furniture being moved across the floors of the adjacent apartment buildings.

I knew that the bathroom was surrounded by a 2½-foot firewall, which was strong enough to stop a 75-millimeter shell. Therefore, I chose to use the bathroom as a "safe room." I put blankets into the bathtub and insulated the tub with towels, so it could serve as a makeshift crib.

The streets remained eerily quiet, and no one ventured outside without a good reason. We ate dinner and welcomed a few surprise visits from our neighbors inside the building. That night as we tried to sleep, the silence outside gave us a pervading sense of doom.

The next morning around 7 a.m., Margit and I looked at one another in mute amazement to the roaring sound of tanks. The Russians were invading Buda!

Quickly, I got dressed and went downstairs, opened the front door a little and saw a convoy of 12 Russian tanks dieseling past me on the right side of the building.

As the last tank passed me, I leaned around the building to watch their progress up the main street. Two trucks containing about 60 soldiers ahead of the tanks were on fire in the center of the street; I heard gunfire.

Some of the soldiers, many afire, stumbled and rolled off the trucks as machineguns from a rooftop pinned them down. Flames licked around the trucks until the vehicles were engulfed in fire. The tanks roared up the street, and the antitank gun from Zsigmond Moricz Square fired off a first shell.

Kaboom!

A direct hit! The remaining tanks roared off toward the antitank position. Another truck filled with troops raced ahead of the tanks.

Whooooooshhhh! A Molotov cocktail exploded on the third truck setting its canvas top ablaze.

Machinegun fire rang out, soldiers ran away from the bed of the burning truck while the sound of a second shell pierced the air.

Kaboom!

Another direct hit! The boys were superb marksmen!

The remaining tanks sped toward the square, firing their shells as they went. I heard a sickening roar behind me. Coming toward me — and toward my apartment building — were six more tanks!

One of the tanks fired toward the building where the machinegun fire erupted.

Kaboom!

The shell barely missed my building! The other tanks lowered their turret barrels toward the surrounding buildings. I slammed the front door shut and bolted up the two flights of stairs toward my apartment.

"I cannot see the boys," I yelled, "because there are at least a dozen tanks out there. Get Laszlo and head for the bathroom!"

Margit grabbed Laszlo from his crib and hurried into the bathroom. She placed him in the towels and gently lay over him inside the bathtub, making sure the pressure over his body was minimal. I followed and lay my body over theirs.

The floor shuddered with thunderous incursions as each tank fired its shells at point-blank range into the apartment buildings. The Russians were here to teach us a lesson about the future of Hungarian independence.

Each new jolt rocked the floor underneath us more and more. The bathtub clanged against the pipes holding it in place. The hinges on the doors complained of their uneasy support.

BOOM!

Plaster crashed down from the ceiling, the floor creaked crazily below us and shuddered violently. Our building was hit! The smell of burnt smoke mixed with the onrush of cold outside air. Dust filled the room, forcing us to cover our mouths and close our eyes. The shell hit the floor underneath us!

We cuddled tighter now. More shells rang out. The floor shuddered crazily with each new explosion; the supports for our building definitely had been weakened.

Finally, the tanks roared off and as the roar of their motors lessened, I crawled from the tub and told Margit to stay put. I emerged from our insulated human cocoon and looked outside through an opening in the window.

The Russian tanks were headed toward Zsigmond Moricz Square. I called down to the lady who lived below me. She was trapped in the bathroom by the debris, but she was okay and had not been hurt.

I crept to the stairway, went downstairs, peeked outside and saw no sign of the Russians. So I ran upstairs and told Margit that she could come out. The two of us unpiled the furniture that bolstered the front glass window and peered outside at the damage.

The freedom fighters I trained were good marksmen, and they managed to destroy two Russian tanks and a truck. The boys were smart enough to flee when they realized their position was going to be overrun.

Two days later, I went up the street to buy some milk from the neighborhood market. In the street were the burned-out hulks of the Russian trucks and the two disabled tanks.

Russian troops were removing their dead comrades from the streets, some of whom were burned beyond recognition. Meanwhile, the bodies of the slain Hungarians were taken away on stretchers by workers from the International Red Cross.

In our densely populated section of Buda, 10,000 people lived in five- and six-story apartment buildings. Every single building within one mile had at least one big shell fired inside of it; some were hit more than 10 times. Russian tanks also went out of their way to destroy private automobiles.

When I got inside the grocery store, nine people were in line, and I asked what happened to the boys.

"They put up a great fight," said an older woman. "Four girls got hold of a machinegun, and after the boys disabled two of the trucks with Molotov cocktails, the girls fired from the roof. One girl was a marksman, because she single-handedly shot most of the Russians.

"Eventually, some soldiers from one of the trucks were able to get behind cover and return fire, and the girl was wounded. She was arrested and taken to the hospital."

"They'll send her to Siberia, or worse," I said. "What happened to the boys?"

"Well," she said, "the Russians found two of the boys hiding in the buildings, and the soldiers beat them with their rifle butts until they couldn't move. While the boys were still conscious, the soldiers threw them onto one of the burning trucks, and we heard them burn to death. It was awful."

I bought the milk and hurried home. For a few days, we stayed inside as the Russians declared martial law. Russian units encircled the city and troops patrolled the streets, arresting anyone who got in the way.

After a week, Radio Budapest told everyone to go back to work. Margit, Laszlo and I walked carefully around the ruins left by the invading Soviets: teetering buildings with complete floors turned into rubble, burned-out automobiles with doors torn off their hinges and plowed-up streets.

The Russian tanks imparted a heavy toll on the city's buildings. Budapest looked like the aftermath of World War II.

As November came to a dreary end, all armed resistance in the country ended, and rumors spread that the AVO (secret police) was searching for anyone who was involved — whether as a freedom fighter or a demonstrator — in the Revolution.

A flood of Hungary's brightest minds was leaving the country across the Austrian border. Many of my neighbors in Buda were leaving. Children who were arrested for fighting the Russians were executed or sent to Siberia.

Although attending mass was risky, Margit and I continued to go to church on Sundays. On December 9, five weeks after Moscow orchestrated the formation of Hungary's new puppet government, we came back from church to find our landlady in a state of visible distress.

"The secret police were here a few minutes ago," she said. "They were looking for my son! Do you think they might be looking for you, too?"

"I don't know," I said. I looked at Margit, and she looked worried. Whoever reported Steven probably saw me, too, since I stayed at the square for over an hour. The visit by the AVO was an unintentional warning that if I didn't want another all-expenses-paid trip to Siberia, I had to leave the country.

As soon as Margit and I were alone, I whispered, "We must leave Hungary!"

"I must talk to Ica first," Margit said. "Maybe she will want to come with us."

"Okay," I consented, "but we better go over there now!"

We took the streetcar to Margit's sister's apartment in Pest and told her that we planned to leave the country. I explained that many freedom fighters were leaving the country across the Austrian border.

"Since Steve and I sold vegetables there in our black-market days," I said, "this is a good place for us to make our escape, too."

"That's dangerous," Ica said. "You should leave Laszlo here with me. I'll look after him."

"Do you know what the communists would do with Laszlo when they discover we are gone?" I asked. "He would belong to the state! No, my son will come with *us*. Either we all die, or we all escape."

I firmly grasped Margit's hand, and she nodded in agreement.

"We won't be able to carry anything with us," I said. "So we'll leave the key on our landlady's dresser. Take anything that you can use — food, furniture. It doesn't matter."

When we got home, Margit and I took turns using the bathtub and attended to Laszlo as well. We both had friends or relatives near the border, and we were confident they would help us escape.

On Monday morning, while Margit put on two sets of clothes underneath her sheepskin overcoat, I put on two sets of underwear, two pair of socks, two shirts, two pair of slacks, a coat, a pair of gloves, an overcoat and a pair of boots. I grabbed my diploma, identification papers and some matches. I put Laszlo inside my backpack; Margit took some diapers and a cooking pan.

We took a streetcar to the South Train Station in Buda and caught a 9 a.m. train to the agricultural and industrial city of Szombathely in the Vas Hills.

When we got off the train, Margit led the way to the home of her distant relative, Gaspar and his wife, Maria, where we were greeted warmly and given use of a bedroom for the night. Gaspar held a high-ranking position in the postal service, which meant his home had a working telephone.

I telephoned Josef, a former schoolmate at the university who worked as a textile engineer in the border town of Koszeg, and asked if he could help us.

"The situation at the border has become tense," he said. "You need to get across as soon as you can."

"Well, we can leave here first thing in the morning," I said. "There's a train leaving for Koszeg early in the morning."

"Don't make it too early," Josef said. "Get here by 3 o'clock. I need to go to work tomorrow so that my routine appears normal; I'll leave a little early. That way, we won't draw attention to ourselves."

The next day, after a half-hour ride to the town of Koszeg where snow-capped hills and mountains signaled the "bottom of the alps" and the Austrian border, we walked to Josef's

house where his wife and parents fixed a big dinner in antici-
pation of our arrival. After he arrived and we finished dinner,
I asked Josef if he wanted to go with us and find freedom in the
West.

"Well, that's very nice of you, Paul, but I'd rather wait out
the Christmas holidays with my parents. Maybe some day ..."

"If we make it," I said, "there will always be a place for you."

"You *will* make it," Josef said. "I'll get you a map so you will
have a better idea of where you are going. As soon as it's dark,
we need to get you started. It's going to be cold tonight. Do
you have any money with you?"

"Yes," I said.

"Good," he said. "We may need it. Next, we need to pick up
two bottles of Russian vodka at the store. I think we can put it
to good use."

We washed up and waited until nightfall and the clock to
strike 7.

We walked surreptitiously through town, and Josef led us
up a narrow paved road that quickly turned into a dirt road.
The road weaved upward past a border checkpoint where
Hungarian guards patrolled regularly. We hid while Josef
walked across; then he waved for us to run past the barrier.

We continued our gradual climb passing a few isolated
houses. Soon, we reached a house that overlooked the dirt
road.

"Stay here on the road," Josef said. "This guy works in my
finishing department." Josef ran up to the house, talked to a
man who answered the door, and then pointed toward us. A
few minutes later, the man animatedly waved for us to come
over.

As we entered the man's house, Josef hurried back to
Koszeg.

"Hello, I'm Peter," the occupant of the house said, and he
closed the front door behind us hurriedly. He took the bottles
of liquor from my bag, and his wife walked up to us.

"Do you have any money?" she asked. I handed her all the
currency from my wallet, and she motioned us past the newly
erected, bare Christmas tree into their bedroom.

"Get down on the floor and hide," she whispered. "The Russians patrol the area outside our back door. Peter will use the vodka to keep them distracted."

The woman pointed beyond the far side of the bed where we would be completely hidden. She lay down on the near side of the bed as if she was sleeping.

From outside, we heard Peter call out, "Hey guys, do you want to talk about wine, women and song? I've got some good Russian vodka tonight!"

Two gruff voices greeted Peter in Russian, and we heard the backdoor open and close. Voices cheered and glasses clinked. We lay flat on the floor listening to the gleeful laughter of three men getting drunk in the kitchen.

"Get ready," the woman warned. She picked a moment when the laughter caused the bedroom picture frame to rattle, and she ran up to the window next to the bed. Quickly, she raised it and whispered emphatically, "Go!"

I crawled out the window with Laszlo in the backpack. Margit handed me the bags with diapers to hold until she made her way outside. Behind us, the window closed as Peter's wife motioned us to hurry away. And off we went, dashing toward the border.

Even though the wind was calm, the night was zero-degree cold. The ground was frozen hard, and a light snow accumulation crunched under our boots. The heavy layers of clothes caused us to perspire heavily.

We ran about 15 minutes until we came to a deep depression in the ground, created by many spring thaws. This foot-deep gully didn't hide our bodies unless we crawled on our hands and knees, which made us grateful that we wore thick insulated gloves in our escape to freedom.

Four hours later as we approached the border crossing, the moon emerged from behind a cloud deck. Ahead of us, I saw the broken barbed-wire fence separating Hungary from Austria!

A flare shot up into the sky. The floating-on-air spotlight turned the moonlit night into day, and the shadows of our bodies spilled into the nearby snow. We played dead until the flare burned itself out, and we could crawl again.

We crawled through the ditch carefully as the border crossing loomed closer. Only 50 more yards to go. 49, 48, 47. I counted down the distance silently as we inched our way to the opening in the fence.

Five yards from freedom, another flare lit up the sky. My hair stood on edge. Something was wrong. "Let's go!" I whispered. "We're almost there!"

The moon and stars disappeared, a bright light shone into my face, and I heard a gruff voice say in Hungarian, "Stop, or we will shoot!"

Chapter 18

AUSTRIA

We stood up and put both hands in the air.

"What's this?" a voice asked. Two hands groped my backpack, and Laszlo gurgled a greeting. "He's got a baby in here!" the voice said.

The light glaring on me turned aside, revealing the uniform of a Hungarian army soldier. These were border guards!

"Do you have a gun?" he asked.

"No," I said. "We just want to go through the border."

"Oh no, you're not," he said. "We're arresting you."

"Oh please, you can't do that to us," I said. "Do you see my son here? He's only a baby. Don't torture all of us by arresting us. You'll destroy us.

"You're a patriot, right? Well, I served in the Hungarian army, but they *still* sent me to Siberia. How would you feel if that happened to you?

"Look, we have money!" I pulled out the thin wad of reserve cash that I had tucked away in my left-hand pants pocket. "Take my watch, take my ring."

The guard looked toward his partner; then the two of them looked from one end of the clearing to the other. "Give them to us," he said, "but be quick about it!"

I handed him the money, loosened the watchband around my wrist and wriggled the wedding ring off my fourth finger.

The guard stuck everything in his pockets. "Alright, you can go," he said. "And if you're asked, you didn't see us."

"Yes, I know," I said.

Margit pushed me forward. "Let's go, Paul," she urged.

We scampered across the snow for 10 minutes until we found a slightly wooded area and the guards were far behind us. We slowed to a casual walk, then stopped.

"Where are we?" I asked. I had lost all sense of our bearings when the border guards stopped us.

"I can't tell," Margit said. "Isn't Austria this way?"

"I think so, but I'm not sure," I said. "Let's sit on this ledge and wait. There is a good view of the entire countryside."

The landscape undulated gradually, and our position and elevation provided a splendid view. We were fully insulated from our several layers of clothes, and we looked over the moonlit terrain for half an hour.

"I see a train, Paul!" said Margit. On the right side of the valley was a brightly lit, 20-car passenger train.

"That's the way we go!" I said. "There's Austria."

In Hungary, trains were not lit up and had to operate in the dark. But in Austria, the trains were well lighted. We walked amiably in that direction and reached a well-used dirt trail. We followed the trail at a leisurely pace as it grew wider and became a road. Two hours later, we strolled around a bend toward a brightly lit Austrian guardhouse.

We approached the shack cautiously, and a jolly-faced stout soldier addressed us in German. "Good morning! Do you know where you are?"

"Austria?" I asked.

"Of course, you are," he laughed. "Welcome to Austria. Would you care for some coffee?"

"Thank you," I said.

"Do you have any tea?" Margit asked.

"Of course," he answered, and he poured a cup of hot water into a ceramic cup and put a teabag next to it on a companion saucer.

The guard handed me a cup of coffee and invited us to sit down in the modest guard shack so we could rest awhile. While we waited, he copied some of the data from my identification papers onto a sheet of paper. Margit shared some of her tea with Laszlo; both of them looked blissfully happy.

An hour later, the guard finished his requisite paperwork and told us to continue on the road descending the hill. Eventually, he said, we will reach the Refugee Welcome Center and be able to register.

I looked at the calendar on the guardhouse wall. Today was December 12, the day I left the communist world behind — and my motherland. We felt happy to be free, but we were sad to have left Hungary.

When daybreak came, we emerged from the forest into the little town of Oberpullendorf. Snow had fallen recently, and our boots crunched satisfactorily as children ran outside to walk alongside us in the crisp, clean air.

A family invited us inside their house to use the bathroom. They filled up a washtub with warm water, which allowed Margit to change Laszlo's diapers and clean him thoroughly. When we got up to leave, they insisted that we partake of some coffee and freshly baked pastry. After our impromptu breakfast, Margit stayed there and breastfed Laszlo while I went to the town hall to apply for refugee status.

When I got back, I told Margit that the registry office made arrangements for us to take the afternoon bus to Eisenstadt, where emergency accommodations for refugees were set up. Our Austrian hosts joyfully congratulated us and said they would fix lunch and have it ready at 12:30 p.m.

We asked if there was a church nearby and were given directions immediately. After promising to return promptly for lunch, we set off down the main street of town and found the church on the south side.

As we kneeled to offer prayers of thanksgiving, I felt relieved and uplifted. Our trek across the border wasn't easy, and we were almost arrested. We had no personal possessions except for the clothes on our back, but we were among friends in a new country who cared about us.

A light snow began to fall as we returned to our house of hospitality, whose inhabitants fixed us a hearty, nutritious lunch. We changed Laszlo's diapers again, thanked our hosts for their gracious hospitality and walked to the bus stop.

A dozen people waited for the bus, and they asked about our welfare enthusiastically. Soon a modern Opel Blitz with about 20 people aboard pulled up.

The bus was warm, so Margit and I removed our overcoats, and looked through large windows at the picturesque mountainsides of Austria. The exhaustion of a difficult night and no sleep caught up with Margit, and she dozed steadily as the bus rumbled cautiously on the two-hour ride.

In Eisenstadt, an industrial steel-producing city of 100,000 people, we got off the bus at a school that was closed to accommodate as many as 700 refugees. A congenial staff worker in the main office examined our temporary refugee visas and assigned us to a private home.

A Red Cross worker gave us some shopping bags to put our extra clothes in, plus a toiletry case with toothbrush, toothpaste, soap, a razor and shaving cream. "You're very lucky, sir," she said. "You have a baby. You get to stay at a private home."

"What's wrong with staying here?" I asked.

"Well," she said, "if you enjoy sleeping on straw in a large dormitory, perhaps I can arrange something."

"I see what you mean," I said. "We *are* lucky. But we are lucky in another way, too. Laszlo is a gift from heaven."

"Oh, aren't you sweet?" she said, and she wriggled Laszlo's nose as it protruded through the blankets around him. Laszlo gurgled in delight as his nose was tweaked.

The staff worker wrote down an address and handed it to me. "You have been assigned to stay with a family at this address," she explained. "This is only temporary. In a few days, you will be assigned to another location in Austria. Enjoy your stay."

She handed us a map of the city and circled our current location plus the location of our assigned house. I also picked up seven pamphlets from various countries that detailed their specific emigration procedures. Each country — Switzerland, Sweden, New Zealand, Australia, Germany, the United States and Canada — looked inviting. After reading about its climate, though, I favored New Zealand.

We reached the house to which we were assigned in half an hour, and our new hosts showed us the way to a small bedroom designed to accommodate a husband, wife and child. A portable crib was used for an infant, and we made ourselves comfortable and cleaned up for supper. Shortly thereafter, we curled up for a good night's sleep.

For some reason, the mantle clock in the living room awoke me when it struck five o'clock. Margit was sound asleep curled next to me, and Laszlo had slept soundly throughout the entire night. Thoughts of our new life rattled through my brain, and I began to worry.

Did I make the right decision to leave Hungary? After all, it was my own decision. I didn't ask anyone before I made it, and

I didn't tell anybody except Margit's sister. My wife supported my decision every inch of the way. Even so, I had put her life at risk, including the life of our newborn baby.

But if we stayed in Hungary, what kind of life would we have had? All the refugees I talked to said we had no choice. Either we live as free people or we live in fear under the Communist regime.

I have been a good Hungarian patriot. I served in the army, fought against the invaders and was wounded. I gave my blood and sweat to my fatherland — my home and my country. And I would give my blood again whenever it was necessary.

But I do not need to go back to Siberia. If the Russians send me back there again, I will be a dead man. I know the AVO is going to find out what I did at the square, even if they have to torture innocent people to get the information.

If I had refused to help the boys use the gun, I would not be on the lam. All I had to say was "No!" But I had to help! Those freedom fighters were going to get killed. Someone had to teach them how to protect themselves!

While I was in Siberia, I lost 2½ important years of my life: time that can never be replaced. Nothing felt as delightful to me as going back to Hungary. And now I am gone again; this time, I am the one to send myself away!

Remember how the only thing I wanted was to be with my Mama and Papa? Remember how glad they were to see me? Papa even cried! I promised myself then I would never leave their side again. Now look where I am! They don't even know that I left the country!

Mama was going to cry, and cry, and cry, because I had left them there alone! Papa would understand why I left, and he would not blame me at all. But my departure from Hungary was going to hurt Mama, I know. I am her only son, and both of my first cousins are dead. Only Steve remains. Maybe he and Irene will visit her and make her an honorary grandma!

The clock struck 7, and Margit stirred, opened her eyes and stared at me. "Paul," she said, "how long have you been awake?"

"Oh, not long," I said. "I was just enjoying the feeling of being in a free country." I told a little lie, I know, but Margit had been so brave and Laszlo so good that it wasn't necessary to share my worries with them.

After four days, a minibus picked us up and took us and another refugee family to the town of Ramsau near the Semmering Mountains, a highly regarded ski-vacation area. I had spent a week here with a group of high-school boys when I was 16, and I had fond memories of skiing on the nearby slopes.

Margit, Laszlo and I were provided with a cozy room in a comfortable tourist motel, and we developed a close friendship with the other family. Zoltan had fled Hungary with his wife, Anna, and five children who ranged in age from 1½ to 15.

Even though governmental agencies and the Red Cross saw to our basic needs, including meals, my pockets were empty, and I was eager to find some work. I learned that a sawmill employing 70 people was located a mile away, and I decided to try my luck there.

The factory made wood veneer for the furniture industry, and I cited my experience in the mountain town of Borsa, which was now in Romania. Nevertheless, the manager appeared hesitant to hire me.

I decided I needed to embellish my past experience a little and told him that I had made veneers before. The manager introduced me to his foreman, who showed me how to secure the logs and adjust the cutting blades. In no time, I had learned a skill and was being paid commensurately.

Meanwhile, Margit contacted a boutique shop in Heinfeld, four miles away, and offered to make sweaters and hats that the store could easily sell. Margit knew how to crochet, and she put Laszlo in the backpack when she walked to the boutique to pick up some yarn. This way, she was able to earn a little spending money, too.

I received my first weekly salary on December 21, and I sent a telegram to my parents to let them know where we were. I also mailed them a gift basket filled with oranges and tangerines in hopes that it would reach them soon after Christmas. I bought another gift basket for Margit, and she bought some mouth-watering Austrian chocolates for me.

We had some money left, and Margit suggested we contact her brother, Bela, who might offer some advice where to emigrate. Bela's travels in Europe had led him to England, and then on to America.

I made the appropriate financial arrangements with the motel owner, who called the overseas operator. Within half an hour, we were speaking to Bela in Cleveland, Ohio. Margit talked to him first, then put me on the phone so that I could explain how we were looking for a country that would accept us as refugees.

"Don't go to New Zealand," he said. "Come to America; I'll sponsor you!"

"Hold on," I said. "I need to talk with Margit about this." I cupped my hand over the receiver's microphone and talked to my wife.

"Margit, he wants us to come to America," I said. "I like New Zealand. What do you think?"

She responded quickly. "Paul, we don't know anyone in New Zealand. It's far better to go someplace where we have family."

"Yes," I said. "You're absolutely right."

Margit told Bela that we're coming to America, and he promised to send a sponsorship letter. After I paid the motel owner for the phone call, we read the U.S.A. immigration booklet eagerly. In it, we learned we have to personally apply to the U.S. consulate in Vienna. We ate dinner excitedly as we made plans for the month ahead.

Although I visited Ramsau as a teenager, I was little prepared for the magnificence of Christmastime. Inside the lobby of the resort motel, the owner put up a bushy seven-foot-tall tree, and he invited all the guests — including Zoltan's family and mine — to spend Christmas Eve decorating it with ornaments, candles and sparklers.

Christmas Eve mass at the church in Ramsau was glorious. The air was crispy cold, the skies were diamond clear, the wind kept still and the stars were ablaze. When the carillon bells rang at midnight, the echoes moved from one mountain to another. The entire church was lit with candles, and the parishioners sang Christmas hymns in unison.

As mass concluded and we proceeded outside, four men climbed up the lofty church tower, where alongside the bells of the carillon, they blew the melodies of sacred Christmas music on trumpets and trombones.

The boys of the town staged a manger scene at the foot of the church, and we engaged in another round of Christmas carols. The glory of declaring my faith in public moved me. I held onto Margit's hand tightly as tears welled up in my eyes.

What a wonderful feeling it was! It had been so long since I had worshipped freely that I forgot that I didn't have to look around for the secret police. I caught myself jumping at shadows, and I had to stop singing long enough to regain my composure.

That night in bed, visions of sugarplums did indeed dance in my head. The next morning, Margit and I exchanged Christmas gifts and kissed one another tenderly. After breakfast, we visited Zoltan's family next door and exchanged gifts with them, including the kids. We then ran outside to play in the snow.

I borrowed a sled from the motel owner and climbed a gradual tree-less slope with Laszlo in the backpack. As everyone watched, I held onto him tight, inside my coat, while he cooed with glee during our descent. Then Margit took a turn in the sled with giggling Laszlo.

Meanwhile, Zoltan's family jumped and played in the snow, making dry snowballs and joining many of the townspeople in sledding runs. Two hours of sliding around in the snow enhanced our holiday appetites, and we enjoyed a magnificent Christmas feast.

New Year's Eve was anticlimactic but fun. The resort motel threw a good-sized party, inviting us to dance to a five-piece band and a brand-new Wurlitzer jukebox. When "Auld Lang Syne" was sung, Margit and I clinked our glasses of champagne together as we welcomed in the New World promise of frost-free Frigidaires and 1957 Chevrolets.

The motel's first mail delivery of the year included Bela's written sponsorship. Zoltan received a letter from his sponsor, too. To say that we were enthusiastic would be an understatement; Zoltan and I were on the next day's train from Heinfeld to Vienna.

We quickly located the American consulate building and applied for a visa and permanent residency, to which we attached Bela's sponsorship letter. Our first trip to Vienna went quickly enough, and we were left with spare time to walk around the gleaming city and window-shop.

Back in Ramsau, I telephoned the consulate each day to check on the progress of our application. Since no one hardly ever answered the phone, Zoltan and I had to go back several more times to make sure our application didn't gather dust on the bottom of some bureaucrat's pile.

On the only occasion I took the train alone, I walked next to the Danube and toured a good portion of the city with six other guys I met while waiting in line at the consulate. We established enough camaraderie to wind up missing the last train to our temporary hosts' lodgings.

Because hotel rooms were renting at a hundred American dollars a night, we tried to figure out what to do. The city practically closed down at 10 p.m. If there were some way we could get ourselves arrested for vagrancy, our accommodations for the night would be assured.

We decided to hang out at a street corner a few doors down from the police station. Once there, we began to talk loudly and sing. Although our voices usually were not off-key, we strained our voices to elicit varying chords of dissonance.

Eventually, a patrolman showed up. "What are you doing?" he said.

"We don't have anyplace to sleep," I said. "We missed the last train home, and we're stuck here!"

"Well, if you don't disperse," the patrolman said, "I'll have to arrest you."

We stood in one line, put our arms around each other's shoulders, and sang, "*O Tannenbaum.*"

The patrolman led us to the station and took us to a cell. My detention seemed to be nothing to worry about. After all, I survived 2½ years in Soviet gulags. Vienna's jail would be a snap!

The next morning, we were "released," and we took the first train that led to our respective temporary lodgings.

Life in Ramsau continued to be idyllic. The food was great, I received a wage that equaled the rate of pay given to the company's Austrians, and Margit knitted sweaters and hats for the boutique.

In mid-January, we received temporary papers from the U.S. consulate and a notice that a bus would be taking Zoltan, Anna, Margit, me and all of our children to Salzburg, an official way station to Bremerhaven, West Germany, where we would board our ship to America.

A week later, we arrived in Salzburg and were taken to an Austrian army barracks that had been converted into a processing camp, where 3,000 people slept on mattresses. Men were put on one side of the camp; women and children, on the other.

Medical tests and interviews took place over four days. Also, everyone was assigned a place onboard the ship. Once Margit and I received our medical clearances, we rendezvoused to visit Salzburg and see the Alps.

As the end of January approached, temperatures dropped to 20 below zero, and a bitter wind blew through the camp. Nothing, though, could dampen our enthusiasm. We were free, we were in excellent health and we were going to America.

Chapter 19

COMING TO AMERICA

"Wake up, wake up," Zoltan's voice bellowed as his hands shook me. "They found us a ship. We're coming to America."

The barracks' lights turned on, and I squinted at his face. "Are we going to Bremerhaven?" I asked.

"Yes," he replied. "A train is already waiting for us!"

I dressed quickly and went to Margit's barracks. She was nursing Laszlo, and I got some more diapers from the Red Cross workers.

The train virtually flew to Bremerhaven nonstop. When the locomotive jerked to a halt at the huge port, we looked out the window to the troop ship awaiting us, the General Nelson M. Walker.

Two thousand of us Hungarian refugees boarded the ship, and we were careful to remember our way around. Men and women were assigned to different areas; Margit was billeted in a partitioned room with a baby crib. All the men were assigned bunk beds once used for American soldiers.

Most of us gathered on deck to watch the departure; a few watched through small portholes from below deck. As the ship steamed toward open water, I shivered slightly from the onrushing chill of sea air. Behind me, the European continent grew fainter as the last rays of sunlight fell into the dark sea. The only sound to be heard was the constant churning of the ship's propellers.

Whatever sea legs I grew were rendered useless in four days. The sea pitched and rolled during the afternoon as if it were angry for the ship's intrusion. Waves from different directions grew in height and volume.

In the huge mess hall, I had to keep one of my hands on the tray constantly to keep it from sliding over to the other end of the table. Beverages spilled from cups and glasses. Meat sauces, soup, iced tea, coffee and water rolled along the bulkhead in a makeshift gravy. A drink from a glass of water meant an instant soaking of one's clothes; a careful sip of hot coffee scalded one's lap.

As the night turned black, the storm grew in fury. The ship groaned as huge waves broke over the ship's bow. The constant pitch, roll and loss of equilibrium resulted in an onslaught of passenger seasickness.

Everybody clutched their "barf bags" tightly as the sound, sight and smell of people vomiting caused formerly strong stomachs to grow queasy. The unbroken hours of rocking up and down, unpredictable rolls from side to side and the fear that we might capsize caused people who were sick to stay that way. Nausea came upon us as surely as the stormy sea, and everyone was miserable.

Conditions on deck grew much worse, and the ship's compartments were locked down. This procedure ensured that if any of the compartments were to become flooded, the other compartments would remain watertight, keeping the ship afloat. Every door was closed, and the ventilation system provided little fresh air.

I slept a few hours that night, awakened frequently by the jolt and roll of angry waves in the North Atlantic. I curved my body into a protective ball so that if I fell off the mattress, I could cushion my fall.

When word came that the lockdown had been suspended and breakfast was being served, I sprang from the bed. Most of the guys were lying on their bunks in misery, but somehow I had managed to keep my stomach settled. I decided to celebrate my victory with a meal of bacon, eggs, potatoes and coffee.

I walked up the steps to get Margit. When I arrived at her partition, she was moaning in bed. "Oh, Paul, I'm so sick! You better go without me."

"Can I get you anything?" I asked.

"Yes," she said, "a new stomach!" She groaned and turned over onto her stomach as another wave crashed across the hull.

The mess hall seemed more massive and lonely, too. Only 12 men had shown up to eat breakfast. Everyone else was sick.

I grabbed a tray and ladled some scrambled eggs onto it as a Chinese cook emerged from the galley, chiding us to "eat, eat, eat, Hungarians!"

I finished my hearty breakfast with a second helping of coffee. I walked out the door leading from the mess hall as I congratulated myself for having a strong stomach. A refugee stepped down from the stairwell from where he sat above me. Suddenly, his eyes rolled back. He flinched, and sprayed a torrent of vomit all over my hair, my eyes, my face and my clothes.

An involuntary sickening feeling rose up from the back of my throat, and as I looked at him, everything that had just gone into my stomach flew back up. I managed to lower my head in time so that I only soiled his clothes, but my impeccable self-assessment was brought down a notch or two.

Eventually, the storm subsided, although Margit was not able to recover from her stomach distress until she received medication from the ship's doctor. Soon we found our sea legs, and took Laszlo to the main deck for occasional breaths of fresh, cold sea air.

The sky was still dark on February 15, but a few of our shipmates awoke everyone. "Come upstairs!" they cried. "See the light! It's the light of freedom!"

A slight mist obscured the shape of the figurine object, and it seemed to glow brighter as our military vessel approached. The sky grew lighter, the sun's rays peeked over the horizon behind the ship and a beam of glistening sunlight spotlighted the immense statue ahead of us: Lady Liberty!

"It's the Statue of Liberty," Anna said, "welcoming us to the Free World."

"Isn't it beautiful?" Margit said.

Zoltan and I stood in mute appreciation as we marveled at the giant raised hand holding up its torch of freedom.

As we steamed our way to the New York harbor, we looked to starboard where cars and trucks traversed the Long Island shoreline. We had never seen so many automobiles at one time, and the vehicles looked like they were flowing across ribbons of concrete.

In New York Harbor, the General Nelson M. Walker slowed and maneuvered past an array of waiting freighters. Finally, the ship picked up speed, and we docked at the Brooklyn Army Terminal. The gangplank was lowered soon thereafter, and our feet touched American soil.

A fleet of U.S. Army and public transit buses waited for us, and we boarded a bus whose marquee advertised its destination: Camp Kilmer. Zoltan and Anna grabbed their children by the hand and followed Margit, Laszlo and me onto an Army bus.

The driver turned the starter, the bus began to move, and we cupped our hands against the windowpanes to eagerly peer through the windows. The bus driver pointed out the buildings by name. There were so many of them! When we came to the Empire State Building, Margit and Anna gasped as they tried to see its roof; the building was far too tall for anyone to see the whole thing.

We passed through Harlem; we noticed that a large number of poor people lived there, and many clotheslines extended from one building to another. Every time the bus turned, the amount of vehicular traffic was overwhelming. How could New Yorkers bear so much congestion?

We crossed the Hudson River over the George Washington Bridge into New Jersey. The size and scope of the highways were beyond anything we expected, and we ran from one side of the bus to another until the driver asked us to be seated.

The buses proceeded south through Newark until we arrived at the vast debarkation and embarkation facilities of Camp Kilmer near New Brunswick. We continued past a guardhouse post and a large number of buildings. Finally, the buses groaned to a stop in front of our assigned barracks.

Men went in one direction; women and children, in another. We went through disinfection procedures, received brand-new underwear, socks and toiletry kits, and cleaned up and showered. Boxes of used clothes were laid out in our sleeping quarters, and we grabbed ill-fitting shirts and trousers from the rapidly diminishing piles.

Next, we were led to an auditorium where we reunited with our wives and children. After we gathered into one large group, we were taken en masse to a massive mess hall where metal trays were filled with meat, potatoes and vegetables, and glasses were filled with pasteurized milk.

Red Cross workers were everywhere, and a volunteer helped Margit make a telephone call to her brother in Cleveland. Bela expressed delight in our safe arrival and said that he would pick us up on the following weekend.

On Sunday afternoon, we were invited to a special reception with Hungarian film star Paul Javor serving as the guest of honor. Javor was known to all of us, because of his captivating performances in Hungarian-language movies prior to the end of World War II. However, because he didn't speak English, he had been unable to find an acting job in Hollywood.

Javor told us how happy he was that we had arrived safely and gave us pointers about life in America. I talked to him privately, and one of the things he said — "The less English you know, the more likely it is that people will spit on you" — haunted me.

As I lay on my bunk bed, I thought, "Surely, the people here will be glad to teach us English." That night, Zoltan, Anna, Margit and I sat together in a small social room and watched our first television programming. Maybe this would be a good way to learn some English.

Ronald Reagan, an American cowboy actor, introduced a drama on "General Electric Theater." The show was called "The Big Shooter" and starred Art Linkletter and Eva Gabor. When Gabor appeared onscreen, Margit said, "Look at how she acts. Is this what Americans expect from Hungarian women?"

"I don't know," Anna said. "I'm not sure if I can say 'darling' the way she does."

"She's just trying to copy her sister, Zsa Zsa," I said. "Look how she moves: the exact same way!"

We watched the program for about 10 minutes before agreeing that the acting was not impressive and turned our attention to the sights and sounds of the New World around us.

The next day, we received used shirts, pants, sweaters, jackets, coats and shoes as well as new underwear and socks from the American Red Cross and other U.S. volunteer organizations. Some of them fit; others did not, but we didn't mind. Some refugees received so many clothes that they couldn't carry them all.

Zoltan and Anna's 15-year-old daughter, Ildiko, picked out a ballroom gown and a bunch of dresses. She went into the ladies' room to change, and modeled each one shamelessly for anyone who would look at her.

On Tuesday, Anna's sister arrived at the camp to pick up Zoltan, Anna and their kids. Our shipmates' paperwork and vaccinations were complete, and they gave us their address in Yonkers so we could write to one another. We hugged each other, and promised to see each other soon.

All week long, representatives from some of America's biggest employers, including U.S. Steel, Republic Steel and United Technologies, visited Camp Kilmer looking for skilled workers. Each refugee filled out a paper listing his education and experience, and copies of these papers were handed out to interested employers.

Many of the refugees received job offers on the spot, and I was no exception. A beer manufacturer's representative interviewed me, because I was listed as a chemist. Within minutes, he offered me a job.

"What do you think?" I asked Margit. "We're here only a few days and now I'm offered a job!"

"I bet we'd have to live near where they are located," she said. "Let's ask Bela what he thinks!"

A Red Cross worker phoned Bela and put me on the line. I explained the job offer to him, whereupon Bela said, "Paul, don't take it! There are many, many jobs here in Cleveland. They need people with your education and background!"

I thanked the beer manufacturer's recruiter for his interest and spent the rest of the week relaxing with Margit. Late Saturday afternoon, Bela turned up at our barracks.

Margit introduced us, and I couldn't believe my eyes. Bela was as short as Margit! He hugged Margit tightly, then shook my hand briskly. "Let's go!" he said.

"Cleveland is 650 miles away," Margit said, "and it's late. Bela, why don't you sleep in one of the vacant cots, and we'll go tomorrow morning."

"No, no, no," he insisted. "Just get in the car, and let's go."

Margit grabbed Laszlo and put him in a blanket. Then she went to her barracks and scooped up a mound of clothes that was given her by the relief workers. Once our arms were full with donated belongings, Bela led us to a shiny dark-blue sedan and opened the trunk.

We squeezed the clothes into the trunk; the items that wouldn't fit were placed on the backseat. Margit and Laszlo rode in the back seat next to the excess baggage, and I rode up front with Bela.

Bela switched on the ignition and started the motor. "How do you like my car?" he asked proudly. "It's a 1951 Dodge."

We presented our papers at the guardhouse. After opening the gate, the guard smiled and waved as we drove past. A couple of hours later, Bela turned onto the New York State Thruway, and we stopped at a service plaza.

"Fill 'er up!" Bela said to the attendant.

I watched in amazement. "Don't you have to pump your own gasoline?" I asked.

"No, not at all," Bela laughed. "This is America; everything is full service!"

A whirring meter on the pump indicated the growing amount of gas going into the car. "This car is great," Bela bragged. "It holds more than 22 gallons."

"Shall I check under the hood?" the attendant asked.

"No, it's alright!" Bela waved off the attendant.

"Don't you check the oil or sparkplugs?" I asked. In Hungary we often had to check the oil and spark plugs of our Opels, Olympias, Volkswagens and Fiats.

"Paul," he said, "I hardly ever open the hood. You don't have to touch these big American cars."

We ate a quick supper and then were back on the highway. Our automobile whizzed across miles of toll road bypassing Albany, Syracuse, Buffalo and Erie, stopping twice more at the highway's service plazas where we were impressed with the clean, modern bathroom facilities. As the first vestiges of daylight illuminated the world around us, we drove into Cleveland.

Bela lived on the southeast side of Cleveland in an area of two-story houses built of wood and clapboard siding with one family on the ground floor and another on the second. The homes were built with brick and stucco, and I found the cheap construction of his building quite unique.

Bela lived in the upstairs apartment, which had three bedrooms, a large living room, dining room, kitchen, bathroom and porch. Two other men shared the apartment, but one of them had moved out recently. Margit and I unpacked our clothes in his now-vacant room.

"Gee, it's cold in here," Bela said.

"Where is the stove?" I asked. "I'll make us a good fire." In Budapest, I always had started the fire in our indoor stove and fed it wood or coal, depending on what fuel was available.

"Come here," Bela said. He walked over to the wall in the living room and moved a lever attached to a thermometer. "You see this? I just turn it on, set it to the desired temperature and heat comes from the basement."

"Well," I said, "heat doesn't come up by itself. You must have a stove or something."

"I don't know how it works," he said. "I just have the serviceman fill it up with oil. The tank is really big, and it goes straight to the furnace. As soon as I move this lever to the desired temperature, the furnace runs until the room warms up."

I was amazed that such a convenience was readily available. "That's modern technology," I said. "I can feel the heat already; that gadget really works!"

"Don't talk about work on a Sunday," a voice said in Hungarian. Wearing a bathrobe and pair of slippers, Bela's roommate, Istvan, emerged from a bedroom, stretched and rubbed his eyes. "Did you have a safe trip?"

"It depends on what part of the trip you want to talk about," I answered. "The voyage was rough!"

Everyone laughed as Bela introduced Istvan. "Give them a chance to get settled," Bela said. "Maybe they would like to clean up."

"Oh yes," Margit said. "We've had nothing but showers lately. Do you have a bathtub?"

"Sure, we do," Istvan said, "and plenty of hot water. Look here." He led the way into the bathroom, and turned on the left spigot from two spigots mounted on the wall. In a minute, the water was steaming hot.

"Bela," I asked in amazement, "where do you get this water?"

"From the furnace," he said.

"The water always comes from there?" I asked.

"Oh sure," he said. "The water is automatically fed to the furnace and heated up. After the water is used, more cold water is heated. Hot water just keeps coming and coming."

"What a nice convenience!" I said.

"Don't take too long in the bathroom!" Istvan said. "Bela and I are going to make a nice American breakfast."

Margit took Laszlo into the bathroom, and we took turns bathing. After we luxuriated in an endless supply of hot water, we put on fresh clothes and walked into the dining room.

"Here you go," Bela said." Plates of bacon, scrambled eggs and white toast were set for each of us. A percolator bubbled furiously on the kitchen table. Margit watched intently as the gurgling from the percolator diminished and eventually stopped, whereupon Istvan poured mugs of steaming, freshly brewed coffee.

"Here," Istvan said, handing a mug to Margit, "have some."

Margit gingerly blew upon the steaming surface of the coffee and hesitatingly sipped some. "Mmmmmmm!" she said. "It's good, Paul!"

I took one sip, then another, and another. "That's kinda weak," I said.

"Oh, Paul," Margit said. "That's good coffee. You're just spoiled from drinking espresso all the time."

"Well, perhaps you're right," I laughed, "but for me, that's nothing but dirty water."

After breakfast, Margit and I talked to Bela and Istvan about our life in Hungary, and they listened intently. Bela told us about his life in America, and Istvan did the same.

Bela arrived in America five years ago and went to work for Republic Steel a year later. He had accepted a clerical job in the company's shipping and receiving department and enjoyed the lifestyle of a single guy.

Istvan was a Hungarian who emigrated to Canada and was a year older than Bela. Istvan worked at Ford Motor Company as a steel-castings pattern maker and was a dependable, stable man who held dual-citizenship status with Canada and the U.S.

"There are plenty of jobs listed in here," Bela said as he brought in the Cleveland Plain Dealer.

"That's a newspaper?" I asked, feeling the weight of the newspaper's contents. "That thing must weigh four pounds! "Is that the newspaper for the entire week?"

"No," Bela laughed. "It's the Sunday paper. There will be another paper tomorrow, but it won't be nearly this big."

"If we're lucky," Margit said, "the newspaper in Budapest consists of 12 pages. That's a lot of news for one day."

"Most of it isn't news," Istvan said. "A lot of it is advertising or junk."

"But how do you tell what's news, and what's junk?" I asked.

"As soon as you learn English," Bela said, "I'm sure you can tell."

I looked through the newspaper curiously and tried to understand the words I saw. From what I had been told so far, learning English was extremely important, and it wasn't going to be easy.

When noontime came, Margit looked in the refrigerator to see what she could cook for us. After viewing its contents, she asked Bela if he would take her to the store to buy some meat.

Bela opened the refrigerator's freezer compartment and took out some chicken. "What do you want to cook?" he asked. "Chicken or pork chops?"

We stood around the refrigerator in awe. Every time we cooked chicken in Hungary, the bird was freshly butchered. And the only freezer we knew was the way we smoked pigs during the height of winter.

Bela showed Margit how to cook frozen meat, and lunch was set upon the table. We ate heartily; then fatigue set in. We had traveled all night without any sleep, and we couldn't stop yawning.

We slept well during the rest of the afternoon. We woke up as the sun was going down, and, to wake ourselves up, we strolled for a few blocks on the snowy streets of Cleveland.

We relaxed in the living room and talked about the latest happenings in Hungary until a little before midnight. I didn't realize how late it was until Margit fell asleep in her chair, and I bade Bela and Istvan goodnight. Margit awoke long enough to put Laszlo to sleep in a new baby crib that Bela had bought for us, and we all slept soundly in our new, comfortable accommodations.

On Tuesday, Bela dropped me off at a factory that advertised in Sunday's newspaper for a textile engineer. I sat in the main office politely, and a secretary showed me into the personnel manager's office.

A jowl-faced man with a cigar looked me over carefully. I was nervous and excited, and I was wearing an ill-fitting second-hand suit that I had gotten at Camp Kilmer.

"I apply for job," I said as I tried to pronounce in English the words Bela told me to say. "Anything."

"Great!" the personnel man said snidely. "Do you know any English at all?"

I looked frantically through Bela's paper, searching for something to say, but nothing I could think up made sense.

Speaking slowly and enunciating sarcastically, the personnel manager stated, "Well, you have to learn English here, because we only train people in English. We don't have any way to teach you anything. You need to go work in a restaurant and wash dishes. Then you might know English, and we can hire you."

I understood enough to be offended. This man wanted me to work in the lowliest job he can think of because I didn't know English.

I sputtered in anger and told him that if this insult reflected his company's attitude, I wouldn't be coming back here for a job. Unfortunately, I could only voice my complaints in Hungarian, and my reaction to his remark only served to amuse him.

I scoured the neighborhood around Bela's apartment looking for work the rest of the day and Wednesday morning. On Thursday, Bela circled a want ad in the newspaper and showed it to me. He convinced me that everyone doesn't have the same attitude toward refugees, and I dressed up in my suit once again.

He drove me to the factory and laboratory of a company called Airco, which had a polymerization plant near downtown. Airco manufactured glues and paint bases for Benjamin Paint and lesser-known companies; therefore, its products weren't textile related. However, I contented myself with the thought that taking a chemist's position with the company didn't mean I was limiting my future to working with polymers.

Bela accompanied me to see the personnel director, who showed interest in me as soon as Bela related some of my work experience in English.

"I have a Hungarian fellow who works for us," the director said. "I will call him to come in here, and we can discuss more of your experience."

The Hungarian worker walked into the office, and the personnel director asked him to translate. "Do you know viscosity?" he asked.

"Using Brookfield equipment?" I replied.

"Oh yes," he said. "That's what we have here."

"I know how to use Brookfield, and I can measure the viscosities for you," I said.

"Follow me," he said, and he led me into the quality-control laboratory where I was shown how the employees did their work. "Can you do it?"

"Give me a solution," I answered, "and I will run it for you."

I measured how many revolutions the spindle made in a given amount of time. I got a pencil and calculated the viscosity. Then I handed the paper to the personnel director.

He looked at the Hungarian who nodded his head to confirm my calculation was correct.

"How soon can you start?" he asked.

Chapter 20

MOWING THE LAWN

I worked 40 hours a week for Airco and was paid $60. The regularity in my work schedule enabled me to enroll in night English classes at an elementary school. Bela agreed to baby-sit Laszlo so that my wife could attend classes, too. English grammar proved to have almost as many exceptions as it had rules, and our lessons proved challenging.

"Why isn't 'door' pronounced like 'poor?'" I asked the teacher one day.

"For the same reason 'sand' isn't pronounced like 'wand,'" she said.

"But why is that?" I asked.

"Look it up in your textbook," she answered.

English isn't easy, especially when your native language is something other than English. Margit and I studied diligently and did our best to speak understandable, conversational English.

Unexpected kindnesses were visited upon us. I was caught in a late season snowstorm at the end of one workday, whereupon one of my co-workers gave me his overcoat, claiming that he had a new one.

In May, my supervisor recognized my level of production and promoted me to the polymer research department, which was worth a $15-a-week raise. I used some of the extra money to buy better clothes, although Bela and Istvan kidded me that I was beginning to look like an American.

Margit took care of Laszlo and prepared all our meals, including box lunches to take to work, on a budget of $30 a week. Each of us kicked in $10 a week, and she used the money to cook meals so tasty that we had to exercise regularly to shed the extra pounds from second helpings.

One Saturday morning toward the end of May, two men knocked on our door and flashed official badges to Bela. "Hey Paul," Bela yelled out, "can you come here?" When I got to the door, Bela whispered in my ear, "These guys are from the FBI."

"That's not quite correct," said a man wearing a neatly pressed dark-gray suit and tie. *"I'm* with the FBI. My associate here is with the CIA."

"What is the CIA?" I asked as I stared at the second man, wearing a dark-brown suit and tie.

"The Central Intelligence Agency," he said. "We're hoping you might help us. We're gathering information about the Soviet Union, specifically about the Sverdlovsk area."

"That's where I was a prisoner-of-war," I said.

"Exactly," one of the men said, glancing into a file folder. "It says here that you spent 2½ years in the Sverdlovsk gulag."

"That's exactly right," I said.

"Well, Mr. Tarko, we're hoping that you might help us. Would you like to be of service to the U.S. government?"

I was flattered. "Of course!" I said. "America took me in as a refugee, gave me a home, gave me freedom! I would be proud to serve this country as the best kind of patriot!"

I invited the two men inside for coffee, and they asked me to sketch the Sverdlovsk area on a large notepad. I drew maps of everything that I had seen: the railway roadbed, the huge area for the building's foundation and the apartments for the people who were to work there.

After I finished answering the agents' questions, one of the men thanked me politely and shook my hand. "If you ever need help or you have any trouble, call us," the FBI agent said. The two men thanked Bela and Istvan for their hospitality and left.

"How are you going to call them?" Istvan asked. "Did they leave a card?"

"Nope," I said, "but I don't care. I was glad to help."

The rest of the weekend was spent exploring and enjoying the city's sizable Hungarian community. Over 50,000 Hungarians filled Cleveland's southeast side where delicacies such as freshly ground sausage, melt-in-your-mouth pastries and an array of European wine vintages could be purchased along Buckeye Road.

Bela usually gave up his free time to drive us around in his Dodge, but it didn't take long before Margit and I wanted to get around on our own. Istvan provided us with a municipal bus schedule so that Margit and I could use Cleveland's public transportation.

Margit and I found the bus stop and took two seats together, talking to one another in Hungarian. The bus driver, a heavy-set black man with huge arms that he used to maneuver the bus perfectly, seemed friendly, so I asked him for directions in broken English.

In perfect Hungarian, he said, "Why don't you speak Hungarian instead of English?"

I stepped back in amazement, and said in Hungarian, "Because I didn't know you can understand Hungarian!"

"Well," he said laughing, "now that you know that I speak Hungarian, I can tell you where to get off and where to go."

In June, Margit and I received English-language diplomas from the adult education program. I was proud of myself on graduation day, because my future as a chemist was dependent upon good communication skills.

I received another promotion at work and began to work with vinyl, acetate, acrylics and glue emulsions. Each week, I studied as much technical literature as I could get my hands on.

One of Margit's distant relatives, Danny, drove into Cleveland in September with two friends, George and John. The three guys were freedom fighters during the Hungarian Revolution and superb athletes who had come to Cleveland in search of a competitive game.

It hurt me that I wasn't able to compete; the long-term effect of my wartime leg injury kept me from running farther than 100 yards. The guys thanked us for our hospitality and offered to put us up at their apartment in Hartford, Conn. whenever we wanted to visit.

The 1958 recession arrived with the cold winds of winter. Bela's union called a strike at Republic Steel; once the labor dispute was settled, he was laid off. Margit got pregnant, and, as the economy worsened, I was laid off too. Fortunately, Bela and I qualified for unemployment compensation, and the checks we received enabled us to pay our share of the rent.

"Don't worry," Margit said. "We're in good shape. I've managed to save some money, so we'll get by."

"You've saved some money?" I said. "How can you save money when you have been feeding us on a budget of $30 a week?"

"I have saved a lot of money," she said. "I have already saved a thousand dollars."

I was flabbergasted. Margit's meals were so good! How did she manage to save so much money?

Nevertheless, a thousand bucks wasn't going to pay all the hospital bills. I needed to bring in some money.

The cosmetics industry appeared to be a big industry in America. All the television programs featured women with blemish-free faces. Perhaps I might make a lot of money if I used my chemist's skill to manufacture some homemade cosmetic cream.

Big department stores sold a small jar of hand cream or face cream for $5 and more. Yet the raw material to manufacture it cost only pennies a jar. This might be my golden opportunity to live the American dream.

I bought a second-hand mixer and the necessary raw materials, and soon I was making cosmetic creams under the label of Tri Chemical. I took a suitcase of little jars filled with my cream door-to-door, selling them for $3 a jar. I didn't get rich, but I managed to eke out a living by selling 25 jars a day.

In order to get an investor for my enterprise, I registered my product with the state health department and the Food and Drug Administration. No one seemed interested, and sales declined while my time was spent caught up in bureaucratic red tape.

By the end of September, I started to worry. My wife was in the late stages of her pregnancy, and I wasn't making enough money for a growing family. I decided to end my floundering career as a cosmetics entrepreneur and began mailing out resumes.

On October 7, 1958, Margit gave birth to our daughter, Eva, while I waited at home taking care of Laszlo. Bela had driven Margit to the hospital and stayed with her until she had fallen asleep.

Three weeks later, a Philadelphia chemical plant, which manufactured emulsions for the backside of carpets, responded to my resume mailing. I bought a round-trip train ticket so that I could be interviewed by the plant owner, negotiated a satisfactory salary and agreed to accept a job offer contingent on a four-week probationary period. I obtained a driver's license and commuted to work in a used 1951 Dodge, since I admired the car that Bela drove.

After my probation was complete, I went back to Cleveland to fetch Margit, Laszlo and Eva, and we moved into a modest Philadelphia apartment. Eight months later, a planned business acquisition for the chemical plant unraveled, and I was laid off again. The owner treated me right, though. He gave me six weeks severance pay and promised to rehire me — albeit at less money — if I could not find other work.

I received my severance check on Friday, the 24th, and I phoned Bela after I cashed it. When he answered the phone, he sounded bored.

"Bela," I said, "I've been laid off again."

"I'm sorry to hear that," he said. "I was called back to work for Bethlehem Steel, but then we went on strike again."

"Well, Bela," I said, "ever since I arrived in this country, I have never taken a vacation. Now I'm being paid to take six weeks off! It's July, and this is a good time to take a vacation. I've got enough money to pay your expenses. Why don't you drive over here, and we will all take a vacation together?"

"A family vacation? That sounds great," Bela said. "Is that all you plan to do: vacation?"

"Let's call it a job-seeking mission and a vacation," I said. "I'll look for work, and we can also visit Canada and New England!"

The next day, Bela called back excitedly. "Paul," he said, "I phoned Danny last night and told him about our plans. He said to tell you that George and John insist that we stay with them in Hartford for two weeks. What do you think?"

I talked to Margit and relayed Bela's words. She nodded her approval, and I said, "Let's go to Hartford!"

On Wednesday, Bela parked his cream-colored 1955 Dodge in front of our apartment building. He stayed overnight with us, and I phoned Danny in Hartford to make arrangements to rendezvous with them.

Danny gave me exact directions on how to get to their apartment house in West Hartford. He also asked what time we expected to arrive.

"Well, Bela will be driving," I said, "so I figure we'll be there around 3 o'clock."

"Well, I'll be working at that time," he said. "So will George. But I can get 'Big Nose' to meet you in front of the apartment house."

"Big Nose?" I said. "Who is Big Nose?"

"Oh, you know him," Danny said. "John! He was with us when we visited you."

"Oh, it's John," I said.

"Sure," Danny said. "I'll tell him to walk up and down the street between 3 and 4. You can't miss him."

The next morning, we threw our bags into Bela's car, gathered Margit, Laszlo and Eva together and headed north.

Unfortunately, I forgot exactly what John looked like, so when Bela's car pulled in front of the apartment house, I didn't know what to do. Several people were walking down the street, and I needed to find the one with a prominently structured nose.

Suddenly, I saw someone with a big nose. I walked up to him, extended my hand and asked, "Are you the 'Big Nose?'"

The man harrumphed at me, eyes ablaze, and walked away without saying a word.

Embarrassed, I looked in the opposite direction and saw an older man with an elongated nose. I ran up to him and asked, "Are you 'Big Nose'?"

The man scowled condescendingly, turned his back and also walked away.

Feeling stupid, I felt a tap on my shoulder, and a voice said, "I'm the 'Big Nose' you're looking for."

I turned around, and John laughed gleefully as I described the two embarrassing moments of mistaken identity. John walked over to Bela's car to help Margit open the door, grabbed some suitcases from the trunk and led the way to the apartment.

Danny soon arrived and hugged all of us. Finally, George came home from work and started making supper for all of us. George was proud of his Hungarian goulash and, from the way we emptied our plates, he deserved to be. A gallon jug of Chianti accompanied the meal, and our laughter filled the West Hartford night. That night, I slept serenely but exhausted.

Friday night was a night out with the guys. While Margit took care of Laszlo and Eva, we visited one of the area's taverns for an evening of food, drink and dance. The next day, we all went to the Connecticut River and took turns looking after the babies and swimming in the cool, clear water.

"Hey, guys," I said, "I think this would be a great place to look for a job. Why don't you get me a Sunday paper so that I can look through the want ads?"

The next morning, George drove me to the newsstand where I bought the Sunday Hartford Courant. I pulled out the classifieds and scanned the Help Wanted columns where I saw an advertisement for a chemist with a textile-and-polymer background.

First thing Monday morning, I called the number listed in the ad, and an operator identified the company as DeBell & Richardson. Within minutes, I wound up speaking to John DeBell, president of the Hazardville-based company.

Mr. DeBell was a well-educated, well-respected French chemist who emigrated to the U.S. after World War I. The U.S. Navy sent him to West Germany after World War II ended, and he had written "German Plastics Practice," a book that precisely catalogued German accomplishments in chemistry.

Mr. DeBell was interested about my experience in the fields of plastic polymers and textiles, and we were able to communicate by speaking half-German and half-English. After we talked awhile, he scheduled me for a personal interview at 8:30 a.m. the next day.

For the interview, I dressed up in a white shirt and dark-gray suit and put on my best dark-blue tie. Everything about this interview felt special, and I asked Bela to drive me, drop me off at the parking lot and meet me back there at 1 p.m.

"But, Paul," Bela said as he pulled into the parking lot, "I want to know what happens. Can't I sit in their waiting room?"

"Bela," I said, "I need to make a good impression. It's better if you check out the town of Hazardville and tell me what it looks like. Relax! Have a couple of beers! I'm sure I will be done by 1:00. Come back then and pick me up."

I walked into the executive office and introduced myself to the secretary. "Oh, you're Paul Tarko," she said excitedly. She rang a buzzer, and it rang back. "Go on in. Mr. DeBell is expecting you."

John DeBell was a couple of inches shorter than me and pleasantly chubby. His energy level was infectious, making it difficult to believe that he was 60 years old. He asked me pointed questions about Hungary and life under communism. There was a kindness about him that was disarming.

He asked about the subjects I took when I got my diploma. He asked about the Revolution. It soon became clear that he cast a favorable eye on me. He spoke with a thick French accent, and he could make it worse when he didn't want someone to comprehend what he was saying.

He offered me a job at a comparatively low rate of pay.

I countered with a much higher figure, and Mr. DeBell began clearing his throat.

"Are you okay?" I asked. "Would you like a glass of water?"

Mr. DeBell waved me off, yet continued to clear his throat. I thought quickly, "What would happen if I lowered the salary figure I give him?"

I lowered the dollar amount, and Mr. DeBell's visible signs of throat distress immediately lessened but nevertheless continued. "Well," I thought, "I'll go just a little bit lower."

I called out the reduced amount, and the sounds of Mr. DeBell clearing his throat ceased.

I spent the rest of the morning filling out forms in the employment office, and by noontime I was done. I waited for Bela; true to his word, he pulled into the parking lot promptly at 1 p.m.

I sat on the hood of his car, and Bela stopped the engine and opened the door. "Hey," he said, "what do you think you're doing?"

"Celebrating," I said. "I start work on August 31!"

"That's wonderful, Paul," Bela said. "It's about time you got a break."

"So," I teased, "are you going to take me to a place where we can buy a beer?"

"You know," Bela said, "I drove all around this little town, and I couldn't find one single bar. This is a dry town!"

"Should I refuse the job then?" I asked.

"No," Bela allowed.

"Then let's go back to where it's wetter!" I said.

We laughed heartily, and on the way home we found a bar and toasted my success.

George had made arrangements to take his vacation during the forthcoming week, and he celebrated each day with us. On Wednesday, George, Bela and John took me aboard their 16-foot boat, on which they mounted an 80-horsepower outboard engine and attached a long rope.

"Paul," John said, "have you ever gone water skiing?"

"No," I said, "but it sounds like fun!"

I imagined myself on snow skis and got ready to fly across the river. The first time the rope grew taut, I skied merrily across the smooth surface of the Connecticut River in their modest boat flying Old Glory on the bow and the Magyar flag astern.

Bela, Margit and I thoroughly enjoyed our visit. The guys promised to send me newspaper clippings listing apartments for rent. And after 10 days marked by divine providence, we drove off to tour New England, Niagara Falls and Shaker Heights in Cleveland.

Bela drove us to our Philadelphia apartment, and we encouraged him to stay as long as he could. We toasted good friends, good family and good wine until I drove off to begin my work with DeBell & Richardson.

Six miles from Hazardville, I found a small motel in the old carpet-mill town of Enfield. I rented a modest room and commuted to and from work each day.

DeBell & Richardson performed contract research work for large corporations, specializing in advanced technology, and was begun by two former Monsanto research directors. The eight other chemists in the lab were quite friendly, and we developed a good rapport. We eagerly took on all challenges, and I found my colleagues to be warm, intelligent and productive.

I used my non-working hours to look for a suitable rental apartment so that Margit and Laszlo could join me. In Enfield, I discovered a two-story house owned by a Polish family whose roomy second floor was available for rent but needed work.

I asked Margit for her opinion, she quickly agreed and we committed to a one-year lease. I used my non-working hours to clean, sand and varnish the wood floor. At the same time, I began to paint all the rooms.

One week before we moved, Margit brought Laszlo and Eva with her, and I picked them up at the Hartford train station. Margit instantly approved of my work and helped me finish cleaning the apartment.

Moving day was exciting and easy, although the 1951 Dodge complained about the hilly topography. After an amusing round of "Pook pook pook," the family car negotiated the last hill into Connecticut, where my family finally had a spacious place with many windows where we could watch the sunshine flow in.

My job went well, our marriage grew and life was prosperous. At the end of our first New England winter, a loan officer at the bank called us up to inquire whether we were interested in buying a foreclosure. The idea suddenly appealed to me, because Margit was pregnant again.

The house the bank offered was a two-story building on the other side of the Connecticut River, with three bedrooms, a living room, dining room, family room, kitchen and a large upstairs bathroom. A three-car garage and a vacant lot added extra value to the $16,500 purchase.

Nonetheless, we were nervous when we signed the mortgage agreement. The bank owner handled the transaction personally and said, "You can enjoy living in the house, but you have to pay the mortgage. If you don't, we'll have to foreclose just like we did with the previous owner. As I recall, the poor fellow committed suicide, so be careful with your obligations."

We gulped, made a $1,650 down payment, purchased our first American house and moved into it on May 1. I had ordered a subscription to the Hartford Courant, and I ventured outside eagerly to pick up our first copy.

The front-page headline screamed about a U-2 pilot named Francis Gary Powers who had been shot down over Sverdlovsk in the Soviet Union! Sverdlovsk was where I worked when I was in the gulag! Sverdlovsk was the place that the FBI and CIA asked me about!

I handed the newspaper to Margit, and she read along in stunned silence.

"I've got to call Bela," I said.

For the rest of the day, my phone line was busy as I talked to everyone that I knew about the ramifications of Powers' Mayday capture.

My first weekend in the house turned out to be sunny and warm, and I examined the vacant lot. The grass had not been cut all year, and its height almost reached my knees. Now that I had a house, I had a good-sized yard to go with it!

"Perhaps," I thought, "I could use part of this lot for a vegetable garden and grow some good Hungarian paprika. The first thing I need to do is get this lot into manageable condition."

Well, I had heard about lawn mowers but never needed one. And I had plenty of experience using a razor-sharp scythe in Hungary. I could think of no faster or more dependable way of cutting this grass to manageable size than by using a scythe. So I went to Agway, a farmers' supply store, and bought a scythe and had it professionally sharpened.

I approached my vacant lot from Third Street, leaned down and began taking slow, deliberate swipes, quickly cutting it down to size. I noticed a few onlookers gathering behind me, and I exaggerated some of my movements.

After finishing a row, I began slashing another one, inconspicuously sizing up the people watching me. I assuaged any feelings of self-consciousness by thinking of the good things I had accomplished.

Whoosh! I have a dream wife.

Whoosh! I have a dream family.

Whoosh! I have a dream job.

Whoosh! I have a dream house.

I repeated these words over and over to myself until only a few feet of the vacant lot remained to be cut.

All of a sudden, my next-door neighbor came outside and naively asked, "Hey, Paul, what are you doing? Cutting the grass?"

I leaned down, took another swipe with the scythe, thought about my confusion concerning nonsensical English expressions, stood up and said proudly, "It's more like mowing the lawn."

Cutting the grass.

Afterward

Chapter 21

A FOREIGNER IN THE LAND
OF OPPORTUNITY

I cut the grass with the scythe a few times, until my neighbor came over a month later and said, "Hey Paul, I see that you don't have a lawnmower."

I replied, "Well, this is what I use," and I showed him my scythe.

"Here is a lawnmower," he said. "I have two more at home. Why don't you use it?"

"It looks good," I said. "I will buy it. How much are you asking?"

"No!" he retorted. "You're my neighbor; take it!"

The lawnmower he gave me was a second-hand machine, and I appreciated his gift. Nevertheless, there were days when I suffered more using it than I did when using a scythe.

Life was peaceful in Suffield. I was very happy, and I started writing letters to my relatives in Hungary to find out how they were doing.

I was sorry to hear that the communist regime responsible for many executions of freedom fighters was still in power.

In 1960, we improved the house by adding a breezeway between the garage and the house. Chick, a carpenter who worked with me at DeBell & Richardson, told me that I could do the work easily.

Summertime was hot, but I started to put the foundation down and get work started.

After I put down the foundation, Chick showed me how to put up the wooden structure that comprised the breezeway. He asked me to get a saw and ladder, and he showed me what to do.

He looked around for my saw and toolset. Not seeing one, he said, "Okay, Paul, where are your tools?"

I showed him the big handsaw that I purchased a week ago.

"Ohhhhhh," Chick said, "that's a Russian saw. Paul, this is America! We don't use this! That's for the Russians!"

He went to his car, and brought out an electric saw. "Paul, this is a saw. What you bought is a Russian saw. Don't use that! You'll take too long to cut with that."

He was right. In this country, time is money. He was 100% right, and later on I bought an electric saw.

On October 9, 1960, Margit delivered a happy baby boy, and we named him Paul Jr., completing our happy family.

And in late November, before the first snowfall, I completed the breezeway and put a roof over it.

My wife didn't work during those days, because a babysitter would have cost her more than she could make in salary. Anyway, I was pleased that I could afford for Margit not to work. She was able to stay at home and take care of our three children.

As we settled in our new house, we started to feel at home. Just like in Hungary, we slaughtered a pig to make sausage with my friends, George, Danny and John.

I was the first one of us to buy a house. They always came over to see us and help us make wine and sausages.

Zoli and Anna Papp, our friends whom we met in Austria and who sailed with us, lived in Yonkers, which was not a great family area. They brought their children out to visit us on frequent weekends. It was great to see them and watch their children breathe some fresh air.

They admired my garden and picked some apples. They enjoyed some of my homegrown green peppers and our fresh fruits. At my house, I had pear trees, a cherry tree and an apple tree, just like the fruit garden Papa tended in Mako.

Laszlo started kindergarten in 1961. I got him into a preparatory school, which was run by the Polish church. He was able to learn English there, because at home we spoke to him in Hungarian.

One night at supper, Laszlo started to sing the Polish song, "Uncle John."

I said to Margit, "I put him into the preparatory school to learn English, and he has started to learn Polish!"

We both laughed, because Laszlo was learning American English, which is a melting pot of many languages.

We didn't have any trouble with him. He was a superior student in elementary school. When I went to ask the teacher to give him some extra attention, because his mother tongue is Hungarian, the teacher told me that he was the best speller of English in school. He was doing well, and he learned English much sooner than I did.

Years continued to go by, and I was still working at the laboratory. At home, we felt more comfortable and more established in the American way of living. However, we still followed Hungarian custom in making wine, killing a pig and smoking the sausages and ham, and, of course, eating well after my 2½ years of starvation in the gulag.

Our journey turned out well, and we were happy. Our life started to shine, and I had a nice family, three kids, a house, a car and a good professional job. I culminated my formal education with a one-year course in polymer rheology at the University of Massachusetts at Amherst in 1963 with Dr. Rudy Deanen, my technical director at DeBell & Richardson.

That year, my mother passed away in her sleep. I was worried about what would happen with my father, because they had been taking care of each other. I couldn't attend the funeral without being arrested, and my father didn't want me to risk an attempt.

Three months after my mother died, John Kennedy was assassinated. Kennedy's dreams and aspirations had inspired me, and I grieved with all Americans during the television coverage of his funeral and the salute from his tiny son.

During the next year, I started making preparations to get my father out of Hungary. There was no one left to take care of him, and I was his only child. I wanted him to come over to America, so he could live with us during his later years. He was entitled to enjoy a better life than he was facing in Hungary.

Margit went to Washington in 1964 and saw U.S. Secretary of State Dean Rusk. She typed up a sponsoring letter, had it notarized, and I had it approved by the State of Connecticut. Then Margit made an appointment to see Secretary of State Dean Rusk, whose signature was required before the communists agreed to let my father out of Hungary.

Papa got here in March 1965, and he really enjoyed living with us. Papa said he enjoyed American freedom, his grandchildren and reading the Boston Globe.

In August 1964, John DeBell retired. I changed jobs and went to work in Leominster, Mass. as a polymer chemist doing research on ABS plastic resin for Foster Grant.

At first, I took a little apartment. Then I rented a house in Fitchburgh next to a golf course and moved the family in before the end of September. We put the Suffield house up for sale, but couldn't get a fair offer. So we rented out the house, which worked out to my advantage.

Nathan Tufts, vice president for Windsor Nuclear, offered me more money than Foster Grant was willing to match, and I returned to Suffield in 1966. Windsor Nuclear specialized in plastics, textile and basic radiation work. My polymer rheology studies helped me with this aspect, and I was put to work on an intensive project.

The head of the company at Windsor Nuclear was somewhat idealistic about the company's projects. We couldn't get enough work, and the company began to flounder financially.

An example of the problem was illustrated when I began a research project for Mobil Oil. I was working on radiation-cured coatings, but the president of Windsor Nuclear wanted to retain patent rights.   Mobil's vice president threatened to cancel the contract.

The conflict adversely affected company morale, and I left the company in 1967 with the intentions of starting my own plastics business. The group of guys that I put together was not committed wholeheartedly to the business venture, and they soon bailed out.

Therefore, I started my own consulting business from my house in Suffield. In 1968, I had taken on a few projects. One of them was at United Technologies where I developed chemicals to absorb carbon dioxide in the astronauts' cabin and lunar module.

I received a contract to make a lithium peroxide compound, which would be encapsulated in a canister. This chemical would absorb the astronauts' exhaled carbon dioxide in a high-surface area and would set off a chemical reaction that would also supply oxygen. This project avoided the need for bulky oxygen cylinders. I used rice-sized pellets that were foamed up so their pores would readily absorb the carbon dioxide.

In 1969, my father died of lung cancer. All the years of smoking tobacco had finally got to him; fortunately, his strength enabled him to survive until the age of 87.

Papa's five years in America was a remarkable experience for him, and the thankful look in his eyes told me I had done the right thing by extricating him from Hungary. To this day, I love to extol the virtues of the Boston Globe, because my father read it religiously.

In 1970, Nixon made drastic cuts in the budget for the space program, and 10,000 white-collar engineers, technicians and NASA-dependent workers were laid off.

The space program layoffs created a ripple effect at United Technologies, too. The Nixon administration didn't give sufficient support for the growing space program, and we lost our consulting contract.

This caused a rocky shakeup in my life. So far, I had made substantial progress as a consultant and made a good profit. I acted fast, and I changed my consultation specialty to plastic processing. I attended an auction where I was able to obtain molding machines at a reasonable price.

I went to the Royal Typewriter auction, bought some machinery and rented a place in Summerville, Conn., where I set up a plant. Half of the business was set up for chemical work; the other half, for plastics research and development.

I started this company at the end of 1968, and the company exists today. Starting one's own business is not easy; there are many things to do, especially for someone without money.

Without a doubt, we were undercapitalized, but I was lucky. God helped me with finding solutions for many of my projects. In 1972 business was good, and I had eight people working for me.

I needed a new plant, though, because our lease in Summerville was terminated. I had no choice, and I bought a place in Windsor Locks, Conn., where we are still located and operating.

At this point, we had to build a plant quickly and needed capital to do so. We had owned the Suffield home for 12 years, and the sale fetched a good price. I took some of the profits from the sale of the house and used the money to build our plant.

First, I constructed a small building to house the molding machine and some of the chemicals. Then I applied for a loan from the Small Business Administration. Once it was granted, I put up a second building in the new Windsor Locks location.

The construction work and reorganization of my business took up a great deal of my time. My children were growing up, but they pitched in and helped us to move the machinery and our household effects from Suffield to Windsor Locks.

Laszlo and Paul Jr. did a good job, and our business began to grow. On some days, we were able to employ 20 people. Our molding business was no longer limited to doing research. Now we were able to concentrate on production, because many of our clients had heard about our expertise with molding and contacted us, which saved us from spending money on advertising.

I hired some excellent mold makers; one stayed with me for 14 years until I sold the mold-making part of the business. I plunged myself into business and spent much of my time and creative energy on our projects.

About 1980, we made another addition to the industrial building, and a year later — in 1981 — I visited Hungary and Transylvania with my wife. In the meantime, Laszlo graduated from the University of Connecticut in 1981 and got a job as a nuclear physicist at Combustion Engineering Co. He bought a house in Windsor Locks close to Margit and me. Paul was still in high school, and Eva had started to work for Travelers Insurance Co.

During the 1980s, I sponsored a few Hungarian refugees who came to the U.S., and I worked with Catholic and non-sectarian sponsoring organizations to find jobs for many refugees.

I received a lot of calls from refugees asking me to find jobs for them. Sometimes, I didn't have any openings, but my better business judgment didn't matter. I needed to help my fellow Hungarians find some work. Perhaps I thought that God would have been pleased by my efforts. Well, He was, because this kind of volunteer work added value to my life.

Nick, one of the refugees I sponsored, romanced my daughter, Eva, and in 1982 they got married. They now have three girls, and my granddaughters visit us often.

I sponsored Silvia Salvary and helped her to settle down in this country. Silvia had a retarded child, Silviu, who could not be helped in Romania. Silvia came to the U.S. in hopes she could find help, but no one wanted to be bothered with her. Because Silvia was not a U.S. citizen and did not pay taxes, the schools could not accept her retarded child.

Consequently, in 1982, I went with Silvia to see Sen. Lowell Weicker, R-Conn., to get school funding for immigrants with retarded children.

Silvia had made a more difficult journey than the one Margit and I did. She came to an unknown country where she felt hopeless during the beginning. Nobody wanted to help her, and she kept running into roadblocks. Sometimes, she and her child did not have a place to sleep.

Well, that's the way life can be when you have children. You're always undercapitalized.

With Margit's help, I was able to establish a life in the U.S. for Silvia, and we took care of her. At least a dozen times, we went to the Immigration and Naturalization Service to expedite her working permit and residency settlement to stay in the U.S.

My wife and I made a commitment to establish her existence in this country. We took her to the retarded children's school in Manchester, Conn., and registered her child. The school accepted him; however, the town told the mother that her son couldn't be accepted, because she was not an American citizen. We tried to enroll Silviu in Hartford, but we didn't have any luck there.

Finally, we tried Enfield. The people here were understanding and helpful. They accepted Silviu into the town's school. We talked with the superintendent, social workers and town manager, explaining the hardships that she had endured. Finally, bureaucracy crumbled in the face of overwhelming humanitarian concerns. The boy was taken care of in Enfield's school.

The next problems to be addressed were housing, employment and establishing a reliable financial base for Silvia. The Baptist church looked around and found a lady who understood her problem and served as an ombudsman.

Once Silvia's son was in school, she was able to work and earn money to pay her expenses. Silvia was a Good Samaritan who dedicated her life to her son.

She is a good cook and wanted to start her own business. We loaned her the down payment to buy a small restaurant. A few years later, she repaid the loan in full. Nowadays, Silvia is self-sufficient, and she expresses her thanks by inviting us to have supper at her very own restaurant.

We are grateful that she is so thoughtful. She thanks us for being a big help to her and patronizing her in this country. I'm glad that God gave me the courage to do this. Maybe later on, God will pay me back for the good things I have done in my life.

John Rozenbersky, also known as "The Big Nose," started his own machine shop business. He was a good, reliable man, so when I needed someone to build machinery for my business, I gave him the contract.

Our harmonic business relationship is characterized by our good friendship, days of making sausages, drinking schnapps wine and enjoying life.

John passed away on October 22, 1999.

One of my wife's best friends, Elizabeth Antal, comes from Vagas, a small Transylvanian village populated by 500 people situated below the Carpathian Mountains. The Hungarian people who live here are called Szekelys, and have been here since the 8th Century. The road leading into the village goes no farther. That's the end of the world, as far as anyone is concerned, because you must come out the same way that you go in.

Elizabeth grew up in the village as a simple, honest woman with two sons, Geza and Frank, and left Hungary alone for America in 1968. Even though she had no skills, she was a hard worker, and my wife helped her find a job in this country.

During her second year here when she earned less than $8,000 a year, she managed to send $3,500 annually to her sons in Transylvania to support them. She knew how to manage her budget.

Eventually, Elizabeth obtained the paperwork to bring her sons to America, and my wife helped her to fill out some of the forms. She prayed every day for their safe arrival, and soon the two boys arrived, reuniting the family. Those boys are the same ages as my sons, and they have become successful in America. We are proud to know them and have them as friends.

I recall an amusing episode with his younger son, Frank, who went to school with my younger son, Paul Jr. One morning Frank called my wife and asked that she call the school and tell them that he missed the bus and can't go to school.

My wife told him, "Get ready, and I will pick you up and drive you to school."

Well, Frank did not like it. But my wife took him to the school anyway. I felt sorry for him, because when I was his age, that trick worked.

Now 15 years later, he appreciates the discipline of those days because he studied the English language and became successful using it. Geza became a successful toolmaker and is renting space from my industrial building to operate his machine shop. This way, once in a while after work, we can have a glass of some famous Hungarian wines, such as Bull's Blood of Eger and the *6 Puttones Takaj Asszu.*

Every week when Elizabeth bakes bread in the Hungarian tradition, she bakes a loaf for our family, too. Each time I eat her tasty home-baked Hungarian wheat bread, I pick up any small crumbs that fall on the table. I can't tell if my habit of picking up the crumbs is due to my time in the gulag or because her bread is so good. Nevertheless, whenever I catch my kids throwing away bread crusts, I get mad at them, because Hungarian bread is truly the bread of life.

In 1988, Bela and I bought a condominium in Florida where we could spend three to four months during the wintertime, making me a "snowbird" from the North.

Our business continued to do well, and in 1991 we added a sunroom to provide solar heat to the house. We continued to modernize the old house to its current five bedrooms. This gives us more room to run around and chase after each other.

I celebrated my 70th birthday in 1992. Very soon, though, I began to experience health problems. I developed a little prostate problem, which required an operation. This took away some of my ability to work.

Paul Jr. said he could take care of the prospering business, which will allow me to retire. This sounded good, so I proclaimed to be retired. But I confess that I'm only semi-retired; once you own a business, you never can retire.

In 1992, my son, Paul Jr., started dating Emese, a beautiful dark-black-haired girl from Transylvania, who was visiting her girlfriend in the U.S. Paul went to Hungary to see her, and a long-distance romance ensued. On October 8, 1994, they married. Two years later, the two of them went to visit Emese's parents in Transylvania. She took Paul to see Dracula's Castle and took a picture with Paul lying on Dracula's bed. Since then, she has helped Paul Jr. run the business and has learned English. They are both successful and happy.

In 1995, when I jumped up on a wooden bench on the deck of my house, the bench broke and so did my ankle. I had an operation, but then three weeks later, I had a heart attack.

God saved me, because the emergency crew got to my house within five minutes of my wife's call. They rushed me to the hospital, and my life was saved.

While I was running my plastics and drainage show booth at the Long Beach, Calif. convention center in March 1997, I had another setback.

Everything about the show had been proceeding smoothly. I was chatting with our customers, many of whom came from foreign countries, including Taiwan, and generally having a good time at the show.

I had gone home for the night and went to sleep. At 4:00 a.m., I felt a severe chest pain. I called out to my wife, "Oh boy, I have a very strong chest pain, and I can't breathe."

She acted quickly. She found my nitroglycerine pills and gave me three. This helped a little bit, but it didn't stop the chest pains. My wife called the emergency number and asked for an ambulance.

Again, with God's helping hand, the ambulance's emergency crew arrived at my hotel room within five minutes, and they helped me. Some people might call the timing "lucky," but I call it "God's helping hand."

Why? Because from my hotel, the fire rescue crew was located only a few blocks away, and they could get there quickly. They took me to the hospital where I received angioplasty surgery, which helped me. While I was recovering, I had a minor heart attack and the surgeons inserted a stint.

I still say that God helped me, because afterward I got well. But my poor wife was stuck managing the rest of the Long Beach show and looking after me while I was in the hospital.

Fortunately, our Taiwanese customer volunteered to man the booth at the show so my wife could visit me in the hospital. A lesson I teach: Good customers help you when you take care of them.

Margit would be able to finish the show without me being there as long as she could drive a rental car. However, Margit had her own Subaru, and she was uncomfortable driving anything else. Now she had to learn how to drive a new car in the Los Angeles metropolitan area, with its vast amount of traffic.

Well, Margit handled everything extremely well.

We extended our stay at the hotel from our initial reservation of three days to 10 days, with the understanding I might be there longer.

I called Bela who picked up my car from Miami International Airport's parking garage and took it to our jointly owned condominium in North Miami Beach, where he greeted some visitors who didn't know of my heart attack.

Six months later, I had another heart attack. Once again, help arrived in time, and I was taken to the Hartford hospital. There, I was given a four-bypass heart operation, and God's helping hand was with me. They got me to the hospital in time, and the surgeons were able to perform the operation in time.

These kinds of things happen. You have to put your faith in God that He will help you. My heart problem seems to have been corrected, and we enjoy life in Windsor Locks and North Miami Beach.

One sad note, though. Zoli Herzeg, my classmate from gymnasium, passed away in 2001. His friendship was another gift from God, and I mourn his loss.

While enjoying my Florida days with some other "snowbirds" from Canada, I discovered a former friend from Borsa, Hungary, whom I knew when I worked in the forestry business in 1942. His name is George Brody, and on winter days we can be found at the Miami Hungarian Club or sitting around the beach reminiscing about the girls of our Hungarian youth in Borsa.

Our good friends and my wife's relatives in Hungary come over here from time to time to visit. At the present time, my medication keeps me in good health and my friends and family keep me in good spirits.

My oldest son, Laszlo, is still happily single and likes to dance. He worked at ABB – Combustion Engineering for 19 years as a nuclear physicist, but he was laid off in 2000. Combustion Engineering had not built any nuclear power plants in the U.S. during the last 10 years and did not need a sizable number of physicists. Laszlo is now at CSC, working for UTC and helping to design aircraft engines.

Eva left Travelers Insurance Co. after working there for 15 years. She was taking care of her three children while they were small. Now she works for Hallmark Card Co. Eva is a wonderful cook, a good gardener and frequently invites us over for dinner or brings us some of her stuffed cabbage.

Paul Jr. has taken care of the business and caused it to grow further. He purchased a new house in 1999, and he enjoys it as much as his first one. Their first baby, a boy with the name of Ryan Tarko, was born on April 29, 1999.

How is it possible for a Hungarian boy to have an Irish name? Well, at first I objected, but now I like it too. Ryan has blond hair and blue eyes, bears the Tarko name and will carry on the family tradition. He trudges happily next to me at we walk along the west bank of the Connecticut River, and he likes to put a paper boat on the water to head south toward Hartford.

God blessed Paul Jr. and Emese again this year. A second baby was born to them on May 30, 2002, a girl named Emily.

During this year on June 14th, while I was writing this book, I celebrated my 80th birthday. Roy White, Jim Cocot and the widow of Stanley Margosiak — my colleagues at DeBell & Richardson — were there. Jimmy gave a speech about our hard work and good times at the company, where we helped each other and worked as a team. Jimmy reminded me of the mischievous nature I could not give up in the workplace.

Stanley and Jim asked me if I could make good plum brandy.

"Sure," I said. "We have the best equipment and distilling apparatus available."

So we bought Prucie-Plume, made the mash, fermented it and began to distill it. We set up two distilleries. One was a synthetic glue for a project we worked on; the other was used for plum brandy. Our supervisor, Sven Richter, smelled the odor, and Jim said that smell came from the glue in the extracting alcohol.

Sven walked away, and we almost cried from laughing. Today, we are friends because of these times, and we still laugh when we remember them.

When I started work at DeBell & Richardson, I was their 39th worker; when I left, the company had 170 workers. This growth shows that we made progress and enjoyed our work.

Chapter 22

GLEANING THE TRUTH
ABOUT THE GULAGS

I have tried to recount my experiences in the gulags, or prisoner-of-war camps. Each gulag was a little different, depending on the personality of the *natchalnik* (camp leader) who determined the camp's rules, prisoner treatment and working conditions. The one trait they shared was the horrid lack of sanitary conditions.

One of the men that I met in Mako during the fall of 1947 told me about his experiences in one of the gulags at the 65th camp in the Briansk area, a waterlogged jungle. The air was filled with mosquitoes, which transmitted malaria and other deadly diseases.

Previously used by Russian partisans, the gulag camp was located underground in bunkers. These bunkers were filled with ticks, lice, bed bugs and other insects. At night, after the lights from the kerosene lamps burned out, the bugs infested the war prisoners. In the morning when the prisoners awoke, their faces and bodies were covered with so much blood from the bites that it was hard to recognize one another.

Into this forest camp, 2,400 men arrived near the end of 1945 with insufficient clothing and shoes for the below-zero temperatures. Although the men wore overcoats, they had worn holes in their shoes from the laborious length of long forced marches. The shoes, therefore, offered no protection for their feet or legs.

With such poor clothing, the men worked eight to 10 hours in the forest cutting timber. At the beginning, the quota was 1 cubic meter of wood for two men. The *natchalnik* promised more food if the men would produce more timber.

He raised the quota from 1 cubic meter to 1½ and then 2 cubic meters in the harsh winter conditions. The emaciated prisoners came down with malaria or got sick with pneumonia and stomach typhus.

The mortality rate was so high that the dead bodies could not be buried. Because it was wintertime, their clothes were removed and thousands of naked bodies were stacked up like firewood.

When the early summer months arrived, the rows upon rows of bodies were sprinkled with lime, kerosene and oil and then set on fire.

What a terrible way to die. Who were the culprits? Modern-era barbarians.

Some people died while at work. They sat on the wood timbers to rest, fell asleep and froze to death while in the midst of a rosy reverie.

When the summer of 1946 began, the man I spoke with in Mako was one of only a couple dozen prisoners remaining from the original gulag assignment of 2,400 prisoners. More than 2,000 died in this hellish death camp. And this is only one of many horror stories that emerged from behind the Iron Curtain.

The humiliation and destruction of so many people was far greater than the soldiers who fought and died at the warfront. And the forced labor camps in Siberia were economically efficient. It didn't cost anything for the Russians to maintain them, not even a bullet.

Many of the calls I received to help arriving Hungarian refugees came from Mary Sanady at the Catholic welfare organization's office. Her husband, Joe, served as president of the local Hungarian-American club, and we knew each other for about 10 years before the topic of Russian gulags came up in conversation.

Joe told me that he had been in Western Siberia. I asked, "Where?"

"In the Sverdlovsk area," he replied.

"I was there too!"

"Oh no! Really?" The look of astonishment on both of our faces was something to see.

I asked him when he left Focsani, and he said at the end of May 1945. I asked him if he came back at the same time that I was transported in 1947, and he said yes.

I asked if he was housed in the same tent camp building where we rested while building the railroad bed, and he said yes. Well, our mutual experiences resulted in the two of us becoming comrades, and we spent many years sharing painful memories.

Joe passed away in 1998, and I said farewell to him as I stood over his casket. Another gulag survivor was gone.

Because of how well my work had gone, we could afford for Margit to visit Hungary during 1974. I wanted to go, too, but I did not dare step foot on Hungarian soil until I was granted complete amnesty by the communist regime.

I received the necessary assurances and, in 1977, visited Hungary with my son, Paul. We had a nice time, and the secret police were no longer openly molesting the people of Hungary. I showed Paul his homeland, we took lots of pictures and lots of old memories came back.

By the late 1980s, Margit and I were going to some Hungarian group picnics. I had hired a number of Hungarian refugees to work in our plastics shop, and the picnics were a festive occasion for everyone to visit with one another.

At one of these picnics, I met Vilma, a lady in her mid-50s who was visiting from Hungary and the godmother/aunt to a Hungarian immigrant, Laszlo Frankovsky, who was working part-time as a welder in my shop.

While I was talking with them, I mentioned that I was in a gulag in Russia around the Sverdlovsk area.

She said to me, "I was in the gulag too."

I asked where she had been imprisoned, and she told me it was Kopejsk, near Cseljabinszk, 300 miles south of Sverdlovsk, and she worked in its brick factory.

When I asked her what part of Hungary she came from, I nearly fainted. It was Temesvár, the closest city to where my childhood sweetheart, Maria, lived!

Vilma confirmed what I had already heard. An overwhelming number of the women in Maria's Romanian town of Nagyszentmiklos died. The Russians used them for sexual pleasure, or sent them to work in gulags, where many of them ended up in mass graves.

In 1991, two years after the communist system collapsed, my wife and I went to my 50th graduation reunion in Mako. Driving on the street, I was looking for the best route to go to the cemetery where my mother's body lies at rest. I stopped and asked a pedestrian for directions.

The man looked at me open-eyed and asked, "Are you Paul Tarko?"

I was flabbergasted. "How do you know me?" I asked.

"You were my role model for how to kick a winning goal. I play soccer, and I graduated the year after you. My name is Stenszki."

I was flattered and pleased to be well remembered, and the moment helped to lighten the moments of grief at my mother's gravesite. It was good to see who was at my high school reunion, and tragic to see who wasn't.

In 1994, I made another trip to Hungary. This time, I met the guy outside Apatfalva who, in 1947, told me about Thomas back in 1947.

He was old, and his eyes retained the hollow look that stayed with most gulag prisoners. He told me about a trip he made to Transylvania where he met the son of one of the prisoners that had been with him and Thomas.

The son had prospered and made a pilgrimage to Tigyina to find his father's remains. Once there, he spent a considerable sum of money to have the area bulldozed. His efforts paid off; he discovered a mass grave. Forty-seven years had passed and the bones of the dead were found scattered together.

I was inspired by this account, and I tried to learn the location of Thomas' body. The only record left by the communists was that the camp where he died was numbered 582. The location of the camp and its mass graves had been expunged from governmental records.

There was no funeral for Thomas. His bones cannot be found. And even if they could be found, there would be no nametags or identification to distinguish his bones from the others. Throughout the rest of my life, I have missed him very much.

If local representatives from the Russian towns would reveal, excavate or make known the locations of these mass graves as a humanitarian gesture, perhaps some day plaques could mark the location of gulags where Hungarian martyrs died.

In 1998, Margit and I went to Budapest to visit the son of Margit's deceased relative in Szombathely, Gaspar Alföldi, whose house we slept in the night before our escape into Austria.

His son, Laszlo, flew in from Switzerland, and we spent an entire day talking about the days when Hungary was not a nice place to live. The next day, we went to the Heroes and Martyrs Cemetery to place a wreath at the foot of the gravestones for two of his comrades.

Laszlo told us that he and two cellmates were sentenced to death during the Rakosi era. During the early morning, the guards took the three of them to be executed. Suddenly, a single guard ran after the procession. The guard stopped Laszlo and told him that his sentence had been changed to life imprisonment. Laszlo spun around, fell, felt dizzy, and was confused and disturbed.

In the cell, he regained consciousness to discover he was alive and his cellmates were dead. More than likely, his reprieve was made possible, because he was the son of a working-class family. Paying respects to his two fallen cellmates was his way of thanking God for saving his life.

The Hungarian government recently unearthed an area of mass graves and individual ones. In tribute to the country's martyrs who died under communist hands, the new leaders turned this area into a memorial and cemetery with marked wooden-post graves.

We paid our respects to Laszlo's cellmates. Then we placed wreaths on Imre Nagy and Paul Maleter's memorial monuments. Whenever I visit Hungary, I go to this cemetery, say a prayer and place a wreath on the marble memorial for the 860 martyrs who died here.

Looking Back

From 1943 until 1955, approximately 450,000 Hungarians vanished in Siberia and throughout Russia.

Writing instruments — pens, pencils, paper — were forbidden in the gulag. I suppose this ban was meant to keep us from writing down the names of those guys who vanished or suffered any of the terrible ways a man can lose his life.

Anything that was written down was confiscated regularly. I managed to remember a few of the guys' names — mostly those whom I buried or hauled to the mass graves — when I came home. But as for the rest, I just couldn't remember.

Many returning prisoners experienced the same phenomena. They couldn't remember all the names, no matter how hard they tried. I could remember the names of some guys that I worked with regularly, like Andy Pokorney or Louis. I knew those very well.

But as far as the other guys, as my captivity dragged on, their names and identifications melted away. I just forgot. I didn't know where they lived, or if I did, I simply forgot.

As far as my captors were concerned, I wasn't a man. I wasn't an individual. I wasn't the embodiment of my ancestors before me.

I was nothing but a number.

I conditioned myself in such a way that I was able to survive a prison camp. But why must life be about survival? How can we call ourselves a civilization when history has given us the Holocaust, gulags, concentration camps, prisoner-of-war camps, nuclear explosions?

Who did all these terrible things? The ruling communists, not the Russian peasants. The Russians were good people, and they suffered as much as we did from the communist system.

Ten days before Christmas 1996, Father Roger Holoubek was celebrating the Sunday mass of Advent in North Miami Beach, Fla. His story is told as follows:

"A long time ago — centuries ago, in fact — in the country of Armenia, there once was an old man and his wife, who did not have any children. Though they prayed to God every day of their lives, lifting their hands, their voices and their hearts to heaven, God did not give them a child. One day the woman said to her husband, 'Let us go to God's Holy City and pray for the gift of a child there, in Jerusalem.' (The women in the town lived a strict religious life.)

"They journeyed for over four months, crossing mountains, plains and deserts before crossing the River Jordan and entering the Holy City of Jerusalem. But now their prayer turned from petition to praise, for the woman was pregnant with child. They rested for a few days, and then began their journey back home. But after traveling for almost nine months, the woman could go no farther.

"They saw an empty shepherd's hut, and entered. Her poor old husband did not know what to do, and said, 'You stay here! And I will go to the village to find a midwife.' So he left her alone, and she gave birth. And then she fell into a deep sleep. The shepherd returned home, and seeing her in his bed wondered who she was. But then the shepherd said, 'I will never have a child of my own. I wish I could have a child.' And so he stole the child — and left a newborn lamb in the woman's arms instead.

"When the husband returned with two midwives, his wife awoke. They all looked in amazement at the little lamb. And then the woman said, 'I asked for a human-child, but God gave me a lamb-child instead.' She raised her heart and voice to heaven, praying out loud, 'Blessed be the Name of God.' And her husband fell upon his knees and — raising his hands, and voice, and heart — also began to thank God. Meanwhile, the two midwives looked nervously at each other, and got out of that place as quickly as they could.

"The old couple did not know what to do. They were looking for the child and the shepherd — but could not find them. They were undecided, confused, worried, embarrassed and anxious.

"When the old couple could travel again, they set out for their village, and as they walked away from the shepherd's hut, along the meadows and the hills, they discovered a very fertile, rich land, where they established their wealth and happiness, what they thanked for the little lambs of God. They arrived 10 months after their departure. No one believed their story. And everyone pitied the old man and the old woman for the unbelievable story they told. But the woman sat on her porch every day, lovingly holding the little lamb close to her.

"One day a shepherd from a faraway district was driving his flock through the village. The little lamb leaped from the woman's lap, and ran to one of the ewes — as if the ewe were its mother. The poor old woman asked the shepherd to return her lamb-child, and the shepherd realized who she was. He told her how he had stolen her child, and begged her forgiveness.

"Quickly the old man and old woman went with the shepherd to a cave in the wilderness. Inside was their little child, having lived only on the milk of sheep. He had been hidden there, and the child never saw the light of day. The woman rushed into the darkness of the cave with her arms stretched wide, calling for her child. The child ran into her arms, and she drew him out from the darkness into the light.

"She and her husband took the child home with them. They fed the child, clothed the child, and most tenderly loved the child. And the child soon grew in both age and wisdom. So everybody was healthy and happy."

As it turned out, God's helping hand was always there! Eventually, the couple found wealth, happiness and satisfaction. Sometimes, His helping hand seems to have disappeared, but this is temporary. These moments are the interruptions, suffering, pain, difficulties, roadblocks, obstructions and frustrations in life.

In the long run, God's help brings its fruits — satisfaction and happiness.

After the Mass and Sunday meal, I was sitting in a chaise lounge, meditating about that story and how it applied to my life. I have journeyed through life during difficult times, as you have read.

As I was engaging in these thoughts, I remembered that there were periods when I was confused and frustrated about God's "helping hand." I decided then to write about my life, because it would open my eyes to something greater.

Why? Because those who perceive and fight for many good things in life, and live through easy and hard times, should chronicle their emotions and impressions. They have collected a wonderful treasure trove, and a written journal will record the joy and happiness in every important moment.

Some old memories were reborn in my mind as I dwelled on this project. Long ago during my late teens, an old shepherd became a close friend.

He grew up in the Hungarian prairie, taking care of sheep, cattle, hogs and horses. He slept in a hot, open barn where he watched the sky, the stars, the moon and the sun.

We often chatted about different things. He was a well-read, self-educated, intelligent man who knew the stars and mathematical equations.

We talked about the meaning of life and whether God exists or doesn't exist.

He said to me, "If I know that there is *no* God, I can live just as well as if I know that there *is* a God. In these instances, you believe what you know. But if you know that God exists and refuse to believe it, then you can't live and die as you're supposed to."

After all these years do I know that there is a God? Or do I only believe it? To believe it *does* mean that I know or don't know.

Well, why are we living? We are living to find the answer to the "big secret": God. We are living our lives so that we not only believe, but know of His existence, too.

What is the goal — the purpose of living? Only to live day-by-day, and then nothing, or God, or something! After that, everything that has happened and once was, is wiped away.

Life has an end, a termination, a completion. Everything that we have done will be left behind. We vanish; we cease to exist. We should know, or make sure, that God exists in our lives.

He wants to do something with us, because sometimes He acts against the law of physics. These moments become known as miracles. If God has plans for us, He will keep us alive. It's all up to Him.

In my life, I came close to vanishing a few times, but God had plans for me and kept me alive. Going through all the horrors and tortures that I experienced, I can say that God's "helping hand" was around. It was never gone!

I was up; I was down; I was happy; and I was sad too.

Somehow, it appears that God still has a plan for me. For some reason, He wants me to live longer. The story you have read is true; it's my life wrapped up in pages of print.

God has His intention for all of our lives. He will either furnish us with His gifts, or He will punish us.

My long, arduous journey taught me never to lose faith. Keep your will strong so that you can survive temporary hardships, suffering, pain and the sweat from your brow.

God's helping hand will never leave you.

The quality of a good life will be enhanced by the difficulties experienced along the way. Your hard work will bring you fruitfulness and satisfaction. And, in the end, you will know true happiness from a life well lived.

My Plea

As you have read this book, it is my life.
I survived!
Yes, I did survive. But humans, stop for a moment!
Think!

Would not life be nicer if we did not need to survive?

Would it not be nicer to live without:
Holocaust
Gulag – Forced Labor Camps
Concentration Camps
War Prison Camps
War – Atom – Hiroshima – Bombs – B-52 – Tanks –
Chemical and Biological Warfare - Rockets

Would it not be nicer to live without:
Fear – Hatred – and Terror.

Men: Do not make another war! Please – Please!

Do not destroy those innocent and poor peoples!
Do not destroy their mud or stone houses, or those nice
architectural and historical buildings.
If you destroy their homes:
That creates: Hatred and Terror

Hatred does not make Peace, it makes War!
You should live in Peace!
You should spend money to eliminate Poverty, educate
the people and put good bread into every mouth!
You should not spend so much money for Weapons!
Please Think!

We do not need Mass Graves with slaked-lime over dead bodies.

I wrote this for the memory of my cousin, Thomas, who as a young doctor ended up in one of those Mass Graves with many other innocent people from the gulags.

There was no funeral for him. His bones cannot be found, because no nametags and no note were put on his body. He just vanished, faded away.

Men, make it so that what I wrote about Life in the Gulag or Concentration Camps **never happens again!**

Politicians, State Leaders, Presidents, Governors: **Do not start War!**

Solve the problems and differences with a glass of wine at white cloth-covered tables!

Glossary

Glossary

Burizs: Wheat or barley that is ground up in its own husk and weeds.

Casha: Corpa that is cooked into bran mush. Used as pig food in Hungary and America.

Clamps: Underground structures for the storage of potatoes.

Corpa: Bran.

Corpaleves: Bran soup.

Csardas: a Hungarian double-step, two-movement dance.

Davaj, davaj: Russian command meaning "go, go, run, move."

Delibab: A mirage caused by summer warmth that gives the appearance that objects on the ground are suspended in mid-air.

Destrophy: Unfit for work.

Drusztutye: Russian cordial greeting, meaning "to your health." Often used while drinking.

Felcher: Medical worker; uncertified doctor.

Harcsa: A large river fish resembling a catfish but lacking the claw-like bone in its mouth. *Harcsa* is commonly found at a weight of 10-12 pounds but tips the scale at 200 pounds when mature. This fish tastes like a combination of snapper and ocean haddock, and is found in the Maros, Tisza and Danube rivers.

Horthy Peak: The Hungarian name for Mount Pietros.

Kadar: A cooper who makes wooden barrels.

Karcer: Punishment prison.

Kharrashow: Good; okay.

Kolhoz: Collective farm.

Komsomol: An official Communist youth organization for aspiring Party members.

Kulak: A middle-class peasant; landowner holding more than 25 acres.

Kurity: The Russian word for smoke.

Lager: Russian-German-Hungarian word for labor camp.

Magyar: Hungarian term for Hungarians; official native language of Hungary.

Mahorka: A Russian peasant-made cigarette of poor quality made up of veins from tobacco leaves.

Makos kalacs: Poppy seed challah.

Natchalnik: A Russian supervisor.

Nyemci: Russian word for Germans.

Pashli, pashli: A polite Russian term for walking, moving or going farther.

Piszagy: A Russian-printed document authorizing a farmer to donate his land to the collective.

Pozdorja: The wooded part of the hemp plant that is broken away to expose the fiber during processing, which is later used for kindling wood.

Pufeika: An overcoat with layers of cloth insulated by cotton or wool.

Pulicka: Romanian blended cornmeal.

Purga: A sub-arctic Siberian blizzard.

Putton: An elongated basket used for picking grapes.

Ribbah: Fish.

Sanitaze: Medic.

Schlivovitz: Plum brandy.

Szervusz: Informal greeting shared among Hungarian guys when gathered together.

Tarrok: A game played with an ordinary deck of playing cards in Hungary.

Tokaji asszu: A Hungarian specialty wine made with dry grapes. The best is called the king of the wines, and is marketed as Six Putton.

Vengerski: Russian word for Hungarians.

Vereb: Brownish blackbirds notorious for eating farmers' crops.

Zabra: The theft of property, especially valuables, during an otherwise legal search.

Zaszlos: Officer.

The Soviet Union's Internal and Security Organizations

GPU: *Goszudarsztvennoje Policejeszkoje Uphavlenyije*
State police highest authority (supreme)

Gulag: *Glavnoje Uphavlenyije Lágerej*
Central Office of the lagers (camps) supreme authority
Headquarters of the lagers (camps) highest authority
located in the largest, strictest prison, Lubjanka, located in
Moscow between 1930-50, responsible for 15-20 million
prisoners.

KGB: *Komisszija Goszudarsztvennoj Bezopasznosztyi*
State security commisszariat

MVD: *Minyiszterszlvo Vrutrennih Gyel*
Secretary of the Interior

NKVD: *Narodnij Komiszariat Vnutrennih Gyel*
Internal Commissariat

VCSK: *Vszerosszijskaja Cshezvicsajnaja Komisszija (CSEKA)*
The Whole Russian Extraordinary Committee

Maros River.

Mako Gymnasium, appearing the same way today as 101 years ago.

Depiction of tank overrunning a shooting ditch and bunker.

Depiction of how bread was partitioned in
Russian POW camps.

Depiction of how prisoners were squeezed together in bunk beds.

Train route from Baja to Temesvar, Focsani and Sverdlovsk.

Partial locations of gulags and concentration camps in the Soviet Union.

Soviet tanks rumbling down Budapest streets to crush the Revolution.

Damaged buildings in Budapest after the battle in the streets.

A little girl carrying home some delicious Hungarian bread.

Bread in Siberia

Laszlo and girlfriend posing in a Hungarian bakery with its shelves of Hungarian bread.

Paul Tarko, as he appears today, displaying his drainage and plastic products.

From left to right, Paul Sr., Ryan and Paul Jr., three generations of the Tarko family at work.